VIDEO GAME OF THE YEAR

A YEAR-BY-YEAR GUIDE TO THE
BEST, BOLDEST, AND MOST BIZARRE
GAMES FROM EVERY YEAR SINCE 1977

VIDEO GAME OF THE YEAR

JORDAN MINOR

ABRAMS IMAGE, NEW YORK

CONTENTS

FOREWORD

or almost half a century, gamers have h̶e̶a̶r̶d̶ others decry their favorite hobby as simple toys for children. Depending on who you listened to, video games were nothing more than bleeps and bloops, destined to rot your brain and lead to a lonely existence filled with lost potential, stunted social skills, and maybe even a criminal record.

But anyone who actually loves games knows how wrong and reductionist that mindset is. Sure, the early years of gaming leaned heavily on high scores and white-knuckle action, but the industry rapidly grew and began offering a massive variety of experiences that evoke the full spectrum of emotional responses. What started as a great way to kill time and munch quarters at the arcade after school became much more.

Landmark titles like *Super Mario 64* and *Metal Gear Solid* caused seismic shifts in the industry and made us rethink what was possible. Tipsy college students filled their dorm halls with the sounds of *Rock Band* as they did their best Slash impersonations. Kids connected with elderly relatives with *Wii Sports* bowling and tennis. Gamers found empathy and relatability in *Depression Quest*, lunacy and laughter in *WarioWare* and *Incredible Crisis*, and even the loves of their lives during *World of Warcraft* raids. In more recent years, a new generation of gamers have replaced the school playground with *Minecraft* and *Fortnite* as their social square of choice. And if you still want some of that good old-fashioned white-knuckle action, it didn't die in the seventies. Those thrills still survive in *Sekiro*, *Destiny*, and countless other titles.

Video Game of the Year offers more than a simple listing of the best game of each year. Jordan Minor provides detailed analysis and contextualization that lets you know why each of these games made an impact on the time of its release. Some of them were the perfect game at the perfect moment in the cultural zeitgeist, and others were just undeniably ahead of the pack in every way.

You'll also hear personal anecdotes from a wide range of gaming industry voices, and see tons of fantastic art from Wren McDonald. This is a true love letter to an industry that so many of us grew up with, and it's eye-opening to see just how far it's come in a relatively short time.

Games are no longer confined to the stereotype of pockmarked teenagers chomping on Cheetos in their basement. They've made massive strides in accessibility, inclusion, and approachability. This book makes that clear as day, taking you chronologically from the simplicity of *Pong* to the surreal examination of choice and fate in The *Stanley Parable*. Gaming is still a relatively young industry, but the story of how we got from then to now is nothing short of fascinating. I hope that Jordan's trip through the years brings you as many smiles and fond gaming memories as it did for me.

DAN RYCKERT, creative director at Giant Bomb and co-founder of the Fire Escape Cast

INTRODUCTION

I have no clue how long I've loved video games. My parents and I tried to pinpoint the exact moment when interactive entertainment consumed my brain, and the closest date I came up with was November 1997, when I unwrapped a Nintendo 64 for my sixth birthday along with **Star Fox 64** and the fancy new Rumble Pak controller accessory. I was just as stoked as the N64 kid in that meme video.

Or was it even earlier than that? Nintendo's first 3D machine might have been the first console I called my own, but I have cherished memories of playing **Contra III: The Alien Wars** and **Donkey Kong Country** on my older sister's Super Nintendo (released in 1991, the same year I was born) or whatever **Teenage Mutant Ninja Turtles** cartridges still worked on her Nintendo Entertainment System (which I adorably called the "Regular Nintendo").

What's special about these anecdotes is that there's nothing special about them. These are the backstories for countless kids who grew up marinating in video games, even if only a handful of them grew up to pursue the extremely real career called video game journalism. From casual fandom to encyclopedic obsession, video game passion persists across multiple generations.

Video games have existed for decades; they're older than many of their biggest fans, yet they still feel brand-new. A fun and fascinating frontier where entertainment meets technology, the video game industry thrives on cutting-edge, youthful, and just plain weird creative energy. But video game innovation doesn't exist without video game history, a proud and inspiring history that artists draw from and build upon, a long and underexamined history that always deserves more celebration. So let's celebrate the amazing games that shaped that history, one year and one game at a time.

As we travel across more than forty years of gaming, you'll read about the best games, the most important and influential games, the games that foreshadowed the most profitable trends, and the games that tapped into the larger cultural and political moment, even if accidentally. Reading honest descriptions for dozens of games back-to-back will also give you a better appre-

...lation of just how uniquely and delightfully bizarre even the most famous games tend to be. The video game industry may finally rival (or arguably surpass) movies and music when it comes to mainstream success, but only in video games can a portly plumber, speedy rodent, and an armor-clad space marine all be equally famous mascots for global corporate juggernauts in a multibillion-dollar business.

I chose this "video game of the year" format for two reasons: the serious answer and the real answer. The serious answer is that I wanted to look back and dive deep into games that could probably sustain entire books all on their own, without sacrificing fun variety or the grand sweep of history. Watching the original pixelated **Legend of Zelda** evolve into the living watercolor painting **The Wind Waker** in fifteen years, with many other games in between, is the radical transformation arc that makes gaming so exciting and unpredictable to follow. Vibrant individual portraits paint the complete picture.

As for the real answer? Gamers love competition, especially meaningless competition. We rack up high scores at the arcade, brag about arbitrary Xbox Live achievements, and take home huge cash prizes at esports tournaments. Arguing why **Final Fantasy VII** is more significant than **Fallout**, or how **Rock Band** is the most important game of the same year that brought us **Call of Duty 4**, are the hills this culture lives to die on. Listen to any game of the year debate from a major website and you'll quickly learn that fighting about rankings is more fun than the results themselves. Since this is my book, my rankings all win, but don't let that stop you from yelling your own hot takes at me through the page. And if my opinions aren't enough, my friends and colleagues from across the industry have graciously contributed their own submissions, too.

The video game business, as much passion as it may stir, does a regrettably poor job of archiving its own past, of preserving old games so curious new players can try them on modern devices. So (legally) getting your hands on some of the games mentioned in this book may be pretty tricky. Still, as a software sommelier, I urge you to try. If people gain a greater understanding of games as a whole, games will get better and our relationship to them will become more joyful. Even for the gaming phenomena you may have already heard of (**Fortnite**, **Minecraft**, Gamergate), I hope you'll realize how they're part of a long trend, a history, of this one-of-a-kind medium intersecting with and influencing our society at large.

Video games are here. They've *been* here. They aren't going anywhere.

1977

▌▌PONG.

THE FIRST GAME OF THE YEAR

SLIDE A PADDLE BACK AND FORTH TO BOUNCE A BALL
PAST YOUR OPPONENT, LIKE DIGITAL PING-PONG.

PRESS START

In 1977, the burning question on everyone's lips wasn't "Have you played video games today?" It was, as the commercial says, "Have you played Atari today?" Few brands dominate their field so completely that their trademark name becomes a stand-in for the entire product. Think Band-Aid bandages or Q-tip cotton swabs. Although its reign was relatively short-lived, at the dawn of video games, Atari wore this crown. The Atari 2600 console brought video games into the home—where they've resided comfortably ever since—and there's one game to thank for that. In what has to be the least controversial pick in this entire list, we begin with **Pong**, the little Ping-Pong game responsible for this medium even existing in the first place.

B.P. : BEFORE PONG

Like many firsts, *Pong* on the Atari 2600 home console was actually the result of many other breakthroughs and innovations bubbling in the background before its debut. Visit the Musée Mécanique, an interactive museum in San Francisco showcasing vintage coin-operated mechanical attractions, and you'll be blown away by how much of this dusty DNA eventually found its way into gaming. You can easily trace the lineage from century-old fortune-teller machines to Mafia-era Chicago pinball tables to the arcade cabinets video games emerged from. Specific early gaming examples deserve recognition, too. In 1958, thirteen years after he helped develop the nuclear bomb, physicist William Higinbotham showed how well computers and screens could simulate the sport of tennis with his popular experimental exhibition *Tennis for Two*.

Pong itself also existed years before the Atari 2600 (which should technically be considered as the start of the *second* generation of video game consoles, not the first, having been preceded by the launch of several primitive home machines, most notably Ralph Baer's 1972 Magnavox Odyssey console). Atari's first game, *Pong*, originally debuted in 1972 as a bulky arcade cabinet. What started as a mere demo by engineer Allan Alcorn became a flagship product through sheer force of fun. It achieved extreme commercial success in its arcade format in North America and overseas. Atari cofounder Nolan Bushnell gained so much clout he also founded the Chuck E. Cheese child casinos in 1977. No one knew what a video game was, but *Pong*'s gameplay couldn't be easier to grasp. No buttons to press, just turn the knobs to move your paddle and hit the blocky ball past your opponent. Everyone recognizes *Pong* now, but to astonished bargoers, it was a fancy, newfangled version of the air hockey tables that also started cropping up around this time.

Regardless, while these musty factoids may be fun for the gaming history nerds, for the vast majority of normal people, video games sprang from the ether in September 1977 when the Atari Video Computer System (later renamed the Atari 2600) flew onto store shelves.

FARAWAY GALAXIES COME HOME

There's something serendipitous about the fact that the Atari 2600 and *Star Wars* launched in the same year. As George Lucas says, "It's like poetry, they rhyme." Beyond being foundational texts for modern geek culture, these were both radical, paradigm-shifting entertainment for mass audiences, too. Their broad popularity becomes even more impressive when you think about just how bizarre these things really are. *Star Wars*' sci-fi galaxy mashed up pseudo–samurai warriors with World War II dogfights and nostalgic 1960s teenage California culture. Meanwhile, if you had never seen a video game before—abstract images on your TV under your command!—they might as well have been from another universe.

To counter any potential discomfort, both *Star Wars* and the Atari 2600 shrewdly used familiar elements to ground audiences and make them feel nice and cozy while leading them through some very strange places. Even if you couldn't wrap your head around his alien home, anyone could relate to Luke Skywalker's struggle for independence, especially when you got hit with the film's lush, classical, orchestral soundtrack. As for the Atari 2600, with its old-fashioned wood paneling and game cartridges purposefully designed to look like 8-track tapes, suddenly this foreign thing called a video game console felt right at home alongside your other entertainment appliances.

As with anything truly new, though, you took a chance if you bought a 2600. Maybe video games simply didn't make sense in the home. Maybe they didn't have enough lasting appeal to be worth the money. Adjusted for inflation, the 2600 cost $850. Maybe the technology wasn't ready yet. For the very concept of the home console to survive, Atari needed to reward customers who made this leap of faith. That reward was *Pong* . . . sort of.

I'M PONG, YOU'RE PONG, WE'RE ALL PONG

The Atari 2600 technically didn't launch with a game called *Pong*. Instead, it launched with *Video Olympics*, later known as *Pong Sports*. This collection not only included *Pong*, but forty-nine other games that were, more or less, slight variations on *Pong*.

It's honestly inspiring how Atari's developers managed to remix their cash cow into so many technically distinct games just by changing a few properties and slapping on a different sport's facade. You like *Pong*? Well, get a load of *Super Pong* with extra paddles, *Quadrapong* with four players, or the single-player *Robot Pong*. Add a smaller goal on each side of the field along with the ability to catch the puck and suddenly *Pong* becomes hockey. Turn the game on its axis for some volleyball *Pong*. The *Pong* buffalo had enough meat to carve into dozens more games.

Pong Sports isn't purely cynical, though. It's a smart acknowledgment of how games at home fundamentally need to serve different needs than games at arcades. At an arcade, you drop in a few quarters for an experience that lasts a few minutes before moving on to the next game. But if you're paying serious money to permanently own a machine for playing games at home, you'll rightfully demand more substance and variety. This now-ancient device's technical limitations meant games could only be so deep, but for *Pong* to have the same smash success at home as it did in the arcade, it had to offer more.

Fortunately, *Pong* is versatile enough to fit into all sorts of variants while keeping its appeal. What makes *Pong* so pleasurable is that simple core act of hand-eye coordination challenging you to move and react better than your buddy, and you can't mess that up even if you tried. Bushnell's Law states that "all the best games are easy to learn and difficult to master. They should reward the first quarter and the hundredth." That's *Pong*. That's how Atari turned the first blockbuster arcade game into a killer app that sold millions of 2600 consoles and brought games to the home for the first time. That's how Atari became synonymous with video games themselves.

A killer app refers to a must-own piece of software so tantalizing, you're willing to buy any hardware necessary to play it. What's so fascinating about *Pong* is that it's more than a killer app. It's a killer concept, too big to stay contained to one mere game. Alongside *Pong Sports*, countless other 2600-era games boil down to "*Pong* with a twist," from *Arkanoid* to *Warlords*. In *Breakout*, you essentially play a solo game of *Pong* to demolish a brick wall. This game's success gave its creators Steve Jobs and Steve Wozniak the foothold they needed in the tech business before establishing a little company called Apple. Before Nintendo dreamed up Mario or even left its home country of Japan, it sold Color TV-Game consoles including, of course, *Pong* clones.

After Atari's *Pong*, video games would evolve in countless exciting and distinct directions, and we'll discuss where they go. But they all had to start somewhere. The first brick in the wall, *Pong* paved the way for not only endless direct imitators but for nearly every single video game that followed from the 1970s onward. *Pong* is the bedrock upon which a console, a brand, and an entire business are all built. *Pong* is more than just the first game of the year. *Pong* is video games, period.

JERRY LAWSON, GAMING'S OWN HIDDEN FIGURE

A huge advantage home consoles like the Atari 2600 had over arcade machines is that consoles let you swap in new cartridges to play different games, as opposed to being one machine dedicated to a single game. By letting consumers buy relatively affordable cartridges, instead of expensive, entirely separate devices, cartridges created the home gaming market. However, this technology didn't debut on the 2600. It arrived in 1976 on the Fairchild Channel F, an ultimately unsuccessful console designed by the late African American engineer Jerry Lawson.

Video games have historically struggled with racial representation. Despite African Americans being a massive segment of the gaming audience, an International Game Developers Association (IGDA) survey found that Black people make up less than 3 percent of game creators. Still, the fact that cartridges, such a cornerstone for video game tech, were designed by a Black man feels like it should be common knowledge. We should shout it from the rooftops every February. Tragically, only shortly before Lawson's death in 2011 did his forgotten story start to reemerge. I'm a Black guy who lives and breathes gaming news, but I didn't learn about Lawson until after he was already gone.

While he didn't write the code or build the rockets that brought us to space, Jerry Lawson is still the video game industry's own hidden figure. He worked under the shadow of giants like Atari. He ran in the same Homebrew Computer Club circles as Jobs and Wozniak. Katherine Johnson and the other Black women NASA pioneers eventually got their movie, so here's hoping Jerry Lawson's full story one day gets its overdue day in the sun.

1978

THE ALIENS OF THE YEAR

SHOOT ALL THE FALLING ALIENS BEFORE THEY DESTROY
YOUR DEFENSES AND TOUCH DOWN ON THE PLANET.

PRESS START

Imagine you're standing on the set of Family Feud. Under the hot lights, a large man with a ridiculous mustache walks up to your podium and asks you the survey question "What do you do in video games?" You want to score that top answer and bring home as much cash as possible. So what do you say?

Here's my answer: In video games, you shoot aliens. You can, of course, find plenty of exceptions, but one of gaming's most enduring tasks is blasting enemies from another world, to the point that it's frankly become cliché. However, we can't forget that even the most common current concepts got their starts as innovative experiments. In the industry's early days, shooting aliens wasn't a lazy trope; it was the bold blast that made Space Invaders truly out of this world.

ARRIVAL

Like so many classic games, *Space Invaders* used the rigid technical limits of its hardware to create an elegantly contained gameplay loop. Waves of tentacled aliens descend from the sky in neatly arranged rows. Controlling a mobile laser cannon from below, you must shoot them all before even one reaches the surface. As the game progresses, the aliens move faster and their rhythms get harder to predict. If you become especially desperate, you may need to shoot through your own protective bunkers to destroy the invader right on top of you. Last as long as possible, and take out as many aliens as you can, to get better scores. With just a handful of elements and carefully placed pressure, *Space Invaders* ratchets up terrific tension. It asks the player to quickly prioritize which threats must be handled immediately to survive versus what must be done to win the game in the long term. Real alien invasions probably wouldn't play out all that differently.

That's a lot of words to describe *Space Invaders*, but you don't really need them. Once you see this game, you get it. Destroy the aliens before they destroy you. It's instinct. Compared with other kinds of games, like card games or board games, video games have a big advantage when it comes to explaining their rules. A video game can teach the player how the game works through the act of playing the game itself. Sure, you might make a few mistakes along the way, and you may need to glance at the tips written on the arcade cabinet. But there's something more viscerally satisfying about figuring out what to do in the heat of the moment as opposed to reading dry instructions beforehand.

This idea, games teaching their rules themselves through gameplay, also allows games to be a shared, universal language, something that became very important in the increasingly international gaming business. Created by Tomohiro Nishikado for Japanese publisher Taito, *Space Invaders* first launched in Japan in July 1978, and came to North America a few months later. Heading into the 1980s, the United States and Japan were set to clash on the economic stage, but video games could transcend something so petty. *Space Invaders* didn't come from another country. It came from outer space! Everyone can get behind pulpy B-movie sci-fi drama like that, a world-unifying threat from an H. G. Wells novel.

Today's games are much more complex and text heavy, ironically making them more like board games. While many games get localized for all regions, if you do import a foreign game you either need to know the language or track down an accurate fan translation. Despite two years of (and average grades in) Japanese language classes in college, I can't understand kanji to save my life. So I can't play, say, an official copy of the vintage dating game *Tokimeki Memorial 3: Yakusoku no Ano Basho de*. But I can still play *Space Invaders*. Destroy the aliens before they destroy me. Got it.

That simplicity, elegance, and fun turned *Space Invaders* into a billion-dollar breakout hit in the arcade, and a game that sold millions more Atari 2600 consoles at home. Despite urban legends, it didn't cause coin shortages in Japan, but it's telling that the legend still persists. Remember that in 1978 the infant gaming industry remained in a precarious position. *Space Invaders'* success was much-needed additional proof that this novelty was in fact the next big thing in entertainment. Gamers weren't going anywhere. The planet belonged to us.

WAR OF THE WORLDS

Why did shooting these aliens feel so fresh and thrilling at the time? Maybe it was because of the aliens. *Space Invaders*' floppy little extraterrestrial cannon-fodder enemies are so iconic that even the most casual gaming fan will recognize them. *Space Invaders*' real revolution, though, was the shooting. If you want to get reductive, you can see the similarity between a game like *Breakout* and *Space Invaders*. They both make players methodically destroy a hostile upper wall, bit by bit, using projectiles. Nishikado studied a broken-down *Pong* machine for months, to learn the game's secrets, before making *Space Invaders*. Still, *Breakout* and *Pong* are about bouncing boring balls. *Space Invaders* is about shooting laser blasts at dynamic living targets. Even if you haven't played the game, you can under-stand why shooting provides a whole different level of gratification. Nishikado understood; his previous game was straight-up called *Gun Fight*. Once gamers shot those first aliens, the chase was on to relive that high and, for the first time, achieve something called a high score.

Like other golden age megahits, *Space Invaders*' out-of-nowhere success birthed an entirely new genre: the shoot-'em-up, or shmup (nerd culture just can't get enough of jargon that would sound absolutely gross in any other context). Nowadays, so many game genres revolve around shooting that attempting to differenti-ate among them can sound like semantics. For simplic-ity's sake, think of shoot-'em-ups as games like *Space Invaders*, *Centipede*, *Defender*, *Galaga*, *Geometry Wars*, and *Xevious*. You view the action from an elevated posi-tion, surveying the endless waves of aliens surrounding you as you best position your spaceship to shoot them down. If you wanted fast, action-packed tests of skill and reflexes, shoot-'em-ups were the genre for you.

Although they dominated in their day, *Space Invaders*' descendants in the shoot-'em-up genre have since settled into a comfortable but narrow niche. Only hard-core fans can tolerate something as brutal as twitchy bullet hell games like *Ikaruga*. While this specific category may have flown off into the sunset, shooters in general flourish in modern gaming. Run-and-gun games, where your character runs on foot while shooting, include classics like *Contra* and *Metal Slug*. On the opposite end of the spectrum from shoot-'em-ups you'll find the first-person shooter. Instead of supercharging your situational awareness with a bird's-eye view, first-person shooters lock your perspective to the limited realistic range of what an actual soldier can see on the battlefield.

I've changed my answer for that *Family Feud* question. Video games aren't about shooting aliens, they're just about shooting. It doesn't matter what it is. All we needed was that first unlucky target, and with *Space Invaders*, the world got one.

CHOOSE YOUR OWN
COLOSSAL CAVE ADVENTURE

Colossal Cave Adventure asked us to use our imaginations to construct more literary gaming worlds with nothing but the written word. Developed by defense contractor-programmer William Crowther and Stanford AI Lab programmer Don Woods from the mid- to late 1970s, *Colossal Cave Adventure* is the first interactive fiction game.

Instead of graphics, interactive fiction gives you text prompts describing what's happening at the moment. Where are you? What items are nearby? What do you do? You then type your own text to control your unseen character. It requires mental effort, not only to picture the scene in your mind but also to make sense of the somewhat obtuse computer logic governing which commands the game can and can't understand. You can't tell the game to move you in or out, but you can tell it to move you north or south. It's all contextual, especially tricky when you can't actually see anything. When this genre clicks, though, it adds a sense of freedom and experimentation to good old-fashioned storytelling that puts any Choose Your Own Adventure book to shame. I walked down to the stream and drank the water because I wanted to, even though it tasted like rocks.

Even today's most expensive blockbuster games add some novelistic narrative justifying all the explosions. But if you trust the power of your text, interactive fiction lets nearly anyone develop widely creative video games without the costly effort of making graphics. Thanks to *Colossal Cave Adventure*, you don't need big budgets to tell a thrilling tale in your video game.

STAR RAIDERS (1979)

Most of my first Atari 800 games were flat, but one sucked me in from the moment I slammed the cartridge into the slot.

Star Raiders transformed my computer into a portal. In those days, we couldn't watch *Star Wars* whenever we wanted. We didn't even have VCRs. But the complex strategy involved as I hopped from sector to sector, flipping radar on and off to save fuel and dodging enemies with their swooping, opinionated AIs, was like being Han Solo every night. This game was 3D, not 2D; dynamic, not static; and vast, not linear. *Star Raiders* yanked you up to the screen and then pushed you back in your chair. You felt the wind in your hair and the g-forces when you banked into turns. It was far more real than any other game you could play at home.

And yet the whole thing fit into 8K of perfect assembly code. The engine, the graphics, the sound and the story: all in under eight thousand bytes. I'm still amazed at how tiny that perfect universe truly was, and how huge it felt.

—SASCHA SEGAN,
mobile expert

OUTER WILDS (2019)

Outer Wilds introduced a beautiful, intricate solar system and then made me watch it die every twenty-two minutes. Each time the sun blew up, everything reset except the information I stored in my ship's computer. The time loop stressed me at first but eventually became freeing. I could crash my spaceship, get swallowed by a giant fish, or disintegrate in a supernova, and then I'd be back, good as new. I was free to screw around for as many lives as I needed or wanted.

Figuring out how to escape the loop was gratifying but paled in comparison to the true revelation of the game: we're all locked in endless cycles of birth, death, and rebirth, but we control what we enjoy and learn along the way.

—PETE HAAS,
social media manager

1979

VECTORBEAM

THE HOT ROD OF THE YEAR

DRIVE DOWN ROADS UNTIL TIME RUNS OUT,
AVOIDING ANY AND ALL OBSTACLES IN YOUR PATH.

PRESS START

So many old video games, bless their hearts, look ugly as sin. Before the 1980s 8-bit era, before developers had the resources and know-how to create genuinely beautiful 2D images, games just looked rough. Games crudely arranged colored blocks into visuals that only barely resembled what they claimed to be if you squinted. Only the lavishly illustrated box art could supply any real answers. Look! Up in what's *supposed* to be the sky! It's a pile of red and blue rectangles in **Superman** on the Atari 2600! Don't blame the creators, blame the comically limited technology. Because games as an art form are so linked to technology, tech advancements dictate how far and how fast games can progress. Sometimes, that change happens slowly and steadily. But other times, tech takes drastic and dramatic leaps forward, and shiny new rides like **Speed Freak** race right alongside it.

TO THE VECTOR GO
THE SPOILS

Even in the late 1970s, when 2D video games were far from reaching their full visual potential, on some level we knew that 3D video games were the future. After all, our real world exists in three dimensions, so for games to properly simulate our world they would eventually have to follow suit. But what options did we have in 1979? Games relied on technology called raster graphics to display visuals. With raster graphics, backgrounds and objects (sprites) are made up of squares called pixels arranged on a grid. Resolution refers to how many pixels that grid can fit. The fewer pixels, the less detailed the image. A 4K high-definition television showcases 3840 x 2160 pixels, but the Atari 2600 could only manage 160 x 192. A simplistic game like *Pong* plays perfectly within those boxy parameters, but between the low resolution and limited color palette, you'd quickly run into problems when trying to do anything more complex. It's hard to feel like you're Superman if you can literally count his gigantic pixels with your naked eye. For games to go 3D, these raster graphics wouldn't cut it. Enter vector graphics.

First developed for the military (like so many tech innovations that eventually find their way into entertainment) vector graphics take an entirely different mathematical approach to visuals. Vector graphics eschew pixels in favor of shapes drawn by electron beams governed by whatever calculations the developer programs. Plotted number coordinates create what we see on-screen. The results look like digital line art, typically monochrome and composed of clean, glowing geometric figures that don't lose any sharp detail as you zoom in on them. What really made vector graphics such an early game changer? Vector graphics could create a crude but convincing pseudo-3D effect. With 3D, the types of games even conceivable opened up immensely. The race was on, and *Speed Freak* zoomed to the front of the pack.

Designer Larry Rosenthal founded Vectorbeam for the sole purpose of developing vector graphics arcade games. Released in March 1979, *Speed Freak* was the company's second game, but it was the first one to apply Rosenthal's patented vector display technology to a driving game. Contemporary driving games like Atari's *Night Driver* and Midway's *Midnite Racer* showed the obvious limitations of raster graphics. Boring sprites slid around a black expanse as obstacles blinked in and out of existence. They were flat and confusing, nothing like real driving. When you got behind the wheel in *Speed Freak* (with the literal, actual steering wheel controller built into the arcade cabinet), you drove off.

With vector graphics, *Speed Freak* harnessed the open freedom of 3D visuals to translate the open freedom of the road. In 3D, the first-person perspective finally made sense. As you try to reach the end of the computer-generated streets as quickly as possible, little visual flourishes catch your eye and add to the immersion. Other cars fly past you. Your windshield might crack. Hitchhikers wave from the side of the highway. You might even see a car crash, or crash the car yourself. The aesthetic, the warping white outlines on black space that define vector graphics, comes across as an intentional, hypnotic artistic choice, not a limitation. *Speed Freak* just looks cool. When colorful vector graphics became feasible in the 1980s, Atari chose to use them for the appropriately flashy arcade *Star Wars* space shooter, as well as the trippy tube tunnel *Tempest*. Vector graphics: the visuals of the future.

TEST YOUR METTLE, AND YOUR METAL

Speed Freak was just one of several vector graphics arcade games from Vectorbeam, which later merged with fellow vector graphics aficionados Cinematronics. The shooter *Space Wars* took inspiration from the massively influential 1962 MIT programming prototype *Spacewar!* to achieve commercial success, while *Barrier* used newfangled 3D graphics to give players an entire maze to navigate. *Speed Freak* stands out, though, not just because it specifically uses vector graphics, but because it represents the larger, ongoing, intriguing trend of racing games being at the vanguard of video game graphics tech, even at the very beginning of the medium and the genre.

Most of us will never get the chance to drive an expensive luxury race car. We'll certainly never be able to own one. So we want that vicarious thrill, which is really what video games are all about—not just simulating our world but simulating the most exciting parts of it, which we'll never safely experience. Since we want that simulation to be as convincing as possible, we push the bleeding edge of technology forward. This holds true for many genres, but it's especially apparent with racing games.

In the arcade, *Speed Freak*'s powerful vector graphics and big, dumb steering wheel controller outshone anything home consoles could do. Eventually, raster graphics struck back with beautiful arcade racers like Namco's *Pole Position*, games that did turn 2D sprites into lush and transportive racing experiences. *Daytona USA* and *Ridge Racer* showed off true, polygonal 3D visuals in the early 1990s. On PlayStation consoles, the popular *Gran Turismo* series committed so hard to realism, its designers meticulously laser-scanned real car parts most players never saw. Apple touted *Real Racing*'s gorgeous graphics to demonstrate the iPhone's gaming prowess. Whenever new consoles launch, racing games typically showcase what the new machines can do. Look at the 4K vistas and fetishized real-world automobiles *Forza Horizon 5*

can pump out at blinding speeds, and feel good about your choice to buy an Xbox Series X. Even the modestly underpowered Nintendo Switch flexed its graphical muscles with the eye-popping *Mario Kart 8 Deluxe*.

PC gamers more than anyone else value high-horsepower hardware. To play games with the fidelity consoles could only dream of, PC gamers drop cash for pricey parts without blinking. They lovingly tune their computers, their rigs, to squeeze every drop of performance from the metal. They form a bond that resembles, more than anything else, the bond between a grease monkey driver and their car. Fans of dazzling race cars and fans of beautiful video games are kindred gearhead spirits. With racing games, they harmonically converge.

Speed Freak—and vector graphics—were, ultimately, the road not taken. The tech requires specialized displays, great for arcades but ill-suited for home consoles. And eventually raster graphics, along with other forms of 3D visuals, grew powerful enough to render vector graphics obsolete. But they blazed such a stylish road to cruise down, a glimpse into what was possible. In their own way, today's stunning racing games and the gaming hardware that powers them still follow this path; they still live their lives the same quarter mile at a time.

THE QUIET BRILLIANCE OF ASTEROIDS

Designed by Lyle Rains and Ed Logg for Atari, *Asteroids*' gameplay setup is simple: Fly your spaceship and shoot asteroids. But *Asteroids* is surprisingly complex and realistic, especially for its time. Think about all the variables to juggle: your ship's speed and acceleration, the dangerous debris that explodes off asteroids when you shoot them, the fact that your ship loops back around when you fly off-screen and throws your trajectory out of whack.

Asteroids is another early game directly inspired by *Spacewar!*. With that scientific context you understand why these games low-key feel like mainstream-friendly physics exercises. Although the game's action, set on a 2D plane, could conceivably work with pixels, vector graphics add that extra space-age edge. It looks like something you might see on a NASA monitor.

Many programs designed to teach novices how to make their own video games, like GameMaker Studio, start their tutorials with an *Asteroids* clone. That's a brilliant choice. *Asteroids* is a game everyone understands, so as a budding designer you know exactly where you want to end up, even if you don't know how to get there. But as the software walks you through the rudimentary development process, you learn how even the most seemingly basic games have a lot going on under the hood. In the quiet vastness of space, *Asteroids* humbles even the cockiest young explorers.

OPERATION: INNER SPACE (1994)

In *Operation: Inner Space*, you navigate through your PC's hard drive structure, entering directories and flying around a space-like environment while rescuing your Windows application icons from viruses. It plays a lot like *Asteroids*, with inertia on your ship. You need to avoid rocks, shoot viruses, and collect power-ups along the way. Your ship can be damaged, repaired, and upgraded. But best of all, there are factions of AI-controlled ships that can either fight alongside you, hold grudges, or become mortal enemies. There's a sexy computer voice. I've never played anything like it on any other platform; it's a forgotten masterpiece.

—BENJ EDWARDS,
creator of Vintage Computing and Gaming

OUTRUN 2006: COAST 2 COAST (2006)

OutRun 2006: Coast 2 Coast does what many other racing games do not: replicate the joy of driving. Ostensibly a racing game, *OutRun 2006* focuses less on placing well among a flock of CPU-controlled, Ferrari-branded sports cars, and focuses more on deftly navigating exquisitely designed tracks based on real-world locales, such as Cape Canaveral and the Great Pyramid of Giza. The goal? Cross the finish line before the descending clock count ticks to zero. That's not as important as it seems.

OutRun 2006 is all about the beautiful journey, with its wild drifting, gorgeous branching paths, hummable music (including the sing-in-the-shower-worthy "Night Flight"), fun Coast 2 Coast mode that adds skill challenges and race variations, and a spirited woman riding shotgun who shouts cheers or jeers based on your driving highs or lows.

A wonderful successor to Sega's groundbreaking 1986 original, *OutRun 2006* is one of the most delightful racing games ever made. Instead of demanding simulation, it celebrates putting the pedal to the metal as you dash toward white sands, blue skies, and the infinite possibilities that come with playing "just one more game."

—JEFFREY L. WILSON,
managing editor at PCMag

1980

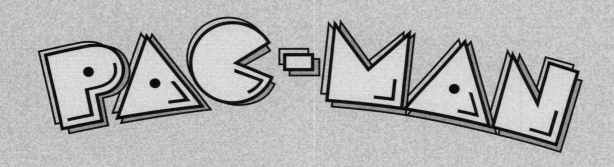

THE MASCOT OF THE YEAR

ZIP AROUND A MAZE TRYING TO EAT UP
EVERY LAST PELLET, ALL WHILE AVOIDING
A QUARTET OF ANGRY GHOSTS.

PRESS START

"Video games, they aren't just Pac-Man anymore." That's the usual opening you'll hear on The Besties, a superb video game podcast. This tongue-in-cheek intro mocks the hopelessly out-of-touch tone consistently seen in most mainstream gaming coverage. You're saying this art form *hasn't* remained stagnant for the past forty years? Shocking. As fun as it is to dunk on people whose views on video games remain hopelessly locked in 1980, Pac-Man is not the punch line. If anything, the joke only works because Pac-Man is spectacular. Pac-Man and his game hit the culture so hard, during such a formative era, that at some point you *would* need to convince people video games aren't just Pac-Man anymore. Pac-Man looms large as not only a beloved game, but the birth of the video game mascot, the first character to give gaming a friendly, hungry face.

PUCK-MAN

As with many a mythical hero, the legends surrounding Pac-Man's origins sound almost too good to be true. And if you learned they weren't true, you wouldn't care, you'd run with that story. You'd believe that creator Toru Iwatani found inspiration for his circular brainchild by looking at a pizza with a missing slice. You'd have faith that he figured a game about eating would appeal to broader audiences more than a game about violence. "Paku" is a Japanese onomatopoeia for eating, and the hockey-puck-shaped Pac-Man was originally supposed to be named Puck-Man, but arcades were afraid of leaving such an easy target for vulgar vandals. That's an incredible, hilarious explanation. The ultimate goal for any brand, gaming or otherwise, is to constantly occupy your brain, for you to willingly welcome that occupation. *Pac-Man* achieved this effortlessly, like no game before it and, honestly, like few games after. Even when you aren't playing *Pac-Man*, anecdotes like this already make it fun to think about *Pac-Man*.

Eventually, though, you'll want to play *Pac-Man*. *Pac-Man*'s legendary status now surpasses any one product, but the whole phenomenon owes a great deal of its success to the sheer quality of that first game. When *Pac-Man* debuted in 1980, its design felt deeper and more deliberate than other arcade games. Gamers appreciated how much thought had clearly gone into the experience before they even put their hands on it. It was a brand-new decade for gaming, and *Pac-Man* arrived with a plan. If you wanted to survive in his maze, you needed to have a plan, too.

Pac-Man's mix of twisting, tight turns and long, thrilling straightaways made you feel like you were in a real chase, where you made life-or-death split-second decisions about which direction to move and when. By eating a power pellet, whether it was out of strategy or desperation, you flipped the script on your ghostly oppressors and took a bite out of them for a change. The mechanic remains the greatest example of instantly transforming player fear into player empowerment, the intoxicating dance between tension and release at gaming's challenging heart.

Pac-Man the character is as revolutionary as *Pac-Man* the game, but because video game characters weren't really a thing yet, *Pac-Man* still had to sell on the merits of its fantastic gameplay first and foremost. Modern mascot games get this backward, hoping a cute or cool enough animal will make up for a mediocre experience. *Pac-Man* couldn't afford to make that mistake.

There's nothing bad to say about *Pac-Man*'s gameplay. It's genius. However, strip everything away and it is essentially another arcade game that asks the player to just look at the screen and maneuver correctly. No one thinks of *Pac-Man* that joylessly, though, and even implying it here feels like a buzzkill. So how did *Pac-Man* get the public to *not* strip it down to its most boring essentials? Now it's time to talk about the genius of Pac-Man, not just as a game, but as a living, breathing being.

FEVER PITCH

The Magnavox Odyssey, the actual first video game console, could display only one line and a handful of player-controlled dots. How do you turn that into a video game? The solution in 1972 involved some charmingly quaint sleight of hand. Included in the box were various colorful sheets of translucent plastic. Players taped these overlays on their TV screens to create rules and context, to create games. Suddenly, you weren't simply moving dots around empty space. Instead, you were a mouse fleeing a hungry cat, a submarine dodging torpedoes, or a baseball star scoring a home run. Games aren't only our mechanical actions, but the larger scene we imagine those actions happening within. Better graphics just do a better job selling the illusion.

With that in mind, now think about Pac-Man. On one hand, he's basically a cursor, a moving dot avoiding other dots. But he's not a dot, and he's not some abstract object like a paddle or a gun. He's Pac-Man! He's a friendly little yellow cartoon boy, a big round mouth man who makes funny noises when he eats fruit. And he's always one step ahead of the bumbling quartet of colorful ghosts named Inky, Blinky, Pinky, and Clyde. Pac-Man is so iconic that anyone can draw his shape. The character illustrations featured on *Pac-Man* arcade cabinets, with their expressive eyes and squishy bodies, wouldn't look out of place hanging out with Mickey Mouse. Pac-Man was gaming's first homegrown mascot, so expertly managed his creators made sure his name couldn't be turned into a swear word. You didn't just play *Pac-Man*, you cared about Pac-Man.

You also spent money on Pac-Man. Players dropped billions of dollars' worth of quarters into *Pac-Man* arcade cabinets. Not only that, as a character Pac-Man existed as more than just a game. He was a full-blown global pop culture event. Mascots equal merchandise. Watch the *Pac-Man* Saturday morning cartoon while you eat Pac-Man cereal and listen to the hit single "Pac-Man Fever" by Buckner & Garcia (RIP). At the height of his power, Pac-Man could even

sell games that definitely did not do the brand justice. The arcade version of *Pac-Man* received a massive downgrade when it got ported to the Atari 2600. Nonetheless, atrocious graphics and borderline unplayable controls didn't stop millions of folks from scooping up a home version of the game.

As a somewhat intangible concept, no one can really own a specific gameplay type, and *Pac-Man* clones arrived fast and furious in the early 1980s. Your character, on the other hand, very much belongs to you, even if someone slaps a pink bow on it. Common wisdom now suggests that 1982's *Ms. Pac-Man* is a better game than *Pac-Man*, with its superior artificial intelligence forcing more interesting and active play at the expert level, as opposed to *Pac-Man*'s fairly rote and predictable patterns. But *Ms. Pac-Man* is only a semiofficial sequel. It began life as an unauthorized modified version of the original made by American developers at General Computer Corporation for publisher Midway, with only vague support and consent from the Japanese creators at Namco. Only in 2008 did all parties involved reach a resolution over legal rights. There is undeniable power in this character, so much so that people were willing to ask for forgiveness, rather than permission, to get a slice of this pizza for themselves.

Pac-Man demonstrates how creators can take stellar but raw gameplay mechanics and elevate them to staggering heights by giving players something to latch on to, by giving people someone to root for. Pac-Man was the first, but he certainly wouldn't be the last video game character to gobble his way into our hearts. Maybe all video games should be *Pac-Man*.

THE DELAYED GRATIFICATION OF ROGUE

Sometimes, a game's impact is obvious and immediate. Other times, a game must wait in the shadows for decades before its true, vast influence fully reveals itself. Such was the fate for 1980's *Rogue*.

Designed by college students Michael Toy and Glenn Wichman, *Rogue* was ruthless. If you died while crawling through *Rogue*'s dungeons, you stayed dead. The unforgiving difficulty made sure you would die a lot. Meanwhile, the game's random algorithm rearranged the level layout before every new run, so you would never crawl through the same dungeon twice. You couldn't memorize your way to victory. You had to rely on pure skill and accrued knowledge of the game's various systems to overcome the merciless challenges.

In 1980, young programmers revered *Rogue* and eagerly shared their own takes on the concept. Years later, like an underground band that inspired a generation of rock stars, *Rogue*'s gameplay philosophy now guides the twenty-first-century independent game scene. Acclaimed hits like *Dead Cells*, *Into the Breach*, *Spelunky*, and *The Binding of Isaac* draw direct inspiration from *Rogue* (brutal challenge, permanent death, ever-shifting levels) while softening a bit of its edges to make a more accessible product. These games are so indebted to this singular reference point that we call them roguelikes, because they are "games that are like *Rogue*." Kudos to this punishing pioneer that now calls an entire subgenre its own. We'll all die, but *Rogue* lives forever.

MISSILE COMMAND (1980)

Pac-Man may be a more obvious choice for 1980. But no coin-op captured the zeitgeist of the time like *Missile Command*. Pop in a quarter, and instead of shooting aliens or driving race cars, you had to destroy waves of incoming ICBMs before they leveled your six cities. To stay alive, you furiously worked the oversize trackball and red-LED-tipped fire buttons for your three missile bases. The relentless attacks included branching missile trails, roving bombers and satellites, and smart bombs that evaded your shots.

As a small kid, I was scared of the game's changing colors. Each pair of levels had its own color scheme, but get good enough to make it to the fifth set and the black sky itself suddenly turned blue, the first in a series of more dramatic changes. It meant things were about to get even tougher. Dave Theurer's *Missile Command* encapsulated the fear of global thermonuclear war in pixels—right down to its frightening last screen, where the words "The End" disappeared in a giant, final explosion, confirming all was lost.

—JAMIE LENDINO,
author of *Attract Mode: The Rise and Fall of Coin-Op Arcade Games*

KATAMARI DAMACY (2004)

An eccentric experience, Namco's *Katamari Damacy* puts you in the shoes of the Prince of All Cosmos, rolling up everything from paper clips to prehistoric beasts to repopulate the night sky with stars. The game itself, with its psychedelic cel-shaded pop art style, is a pretty simple puzzler that puts you in control of the katamari, a sticky ball that grows as you pick up more and more junk.

But that isn't what makes *Katamari Damacy* shine. It's the heartbreaking story that cuts through the wonderfully painted world: Those stars you make are all an effort to clean up the mess made by your drunken, melodramatic giant of a father, the King of All Cosmos. *Katamari Damacy* can be the fun, low-stakes time sink of your dreams, or an Oedipus-like tale speaking to a generation of gamers. Either way, nothing beats a "good job" from your dad, even if he's a little hungover.

—PATRICK LUCAS AUSTIN,
technology columnist at *Time*

1981

DONKEY KONG

THE IRREPLACEABLE GAME OF THE YEAR

RUN UP STACKS OF TREACHEROUS SCAFFOLDING,
LEAP OVER AND HAMMER THROUGH BARRELS AND OTHER
OBSTACLES, AND RESCUE THE DAMSEL IN DISTRESS.

PRESS START

For such a lovable lunkhead, Donkey Kong sure provokes a lot of thought. **Donkey Kong** is 1981's game of the year, obviously, but trying to crystallize a unified thesis explaining why proves almost impossible. **Donkey Kong** is so important, such a lynchpin for gaming as we know it, that there are just too many different things to talk about, too many different approaches, too much to praise. **Donkey Kong** inspires too much awe to form coherent analysis, and not just because a gorilla wearing a tie is objectively hilarious.

What can be stated without hesitation, however, is if you erased **Donkey Kong** from existence, you would render gaming history absolutely unrecognizable. Let's appreciate the fact that we have **Donkey Kong** by imagining how dark this alternate gaming universe would be without it.

IT'S A WONDERFUL KONG

Founded in 1889, Nintendo spent just under a century running a business that had nothing to do with video games. The company made playing cards and dabbled in food and spicy love hotels, and the Nintendo video games that did eventually precede *Donkey Kong*, like the Color TV-Game console and Game & Watch handhelds, never spread beyond Japan and certain parts of Europe. So when *Donkey Kong* became a smash arcade hit all over the planet, it introduced Nintendo to the world, and introduced it as a video game company. No *Donkey Kong*, no Nintendo. Decades' worth of consistently acclaimed, massively influential, and fiercely beloved video game software and hardware simply would not exist without this barrel-tossing jerk. But let's expand our scope. No *Donkey Kong* also means no Shigeru Miyamoto. No Gunpei Yokoi. No platformers. No home consoles. No Mario!

Donkey Kong began as an attempt to salvage and rework a previous failed Nintendo arcade game, the *Space Invaders*–esque *Radar Scope*, into something that might sell in America. An old game doesn't morph into a new game all on its own. People do that work. In this case, those people were untested art-school-graduate-turned-director Shigeru Miyamoto and veteran producer Gunpei Yokoi. An undisputed game design god, Miyamoto went on to create some of the most important franchises for both Nintendo and gaming at large including *Mario* and *The Legend of Zelda*. Meanwhile, the late Gunpei Yokoi would go on to create cooler, hipper Nintendo games like *Metroid*, as well as hardware innovations like the Game Boy handheld. Without the big gorilla launching their careers to new heights, gaming loses two of its most cherished luminaries.

Donkey Kong is also the first Mario game, the first taste of the powerful leaps players would later enjoy across dozens of platforming masterpieces. Mario, originally named Jumpman, is gaming's most important mascot, and his cheerful omnipresence also extends to kart-racing games, sports spin-offs, role-playing games, party games, and whatever other

quality product Nintendo slaps his mustache on. Mario and Donkey Kong may be friends now, but their initial bitter rivalry (at one point spilling into a blood feud with Donkey Kong's son) birthed Mario in the first place. Gaming's most famous face owes an unpayable debt to the ape.

Because of Mario's success, in *Donkey Kong* and elsewhere, other games decided that they, too, should be about characters who jump. Maybe you jump by flying a giant ostrich like in *Joust*. Maybe you jump while shooting like in *Ghosts 'n Goblins*, jump in limited 3D space like in *Crash Bandicoot*, or jump while solving puzzles like in *The Lost Vikings*. Maybe you run and jump endlessly, like in *Canabalt* or your favorite mobile game platformers. Maybe you even jump while running at high speeds like in . . . a certain blue hedgehog's game we'll get to later. Donkey Kong's own platforming series, *Donkey Kong Country*, revitalized Nintendo at a low point. We celebrate the platforming genre for its wide range of characters, agile reflex challenges, and wellspring of creativity. Take away *Donkey Kong*, and that all gets snuffed out.

When *Donkey Kong* released in 1981 for arcades, the Atari 2600 still had the home console business on lock, and in 1982 *Donkey Kong* even got a (bad) Atari port. But the next year, Atari and the console market it propped up would flame out in the Great Video Game Crash of 1983. The wreckage left a vacuum that needed to be filled with a new home console leader, and Nintendo stepped up to the plate with the Nintendo Entertainment System. Would that have still happened without *Donkey Kong*'s success? Would video game home consoles as a concept have died forever? Is *Donkey Kong* responsible for PlayStation and Xbox even being a thing? Yes!

You can wake up now. Don't worry, *Donkey Kong* and the video game industry it changed forever are thankfully all still here, but this exercise illustrates just how irreplaceable *Donkey Kong* is, how trying to boil down its importance to one thing doesn't do the game justice.

As intriguing as that all sounds, it's for the best that *Donkey Kong* happened exactly as it did. It had to be fate. *Donkey Kong* is gaming's destiny.

FROGGER'S FOIBLES

Surprising no one, a game about a frog features some pretty fantastic jumping. In Konami's *Frogger*, you don't jump to save the girl, you just jump to avoid oncoming traffic. Designer Akira Hashimoto literally saw this scene play out in nature, a frog jumping between cars, and decided to make a game about it ... after helping the real frog.

A famous *Seinfeld* episode revolves around a *Frogger* arcade cabinet, and like *Seinfeld*, *Frogger* creates irresistible entertainment from a premise that sounds like nothing. Hop a frog across the street? Sign me up! Between their sketchy business models to their one-handed simplicity, today's popular mobile games parallel arcade classics in many ways. So it's not shocking that a stellar mobile game, *Crossy Road*, is just *Frogger*.

Frogger is the gaming equivalent of a high-concept movie. It instantly sounds understandable and appealing with just a few words. Sure, the idea probably couldn't sustain a longer, deeper platformer, but it doesn't have to. It shines as the endlessly replayable arcade game that it is.

STARFLIGHT (1986)

Decades before *No Man's Sky*, a game came out that tasked the player with exploring a simulated world, flying through space to hundreds of systems and landing on almost a thousand enormous planets, populated with hazards, resources, ruins of lost civilizations, and even alien life. This abundance of content fit on *Starflight*'s single 3.5" floppy disk, thanks to the magic of procedural generation. This expansive game gave me a false idea of what video games were normally like, but inspired a lifelong fascination with the idea of creating content from code.

—**JOHNNEMANN NORDHAGEN**, game developer

KENTUCKY ROUTE ZERO (2013)

At first one might be forgiven for thinking that *Kentucky Route Zero* is a throwback, retro nostalgia game. It appears to have a simple look and an old-fashioned adventure game interface. And then, again and again, the designers surprise and amaze you with narrative innovations, a magic realist world, tricks from live theater, and multimedia interludes that make this one of the most interesting and mind-expanding games ever made. The art and visual techniques are like nothing ever seen in games, the story is timely and timeless in the way of the best tragedies, and the music is transcendent.

—**JOHNNEMANN NORDHAGEN**, game developer

1982

PITFALL!™

THE THIRD-PARTY **GAME OF THE YEAR**

RUN AND JUMP YOUR WAY THROUGH A TREACHEROUS
JUNGLE, SWINGING OVER QUICKSAND AND
CLIMBING AWAY FROM FEROCIOUS BEASTS,
WHILE COLLECTING AS MUCH TREASURE AS YOU CAN.

PRESS START

When you play a game, you want to win. If there can only be one winner, you better take out everyone else. However, if there was no one else there, if it were only you, would it even still be a game at all? The beauty of competition is that there are competitors, plural. The video game industry, like all businesses, is just another big (highly profitable) game. But before it could truly expand, this game desperately needed more players. Atari may have made the hardware, but we needed a game to show us that incredible software could also come from outside sources, sources that would have otherwise stayed locked away on the inside. In 1982, Pitfall! was that game, the third-party game first in our hearts.

TOO BIG TO FAIL

In 1979, Atari had a monopoly on the video game market—not just the machines you used to play the games but also the games themselves. You bought an Atari 2600 to play games made and published by Atari. Like vertically integrated golden age Hollywood film studios that owned their own theaters, it was Atari all the way down.

There's nothing inherently wrong with companies making their own games for their own hardware. Far from it. When you fully understand a piece of technology, you can make the best use of it as you develop your game. And who knows technology better than the company that made it? Even today, some of the most acclaimed games are the first-party games that console manufacturers like Microsoft, Nintendo, and Sony make for their own systems. These games need to be fabulous because they don't just sell themselves, they sell consoles.

The problem was, in its first years the Atari 2600 didn't have distinct first-party games. All games were Atari games whether you liked it or not, and the company had absolute control over its money printing platform. It was a harmful arrangement, robbing consumers of potential choices they didn't even know were possible and causing console game development innovation to stagnate from lack of competition. Even worse, anecdotes suggest that the culture inside Atari had rapidly declined, with reports and allegations of rampant drug use and gross sexism. Without anyone to challenge them, though, why would Atari's bosses change? First-party games shine because they know their home hardware so intimately, but when disgruntled employees know their company intimately, they know how to burn the house down and shine on their own.

ACTIVE VISION

Video game companies have historically been terrible at highlighting the immensely skilled artists, programmers, and testers—the real human beings who craft the products that get all the love and money—a problem that still plagues the industry today. The key creatives behind the most famous games of all time remain largely anonymous. Old 1980s games even featured fake credits to stop star workers from being poached by rivals. Even this book, unfortunately, will mostly give credit to individual designers for work done in reality by their large, talented teams. Today's union organizers have all sorts of advice for video game workers looking to collectively organize their labor to improve conditions, but in 1979, David Crane and his partners had far fewer options.

Crane joined Atari just as the 2600 truly began taking over the world. Flush with cash thanks to a Warner Bros. buyout, Atari put its programmers to work making games to rake in even more cash. And rake in cash they did. After reading a marketing memo, Crane realized his own games made fully by himself, like *Outlaw* and his console port of Howard Delman's arcade game *Canyon Bomber*, had brought in $20 million. So why was his salary still $20,000? Crane then combined his games' profits with games from three other colleagues: Larry Kaplan, Alan Miller, and Bob Whitehead. Turns out this Gang of Four was responsible for 60 percent of Atari sales. In a world where all home console games were Atari games, that number becomes even more staggering. Unfortunately (if unsurprisingly) corporate bosses saw no need to reward the creators actually responsible for the company's success. They weren't rock stars to be celebrated, just cogs to seemingly be exploited. So these guys, unlike cogs but very much like rock stars, up and quit Atari with no clue what to do next.

What could they do next? How do you start a home console video game business after you just quit the only home console video game business? Ultimately, early video game history doesn't differ that much from early computer history. It's a lot of the same nerdy people with a nerdy set of skills and a rebellious hacker ethos. The Gang of Four just had to hunker down in a garage and build from scratch something that had never been built before. Like any good Silicon Valley tech start-up, the gang even had a benevolent venture capitalist helper, their attorney, Jim Levy. Together, Crane,

Kaplan, Miller, Whitehead, and Levy formed Activision, short for Active Television, which honestly might be a better name for video games than "video games."

Using knowledge gained from their time inside Atari, where they had apparently made the most popular games, the gang pushed the 2600 further than it had ever been pushed. The team made beautiful games, games you would never get from Atari itself. The company made a splash at the 1980 Consumer Electronics Show, despite a smear campaign from Atari and whispered threats against retailers who considered carrying Activision games. When underground tactics didn't work, Atari sued Activision, claiming the reverse-engineered business model violated nondisclosure agreements. If Activision wanted to make games so badly, it could go make its own console instead of hijacking Atari's.

Fortunately, the courts disagreed. Expert witnesses, including Jerry Lawson, demonstrated how one could develop for the 2600 without stealing secrets. Instead of going away, Activision simply had to pay Atari licensing fees to keep making Atari 2600 games. Third-party developers still pay similar licensing fees to put their games on consoles. Third-party video games became a real thing in 1982, and in that same year *Pitfall!* proved why they were worth the wait.

NABBING THE TREASURE

The pressure of Activision's dramatic creation led to quite the diamond with *Pitfall!*, a game where you collected diamonds along with gold, silver, and cash. You'd never believe the system you played *Pong* on could also play a game like David Crane's *Pitfall!* The game earned its exclamation point. The jungle threw so many thrilling challenges to overcome, from swinging on ropes to staying out of crocodile jaws. It was a huge adventure on a console where some other games could barely put two blocks together.

Pitfall! also looked like an adventure. The lush, foliage-filled scenery created an atmosphere and vibe wholly different from first-party Atari games. The box art featured a rainbow trail coming from the swinging

hero, and the game's actual color palette didn't disappoint. Speaking of that hero, *Pitfall!* also gave us Pitfall Harry, a dashing adventurer in a time when most game characters were, again, nothing but literal squares (like in *Adventure*). He traveled through uncharted lands before Nathan Drake and raided tombs before Lara Croft. The same way the Atari 2600's release paralleled *Star Wars*' release, *Pitfall!* came out one year after *Raiders of the Lost Ark* and took much inspiration from Indiana Jones's pulpy, two-fisted debut.

Activision's founders already knew their games made money. With *Pitfall!*, now they got to keep it. *Pitfall!* sold four million copies on the Atari 2600, making it one of the top-five bestselling games on the system and putting it far ahead of many Atari-developed games. Several other Activision games also cracked the one million mark. These games were individual winners, but in reimagining what games could be they also improved gaming as a whole. They made room for more players to compete. Like Jerry Lawson's cartridges, third-party games were vital for opening video games up into a real market and ecosystem for everyone, not a closed-off monopoly subservient to one shortsighted bean counter.

First-party and third-party games now coexist in peace. We even have second-party games, games technically made by external studios but in close collaboration with first-party companies. Activision is also no longer the scrappy, inspirational upstart it once was. It has become its own big, bad behemoth, capable of great games but seemingly even more ruthlessly obsessed with chasing profits at the expense of human labor than Atari was. The company's culture allegedly became so toxic it prompted a lawsuit from the State of California. Numerous stories poured in from workers alleging widespread systemic abuse. Microsoft moved to acquire Activision, absorbing the original third party into a first-party juggernaut, but there's still much damage left to repair.

Still, without third-party companies like Capcom, EA, Konami, Ubisoft, Square Enix, indie publishers, and, yes, Activision, gaming would be a whole lot smaller, duller, and less diverse. *Pitfall!* is a real treasure.

E.T. CRASHES AND BURNS

Third-party games can, regrettably, cause as many problems as they solve. Jealous of Activision's success, new third-party publishers flooded the Atari 2600 market, hungry for moola and with little appetite for quality control. These games were trash, otherwise known as shovelware, because cynical publishers think shoveling games in bulk at poor customers will turn a profit no matter how bad the games are. The most high-profile, and most damaging, piece of shovelware came from attempting to cash in on *E.T.*, one of the best movies of all time.

In the summer of 1982, Steven Spielberg directed *E.T. the Extra-Terrestrial* with the care and craft of a master artist. He got audiences to fall in love with a boy bonded to an alien. Warner Bros. wanted to turn that love into dollar signs by rushing an *E.T.* video game onto store shelves just a few months later, that Christmas. Programmer Howard Scott Warshaw got paid a hefty sum to make the impossible five-week deadline all by himself. He had only thirty-six hours to figure out the concept, the length of today's intentionally high-pressure self-imposed game jam development challenges. Although Atari published the game (proving that first-party games can also be shovelware), *E.T.* was conceived of by businesspeople, not game developers.

Unlike modern games, simple retro games didn't always need multiple years to finish development. That said, *E.T.* began the dubious trend of terrible licensed movie games being terrible because they were so clearly half-baked. In theory, *E.T.* the video game has you trying to collect phone parts while avoiding government agents. In practice, the game is an unplayable, incomprehensible mess where you constantly fall into pits and spend what feels like hours stretching out E.T.'s neck to float back up. You do at least eat Reese's Pieces.

Atari was so convinced *E.T.* would be a smash hit, the company didn't even bother to test the game before producing millions of cartridges. The disaster that followed changed gaming forever. No one wanted this awful game. The poor kids that got duped into buying it returned it as fast as they could. Atari took a financial hit so devastating the company went into debt. The shock caused the video game industry as a whole to crash in 1983, and it largely stayed dead until Nintendo revived it in 1985. Atari got stuck with so many unsold *E.T.* cartridges the company had to bury them in a secret New Mexico desert landfill. The lesson? Corporate hubris can turn even the cutest alien buddy into the angel of death for an entire nascent art form.

1983

DRAGON'S LAIR

THE CARTOON OF THE YEAR

GUIDE BRAVE KNIGHT DIRK THE DARING THROUGH
A GAUNTLET OF MEDIEVAL TRAPS BY CAREFULLY
OBSERVING ANIMATED SCENES AND PRESSING
THE PROPER BUTTON IN TIME.

PRESS START

Video games as a medium crave respect. Gaming doesn't just want to make more money than movies and music and books, it wants the same level of mass praise and critical appreciation. It's a young, hungry medium eager to be taken seriously. Sometimes, this manifests as jealousy for more established art forms. So when a game especially wants to prove its worth, it may grab elements from other "serious" sources for some secondhand prestige. However, while some art forms can easily turn into one another, on a fundamental level video games aren't movies. When games try to be something they're not, that clash produces strange, not fully successful, but still fascinating final products. It produces Dragon's Lair, our game/cartoon of the year.

THE SECRET OF BLUTH

In 1979, disillusioned animation director Don Bluth had just quit Disney and was ready to take some risks. Having worked on classics such as *Sleeping Beauty*, *The Jungle Book*, and *Winnie the Pooh and Tigger Too*, Bluth felt confident enough to form his own animation studio and dream up new cartoon classics out from under the mouse's thumb. In 1982, his team released its first feature, fantasy film *The Secret of NIMH*. Even if Bluth's name never became Disney-level famous (especially as his films became overshadowed by the Disney Renaissance films of the 1990s), he carved out a nice niche in the animated landscape with films like *An American Tail*, *The Land Before Time*, and *All Dogs Go to Heaven*. Shout-out to *Titan A.E.* fans.

When game designer Rick Dyer watched *The Secret of NIMH*, he didn't just become a Bluth fan, he became Bluth's partner. Dyer and his company Advanced Microcomputer Systems had been struggling to fully realize their new arcade game concept. They wanted to combine the adventurous fantasy storytelling of *Colossal Cave Adventure* with the untapped interactive filmmaking potential of a radical new technology called LaserDiscs. With the hiring of Bluth's team to work on *Dragon's Lair*, all the pieces finally clicked into place.

You don't ask a classically trained animator to draw a bunch of low-res sprites, so how would Bluth apply his talents to a video game with 1983's visual limitations? *Dragon's Lair*'s big innovation was how it took advantage of LaserDiscs. The ancestors of optical discs like CDs and DVDs, LaserDiscs could fit far more data in smaller packages compared with competing storage options at the time. With more memory, arcade machines with built-in LaserDisc players could include more content. So what did *Dragon's Lair* include? Lavishly animated cartoon sequences crafted by Bluth and his team. Dirk the Daring traveled the castle with style and fought over-the-top monsters. Animators referenced *Playboy* photos to bring Princess Daphne's buttery-smooth movements to life, and boy, did that show. It's no surprise the game

got published by Cinematronics, who had previously championed the game-changing visual power of cutting-edge vector graphics tech. Hollywood production value meets video game fun. That mix sounds like chocolate and peanut butter, but the reality was more like oil and water.

MORE VIDEO THAN GAME

Here's how *Dragon's Lair* actually works: You drop in your quarter and watch a few seconds of feature-film-quality animation. Dashing knight Dirk the Daring walks up the bridge to the looming castle as he sets out to rescue Princess Daphne. Suddenly, he falls through the bridge and gets attacked by a sea monster. Here's where you, the player, come in. With lightning-fast reflexes, you must press the proper button that makes Dirk attack. Since you can't really control the cartoon, pressing the right button actually plays the triumphant footage showing Dirk successfully fending off the beast. If you fail, the game instead spins up a clip showing Dirk meeting a PG-rated death and turning into a skeleton. That's *Dragon's Lair*. The whole game consists of these vignettes strung together. Guide Dirk through the door on the left. Make sure he doesn't fall into the bottomless pit. Run him up the chessboard to defeat the shadowy enemy. Do it all by watching the animation and nailing each cue.

If that only barely sounds like a game, it's because it *is* barely a game. *Dragon's Lair* is Simon Says, but you have to intuit the pattern instead of having it explicitly told to you. It's a movie, so you have to stick to the script. But also, that script isn't always clear. The connection between the action on-screen and the inputs players must enter don't always sensibly sync up. Why do I need to hit the same button multiple times to avoid one trap? That's probably intentional. If you memorized *Dragon's Lair* perfectly, you could watch all the animation in less than half an hour. So it's no wonder the game uses the classic retro game trick of artificially increasing the difficulty to keep players playing (and paying) longer.

Despite this format's flaws only growing more glaring with time, *Dragon's Lair* truly did look like nothing else in its era. Like vector graphics, cramming a whole Don Bluth cartoon onto a LaserDisc blasted the game into the future, however unsustainable that future was. In the arcade social setting, even watching the game was a delight. Arguably, *Dragon's Lair* was more fun to watch than to play. Watching was kind of the whole point.

MOVING PICTURES

Dragon's Lair found an audience and soon became a full-blown franchise. While they had to sacrifice the LaserDisc animation, *Dragon's Lair* ports and spin-offs were released on everything from the Mac to the Game Boy Color. In 1984, Dyer and Bluth teamed up again for *Space Ace*, a sci-fi *Dragon's Lair* follow-up.

Other developers tinkered with *Dragon's Lair*'s interactive movie concept. The infamous full-motion video (or FMV) genre took the *Dragon's Lair* format but replaced the expensive animation with cheap, live-action footage. Games like *Mad Dog McCree*, *Sewer Shark*, and *Wirehead* are the closest things video games have to schlocky, *Mystery Science Theater 3000*–tier movies so bad they're ironically hilarious. In 2015, Sam Barlow finally pulled off the impossible and made a legitimately fantastic FMV game called *Her Story*, an engrossing detective thriller tasking you with searching a database of live-action interviews to crack the case with the power of your own reasoning.

A whole game of nothing but responding to videos may get old, but modern developers realized they could just sprinkle little bits of these sequences into their games to make even the passive parts of their stories feel more active. In a game, cutscenes refer to movies that typically happen in between levels to advance the stories. Gamers tend to dislike cutscenes because they buy games to play them, not watch them. However, a quick time event (QTE) is a cutscene where players must press a corresponding button to make sure the cutscene happens as it should.

When Kratos rips open a Greek deity in *God of War*, you have to hammer on the X button until the bloody spine fully pops out. QTEs also don't get much respect from gamers, who see them as a relatively lazy excuse for gameplay. Still, QTEs are basically brief snippets of *Dragon's Lair* happening inside otherwise normal video games, so it's not like the idea doesn't have a historical precedent.

Besides, no one should gatekeep what is and isn't a video game. *Dragon's Lair*—and the interactive movie genre it started—absolutely has fans. Some people will play these games so much they memorize their patterns perfectly, and that's no different from chasing high scores in any other arcade game. On a first date, I took a woman to a Barcade (a bar with arcade games in it) and watched her play an impressively long game of *Time Traveler*, a hologram-based FMV game designed by Dyer but not Bluth. I married that woman. Don't hate on FMV games.

Video games combine all sorts of creative fields: visual art, music, writing, design. So it makes sense for game developers to draw from other art forms; that's how the medium grows. By creating an entire Hollywood cartoon only to retrofit it into a barely interactive and borderline unfair arcade game, *Dragon's Lair* perhaps took too big a bite from another medium for its own good. But it's important to test those boundaries. Flaws and all, nothing as weird, memorable, or ambitious as *Dragon's Lair* could ever be a mistake.

ULTIMA III IS ULTIMATE

In 1983, if you wanted the deepest take on fantasy gaming, the *Ultima* franchise had the games for you. Legendary designer Richard Garriott, known by fans as Lord British, spent years trying to translate the role-playing mechanics of tabletop games like Dungeons & Dragons into video game form. With each new entry in his *Ultima* series, he got one step closer to replacing pen and paper with pixels.

There's probably a case to be made for crowning almost any *Ultima* as game of the year, but *Ultima III: Exodus* stands out for a few reasons. It was the first entry Garriott published under his own new company Origin Systems. With fully animated characters and a musical score, the game looked and sounded better than any PC RPG before it. You now controlled four party members instead of one, which vastly deepened your role-playing options, and the game's story marked the end of the Age of Darkness, the first third of the overall narrative.

Six more games followed for a total of nine mainline *Ultima* games. The series had a massive impact on the burgeoning RPG genre. Meanwhile, the revolutionary 3D dungeon locales in spin-off *Ultima Underworld* eventually morphed into the first-person shooter genre. Origin Systems may be gone, and Garriott is currently too busy flying into outer space to make games, but *Ultima* remains ultimate.

CHRONO TRIGGER (1995)

My gaming life is split into two distinct phases: life before *Chrono Trigger*, when I'd play just about any platformer or fighting entry you'd throw at me, and life after *Chrono Trigger*, when I started demanding actual narratives and compelling characters. *Chrono Trigger* made me a lifelong RPG fan, but it also cursed me with the knowledge that nothing will ever re-create the experience of playing it, not even its sequel *Chrono Cross* (though *Xenogears* came achingly close).

Like the mysterious End of Time, *Chrono Trigger* is something I always come back to, be it for the comfort of its epic story, its unmatched Yasunori Mitsuda soundtrack, or the (perhaps naive) idea that you and a bunch of friends can prevent an impending apocalypse. In uncertain times, hope can take many forms. For me, it's an RPG from 1995.

—DEVINDRA HARDAWAR,
senior editor at Engadget

XENOGEARS (1998)

There is a war going on inside of you. You are, every day of your life, swimming with no life jacket in the sea of your subconscious, grabbing at whatever bubbles up and clinging to it like a sailor flung from a ship in a storm. "See!" you say as you grab the next object, before you even know what it is. "This! This is truth!" before it slips away from you, sinking back down into the depths, only to be replaced by something else you can't quite identify moments later. It is a cyclical struggle that would drive you mad if you didn't have more important things to consider, like whether or not you were about to die.

And all for what? What is the meaning of all this? Where does it lead? The war inside you rages on, day after day, leaving you confused, helpless. Hopeless.

The solution to this dilemma? You are going to kill God.

Welcome to *Xenogears*. It's not a game. It's a literal journey into your subconscious, and you've got a ticket whether you want one or not.

—JOE ZIEJA,
voice actor, author, and musician

1984

TETRIS®

THE COMMUNIST GAME OF THE YEAR

ARRANGE FALLING BLOCKS INTO SOLID LINES
AT THE BOTTOM OF THE SCREEN. ONCE YOU FORM
A LINE IT DISAPPEARS, BUT IF YOUR SCREEN
COMPLETELY FILLS UP, IT`S GAME OVER.

PRESS START

Tetris is perfect, the only video game with truly no flaws whatsoever. From an empire at the end of its rope emerged an incredible, immaculate, enduring object that transfixed the world. The only way to make **Tetris** better is to spread it farther, put it on devices you can take with you no matter where you go. Few games receive the acclaim and success of **Tetris**, but then again few games deserve the acclaim and success of **Tetris**. Like a left-wing collective, **Tetris**'s individual, fragmented pieces come together with a common purpose to create an unbreakable whole.

THE SOVIET MIND GAME

The book *1984* paints a picture of a dystopian future where an authoritarian regime (similar to Stalinist Russia and other totalitarian dictatorships) represses the truth and rules society with an iron fist. In the actual year 1984, the USSR was only a few years away from collapsing, clearing the way for American capitalism to be the only hegemonic global superpower. Hooray. But people, not states, are what really matter in this world. In 1984, Russian computer engineer Alexey Pajitnov was tinkering with new ways to entertain people with the power of technology.

Inspired by childhood puzzle pastimes, Pajitnov designed a game about arranging tetrominoes, or shapes made of four squares. Tetrominoes include blocks shaped like *T* and *L*. He combined the words "tetra" and "tennis" to create *Tetris* on the Electronika 60, a type of computer used by the Computer Centre of the Soviet Academy of Sciences. Since the Soviet Union didn't believe in intellectual property, *Tetris*'s journey to the rest of the world took many forms and involved many legal disputes. However, in the post-USSR world of 1996, Pajitnov eventually teamed with Henk Rogers, the entrepreneur who helped get *Tetris* on Nintendo platforms, to create the Tetris Company, where he could finally receive compensation for his groundbreaking work.

Tetris never hid its Russian roots. Western marketing pitched the puzzle as "The Soviet Mind Game." But the game's specific cultural identity is more than just a fun Easter egg anecdote, or an explanation for the game's distinct music and box art featuring Moscow's St. Basil's Cathedral. *Tetris* has collectivist—dare I say communist—ideas built into its very design. This may be butchering a semester of art history class, but Russian Constructivist philosophy prized art that could actually be enjoyed by common working people as opposed to decadent and detached elites. Art should serve a function in society, as should technology. Society needs entertainment, and with *Tetris*, Pajitnov used technology to create art that served that purpose for millions of people from across all classes.

Tetris's whole gameplay loop also feels satisfying in a socialist way. It's your job to put together these flailing, disconnected pieces into a strong, uniform whole. That's not the same thing as devaluing individuality. In fact, the optimal way to quickly determine how a tetromino can complement the others, how it can best achieve the collective goal, is to understand and appreciate the shape's individual qualities. Which blocks will best fill which gaps? Every *Tetris* player knows the long piece is the lifesaver. *Tetris* started out in black-and-white but eventually used color to make each tetromino look distinct. Seeing all the different colors as you build your stack further demonstrates how *Tetris*'s cerebral victories come from many working together as one. Some angry gamers insist that video games shouldn't be political, that anyone claiming otherwise is just trying to push a nefarious agenda. But *Tetris* is proof of how every game, every work of art, can't help but absorb the politics of its surroundings. This simple game about blocks demands more brain power than you think. The Soviet Mind Game, indeed.

HOOKED ON A FEELING

Tetris got remade, remixed, and rereleased many times over the years. In keeping with the game's collectivist themes, some of the best new versions of *Tetris* came up with new ways to expand the game's multiplayer modes. In typical *Tetris* multiplayer games (like the delightfully named *Tetris: The Grand Master 3 Terror Instinct*), whenever you clear lines, you send "garbage blocks" to your opponent's field to clutter up their board and give them less room for error. However, if your foe can skillfully clear these garbage blocks, you'll get garbage blocks dumped on you, making for dramatic reversals of fortune.

Imagine the chaos then if ninety-nine *Tetris* players all competed at once using those rules. You'd get *Tetris 99*, combining *Tetris*'s singular joy with battle royale mass mayhem. Outlasting every other opponent through sheer block-stacking grit feels like blood-pumping euphoria. For a different, chiller kind of euphoria, Tetsuya Mizuguchi's *Tetris Effect: Connected* slathers the familiar game with gorgeous, trippy, neon visuals and trance music to guide players on a personal journey of synesthesia. It turns *Tetris* into something downright spiritual. In the game's sublime multiplayer cooperative mode, each player begins on their own separate board. Eventually the music swells, and all three boards combine, allowing the teammates to help each other in the same shared space. More socialism! You'll start crying as the game's soothing theme song says, "It's all connected, we're all together in this life."

When you play any good puzzle game, you get pulled into the zone. *Tetris* is such an unbelievably incredible puzzle game, scientists literally created a term for how it rewires your brain to perceive its patterns even when you aren't playing. If you see falling blocks in your sleep, you're experiencing "the Tetris effect." That's sacred geometry, game design that shatters any barriers between your brain and hands and pure reflexive instinct. The best, smartest *Tetris* players can operate at blazing-fast speeds even with invisible tetrominoes, inventing new handgrip techniques to shave milliseconds off of world records. Aside from endurance, the only thing stopping you from playing *Tetris* forever is that the game's algorithm inevitably spits up too many S and Z blocks to neatly fit together in time. But you feel like you could play *Tetris* forever, which speaks to *Tetris*'s captivating, perfect power.

THE PERFECT COMPANION

One way to play *Tetris* forever is to always have it with you, and you can do that only if you have a portable video game system. *Tetris* launched on all sorts of devices, but the 1989 Nintendo Game Boy version has to be the most significant. After Atari proved that people wanted to play video games at home, Nintendo designers Gunpei Yokoi and Satoru Okada asked if people wanted to play video games on the go. With *Tetris* on Game Boy, we got a resounding yes.

The Game Boy—a gray brick with modest 1970s calculator tech and a pea-soup-green screen—couldn't do that much. But it could let you play *Tetris* on a plane, on a bus, or in bed. Really, what more did you need?

Tetris, which was often bundled with the system, is the best-selling Game Boy game (more successful than even *Pokémon*) at 35 million copies sold. Everyone played Game Boy *Tetris*. There's a picture of Hillary Clinton playing a Game Boy, and you know she was playing *Tetris*. There's even a Game Boy on display at Nintendo's New York museum that survived a Gulf War bombing, and while the exterior is charred, the *Tetris* game inside keeps on ticking. The pair can survive anything, anywhere. With *Tetris* as a system seller, the Game Boy's massive sales (118 million units) popularized the idea of handheld gaming alongside console gaming, arcade gaming, and PC gaming.

Without handheld gaming, without the Game Boy's successors like the Nintendo DS or PlayStation Portable, we also wouldn't have mobile gaming, where hundreds of millions of people discovered the convenient joys of playing games on the phone they already carry with them every day. Puzzle games especially excel on mobile as short portable time wasters you can't put down. Next time you whip out your phone to match gems in *Bejeweled* or bounce balls in *Peggle*, thank Game Boy *Tetris*. You can also just play *Tetris* on your phone. EA sold more than 100 million paid copies of *Tetris* on mobile, making that version alone one of the best-selling games of all time.

Tetris is perfect. There isn't a single thing you could do to make its core puzzle fundamentals any better. It's that magnetically attractive and mathematically sound. That's not to say all video game quality should be treated like a sterile number problem to solve. Games messier than *Tetris* may also display more passion and ambition than a puzzle game is capable of. But with *Tetris*, all the pieces come together like an expertly argued manifesto. You carry it with you on your portable device because you want it to become a part of you. *Tetris* makes you whole.

AT THE MOUNTAINS OF MARBLE MADNESS

Marble Madness gave us fun with smooth spheres. Designed by Mark Cerny, who later went on to become an architect of Sony's PlayStation consoles, *Marble Madness* dared players to guide marbles through each level without falling into the abyss. These isometric levels were M. C. Escher–esque realms full of ramps and pyramids and seemingly impossible checkerboard architecture. Just trying to make sense of the environment was half the challenge.

The other half of the challenge was guiding the marble itself. While other arcade games used buttons or sticks or other digital movement, *Marble Madness* used a mouselike trackball control for analog movement. Analog movement doesn't see inputs in binary on-off states. You didn't just move the marble left or right. By spinning the physical trackball at various speeds in different directions, you could roll the marble quickly or carefully inch it forward. Accurately translating fluid analog movement and acceleration would eventually prove essential for controlling games in 3D. It also just felt fancy and cool.

Video game controllers have now become basically standardized. A handful of buttons, a couple of analog sticks, a few triggers, and maybe a social media button. But not all games have the same needs. Fighting games need fight sticks. Virtual reality needs motion controls. *Steel Battalion* needs its comically massive, forty-four-button giant robot mech suit controller, complete with windshield wipers. And *Marble Madness* needs a trackball. When we're willing to rethink how we control games, we embrace infinite new possibilities for games.

SUPER HEXAGON (2012)

Begin. Tap at the screen, feel the pulse, let the rhythmic beat envelope you. Get into that high-flying fugue state. Steer your orbiting avatar precariously between screen-sweeping barricades. Let the downplayed tones of writer Jenn Frank's narration lull you into a cradled calmness, a centeredness.

Game over. Hit Start again without skipping a beat. Nothing can keep you from the task, from the journey straight down to the center. I'm guiding my indefatigable little pyramid, skimming across the shifting event horizon into an unknown place, a high score without shape or dimension. Aiming not for leaderboard boasting rights but escape: An escape from the tedium of the world. Escape from the rocking cacophony of the subway car I'm sitting in. Escape from the work and drudgery that this train car is carrying me toward. The hexagon leads me away from that fluorescently bright, harshly clinical reality, toward a comfortingly dark center. Not a place of fear, but of comfort, sketched with mathematical precision.

I will be endangered, threatened by the blockades appearing ceaselessly in front of me. I will be enveloped, swallowed whole by their frenzied encircling. But I am centered, I do not die but am folded within, strung through and latticed like a perfect cat's cradle. On the other side I feel wrung out and smoothed over. I feel the horizon perceptibly widen, as the thrumming bass drives me forward, as the shapeless voice beckons me home.

—YUSSEF COLE,
artist and game critic

1985

THE CITIZEN KANE OF THE YEAR

RUN AND JUMP THROUGH SIDESCROLLING LEVELS,
USING MARIO`S NIMBLE PLATFORMING
CONTROLS TO OVERCOME TRICKY OBSTACLES,
IN YOUR QUEST TO RESCUE PRINCESS PEACH.

PRESS START

hat is the Citizen Kane of video games? Blame gaming's ongoing pursuit of prestige and desire to be treated like "real art" for the greatest and dumbest argument among people who think about this hobby for a living. In the world of cinema, Orson Welles's 1941 masterpiece sits on a lofty perch, not only because of its undeniable quality but because of what it did for filmmaking as a whole. Citizen Kane expanded the artistic possibilities of what a movie could even be. Calling it the greatest movie of all time is maybe a safe, almost cliché answer now, but think about how amazing something has to be that decades later folks are tired of saying how amazing it is.

What has gaming offered that even approaches this level of quality and importance within its own medium? The gamer hive mind has debated this issue for years, sometimes proposing that video games don't even have a Citizen Kane equivalent yet, and we need to work harder until that mythical game comes to pass. I disagree. I've felt extremely confident about my personal answer to gaming's Kane conundrum for quite some time now. What's the Citizen Kane of video games? Easy, it's Super Mario Bros.

TROJAN TOYS

The year was 1985. Orson Welles had just passed away, shortly after voicing Unicron in *The Transformers: The Movie*, a toy commercial with way more artistry than anyone could've imagined. The video game industry remained in a financial slump following Atari's *E.T.* calamity and the subsequent Great Crash of 1983. Arcades still chugged along, but nobody knew if home console gaming would survive or if the Atari 2600 was the beginning and end of that era. No one was rushing out to buy an Atari 5200 or Atari 7800, that was for sure.

Nintendo, however, still believed console gaming had a bright future ahead of it. Nintendo's president Hiroshi Yamauchi tasked engineer Masayuki Uemura with constructing a device to bring arcade games home. In 1983, the company launched its 8-bit console the Famicom (or Family Computer) in Japan. After some initial technical difficulties, the product became a huge success in its home region. So bringing it over to North America was only a matter of time.

How could Nintendo crack such a hostile market? Originally, the company planned to partner with Atari to distribute the console. However, the deal fell through due to seeming violations of exclusivity agreements after rival ColecoVision showed off *Donkey Kong* running on its next-gen home computers. Besides, given Atari's ultimate fate, Nintendo probably dodged a bullet there. Meanwhile, retailers (still burned from the *E.T.* fiasco) had zero interest in devoting valuable shelf space to dumb video games nobody wanted. So how did Nintendo convince the United States to give video games a second chance? Just like *Transformers*, they smuggled in artistry under the guise of a toy commercial.

Duck Hunt and *Gyromite* may be the most fun Trojan horses in video game history. On their own, they're fine enough games. In *Duck Hunt* you aim the Zapper light gun controller at your TV to hunt ducks or else a dog will laugh at you. When you press the trigger, the screen flashes white, allowing the gun's IR sensor to transmit its position. *Gyromite* uses a similar IR technique to send commands to a toy robot, Robotic Operating Buddy (R.O.B.), so players can pick up and stack physical blocks. These were cool hardware gim-micks, something Nintendo would become increasingly known for over the years, but the real genius of these accessories is that they allowed Nintendo to market its console as a cool toy rather than a lame video game box. The renamed Nintendo Entertainment System (NES) came with the Zapper gun and R.O.B. robot packed in, making it much more alluring to skeptical retailers. Remember how the Atari 2600 looked like any other piece of 1970s tech to make users more comfortable? The NES pulled off a similar scheme. Unlike with the Famicom, where players had to plop in prominent cartridges up top, NES players inserted cartridges through a slick front-loading slot that felt a lot like using a VCR. Just make sure to blow on those cartridges first (don't actually do this).

These tricks got the NES into potential players' hands, but sooner or later those players would realize they had actually bought a video game console and not just some weird, plastic Japanese electronics. To truly make people care about video games again, Nintendo's flagship title couldn't be a toy—it had to be a game better than anyone's wildest imagination. And boy, Shigeru Miyamoto's *Super Mario Bros.* sure is that game.

THE MUSHROOM XANADU

Citizen Kane didn't invent movies. You may argue it reinvented them, but nearly half a century's worth of amazing films, the entire silent era and early talkies, had already hit theaters by the time Welles decided to go from broadcasting fake alien invasions on the radio to dunking on William Randolph Hearst on-screen. Likewise, a vibrant era of gaming history predates *Super Mario Bros.* Nearly a decade's worth of incredible, influential games brought us to this point. *Super Mario Bros.* wasn't the first game starring Mario. That was *Donkey Kong*. It wasn't even the first *Mario Bros.* game. In 1983, Nintendo released a *Joust*-esque arcade game simply called *Mario Bros.*, where you control the plumber and his brother, Luigi, traveling through pipes and hopping on enemies within a single screen. *Super Mario Bros.* didn't invent video games, but it did reinvent them.

Like *Citizen Kane*, *Super Mario Bros.* absolutely blew up the shared assumptions of what a video game could even hope to achieve. It opened the door to a wondrous world with its Mushroom Kingdom, filled with curious blocks and sinister turtles and Koji Kondo's catchy city-pop-inspired music. No offense to *Pac-Land*, but there had never been a 2D sidescrolling platformer as athletic as *Super Mario Bros.* before. No longer confined to a single fixed arcade screen, players freely traveled left to right through expansive seamless levels where new joys and new dangers always waited just out of sight. Due to memory limits, once you moved forward, you couldn't move back, but why would you want to?

To teach players how to survive and thrive in this foreign land, *Super Mario Bros.* employed game design so genius that any serious modern developer still studies it to this day. Without you even realizing, the very first seconds of the game tell you everything you need to know about jumping on enemies, collecting power-ups, and bashing through blocks. From there, level layouts wordlessly communicate concepts in safe contexts before removing the guardrails and testing the player's skill. The game demands you master Mario's elegant, endlessly enjoyable movement controls, and entices you with rewarding secrets. Run to build momentum as you vault over pits you thought looked impossible to cross. Shoot a fireball to knock the enemy Lakitu out of his cloud and ride it yourself. Hop over the false ceiling to find the hidden Warp Zone to skip entire worlds. You couldn't play this with a basic Atari joystick. You needed the NES controller, with its two face buttons and game-changing plus-sign-shaped directional pad.

From a technical perspective, *Super Mario Bros.* was an impressive feat in the early days of 8-bit consoles. But those technical breakthroughs were in pursuit of a larger goal, of fulfilling a vision. *Citizen Kane*'s Gregg Toland didn't use revolutionary deep focus cinematography techniques just because they looked cool—they served the larger artistic purpose of showing the full sweep of Kane's life. *Super Mario Bros.* used the NES console's capabilities to create another *Pong*-tier leap forward, an unprecedented paradigm shift for gaming as an entertainment art form.

THE PLUMBER PROPHET

The rest is history. *Super Mario Bros.* and the NES became smash hits in North America, just like they had in Japan. Nintendo ushered in a new age for console gaming—for gaming, period—that continues strong to this day. Mario became not only Nintendo's mascot but the face of video games as a whole. Even if you don't care at all about video games, chances are you know Mario is a big deal. And to think, so many of Mario's signature qualities (mustache, hat, overalls) are there only because they made his details easier for Miyamoto to draw on primitive hardware. Mario's iconic Italian American identity is incidental bordering on accidental, a wonderful example of how game design choices lead to utterly bonkers yet totally logical end points.

Even if you are a gamer, you may take for granted just how deep Mario's influence runs. It's so all-encompassing, you just don't notice it anymore. I'm not talking about seemingly blatant rip-offs like, oh, *The Great Giana Sisters*. I'm talking about how basically any video game from 1985 onward that's about moving from left to right and jumping, sometimes while dealing with enemies, would look drastically different without *Super Mario Bros.* That's a lot of games.

Super Mario Bros. established such a universally understood gameplay language that one of the best ways to teach game design is through *Super Mario Bros.* Nintendo's Wii U console may have failed financially, but it had plenty of wonderful games, and arguably the best one was *Super Mario Maker.* This level editor gives you all the tools you need to make your own custom 2D sidescrolling Mario levels. As you live out your fantasy of designing your own Mario game, you'll educate yourself on everything you need to know about making any great game, from balancing the difficulty curve to properly introducing and expanding a mechanic to the satisfaction of surprising and delighting the player. It's all right there in *Super Mario Bros.*

Citizen Kane analogies have always been hacky, bordering on insecure. What actually matters is that *Super Mario Bros.* isn't just famous. It revolutionized its own medium like no video game before it.

HEADING OFF ON THE OREGON TRAIL

If you want to learn about American pioneer life and antiquated diseases on your school computer, start your trek across *The Oregon Trail*. The game began life in 1971 as a pure text adventure by Paul Dillenberger, Bill Heinemann, and Don Rawitsch. The 1985 version by R. Philip Bouchard added a brand-new graphical interface, along with substantial new content, creating the educational classic we all remember.

As players young and old headed west in a digital version of the nineteenth-century USA, they contended with simulated versions of real hardships. Hunt for food, travel through harsh weather, and do whatever it takes to make sure the community survives. Simple visuals made the evocative text more immersive. Sure you received a score, but just reaching the end in one piece after hundreds of miles was its own victory.

Death-by-dysentery memes aside, *The Oregon Trail*'s ubiquity did a great service for gaming by demonstrating the educational value of the medium. It's one thing to read about history, but you'll really remember frontier life if you have to act it out yourself. Educational games are an underappreciated video game cornerstone. They remind us that games, especially games for kids, can offer experiences more valuable than just scary violence. Don't disrespect Carmen Sandiego.

As our understanding of real history grows, our historical games should grow alongside them. The most recent version of *The Oregon Trail* features much more input from Indigenous historians, who provided insight on language and music and hairstyles, which honestly makes it cooler and more accurate than 99 percent of other, more "realistic" games that take place in this country.

RED DEAD REDEMPTION (2010)

Rockstar gambled big-time on *Red Dead Redemption*, the now-classic Wild West game that could be all things to all people. You could be Zen and travel the land by foot or on upgradable horses, stopping atop a mountain to envision the gobsmackingly realistic sunset vistas of America's canyons and rivers. Or you could sling your gun as you uncovered the story of John Marston. In the downloadable content's Sasquatch quest, Rockstar turned the tables. You kill four, then find a fifth bigfoot under a tree, head in hand, full of the constant sorrow that comes with genocide. He cries that someone has killed off the rest of his kind. You may as well kill me, he tells you. Think about it. The same *Grand Theft Auto* maker that made it easy for you to kill was now asking you to think hard about what killing means.

—HAROLD GOLDBERG, founder and editor in chief of the New York Videogame Critics Circle

RED DEAD REDEMPTION 2 (2018)

I played *Red Dead Redemption 2* during a very tumultuous period in my personal life, and it was just the thing I needed to escape from myself for a bit. There is so much within the game that is never meant to be truly beaten or solved. Things that are only there to add flavor or open up more questions about the world.

Red Dead Redemption 2 is a game that is all about coming to terms with the choices you've made in your own life. The hero of its story must learn that it's never too late to choose to try to be a better person, even if it's to no avail. And sometimes, don't we all need a little reminder that the stories we tell ourselves and the ways in which we see ourselves are never set in stone?

—ABBY RUSSELL, comedian and producer known for her work at Giant Bomb, G4's *Xplay*, and more

1986

THE JAPANESE ROLE-PLAYING
GAME OF THE YEAR

TRAVEL A FANTASY LAND, HELP VILLAGES IN NEED,
AND FIGHT MONSTERS IN TURN-BASED BATTLES.
GROW STRONGER AS YOUR QUEST CONTINUES AND
TACKLE TOUGHER CHALLENGES UNTIL YOU CONFRONT
YOUR ULTIMATE FOE, THE DRAGONLORD.

PRESS START

erds love stories, and nerds love math. It's no surprise then that we love tabletop role-playing games, or RPGs, since they seamlessly combine the two. Experience your imagination's most epic fantasy adventure alongside your friends? All governed by dice rolls, complicated equations, and a lot of reading? Dungeons & Dragons still reigns supreme after nearly fifty years with that winning formula. As video games became nerds' new preferred pastime, though, tabletop RPGs needed to embrace this new interactive environment. But how?

Descended from centuries-old war-gaming, tabletop RPGs thrive with pen and paper (or as podcasts). But how would you adapt them into a video game? In 1986, every strength gaming provided came with a caveat. Games could easily crunch numbers more efficiently than human players, but rigid technology didn't allow for the communal impro-visation participants craved. With a video game, you could see your character and all their weapons and loot, but that took away just a little magic from the version you dreamed up in your head. Tabletop RPGs offered a fantastic foundation on which to build a new genre, but the video game console RPG clearly needed to be its own unique, special thing. Few games are as unique and special as Dragon Quest, the Japanese RPG that first solved this riddle.

THE LUMINARY

Developers had tried turning RPGs into video games well before 1986. The genre's nature, from its patient gameplay to its text-heavy narratives to its long play sessions, made it a poor fit for the arcade, but Western games like *Ultima* and *Wizardry*, with their labyrinthine dungeons and first-person monster battles, appealed to the types of people willing to learn how early PC gaming worked in the 1980s.

One of those people was Japanese game designer Yuji Horii. After cutting his teeth making games for Nippon Electric PCs, Horii wanted to make an RPG like those aforementioned classics. However, instead of developing the game for computers, Horii believed that a console game could greatly expand the genre's audience. Consoles sat at the perfect intersection between PC depth and arcade immediacy, so Horii's console RPG would deliver the same substance but in a far more accessible form. Plus, Japanese players couldn't get enough of the wildly popular NES. Working with developer Chunsoft and publisher Enix, Horii created *Dragon Quest* for the NES, the first Japanese console RPG (now known as JRPGs). His design was so smart, you'd swear RPGs were built for console gaming all along.

REALMS OF REVELATION

Like the tabletop games that inspired it, *Dragon Quest* revolves around a battle system that expresses exciting fantasy adventures as cold hard logic. When you play an RPG, you make many choices about attacking and defending and using items. Your decisions matter. However, numbers play an arguably larger role in determining your success or failure. In *Dragon Quest*, your skills are subservient to statistics. How much damage you deal, how much damage you take, how many magic spells you can use, how often you can dodge enemy attacks. It's all a roll of the digital dice, all part of the role-playing metaphor that reflects how skilled your character is supposed to be in the fiction.

This conceit alone gave *Dragon Quest* a vastly different feel than other console games at the time. Many games like to test the player's real-world reflexes. They challenge you to shoot or jump or solve puzzles as quickly and skillfully as you can. Traditional RPGs don't care about that. They just want you to explore the world at your own pace. While other games forced you down linear levels, *Dragon Quest* set you free in an open kingdom where you could go in any direction. As you traveled, unseen monsters picked fights with you without warning. But when these battles (random encounters) actually began, players and enemies took turns attacking each other, no rush. Consider all your options and savor the experience.

RPGs are still games, though, and games need challenges to keep players engaged. So how did *Dragon Quest* keep players constantly striving to be the strongest warrior possible? A controversial technique called grinding. Remember that everything in an RPG is just a collection of competing numbers and equations. A *Dragon Quest* enemy was only hard because its attack and defense stats were higher than yours. As you slayed monsters, you earned experience points, and once you earned enough points you leveled up and increased your stats. With higher stats, you could demolish foes that had previously wiped the floor with you. Later RPGs let you funnel upgrades toward specific attributes for you and your party, allowing even greater character customization.

So why is grinding controversial? RPGs often test your patience more than your skill. Some players think having to kill the same low-level skeleton creatures over and over again to improve themselves is a tedious and arbitrary endurance test, not meaningful gameplay. That's the downside. The upside is that with enough time, any player can theoretically grow strong enough to beat the game if they just keep playing. Not everyone can or wants to become good at games through raw real-world reflexes, and grinding gives them an achievable (if longer) path forward. Before, video game characters only became strong through temporary power-ups like magic mushrooms or goofy guns, but grinding permanently made you more powerful. Think of grinding like exercising, two activities many folks find relaxing rather than tiresome. Again, these are all well-understood concepts now, but not when *Dragon Quest* launched. The JRPG asked brave console players to approach gaming just a little differently, and rewarded heroes for keeping an open, adventurous mind.

CHAPTERS OF THE CHOSEN

As a video game, *Dragon Quest* couldn't be a tale told around the campfire the way tabletop RPGs are. While players had some freedom, the overall experience had to be much more authored. So if players must hear this one story, Horii wanted to ensure it was a story worth hearing, or rather, worth reading. Fortunately, Horii had the perfect background for this task. His previous game, *The Portopia Serial Murder Case*, was a text-driven adventure game. It was also an early example of the Japanese visual novel genre, a type of interactive fiction all about guiding players through a linear literary narrative. Horii just swapped one familiar set of tropes with another. Goodbye, murder mystery; hello, fairy tale.

The original *Dragon Quest* didn't feature much of a story beyond its epic high-fantasy archetypes. Defeat the evil Dragonlord to reclaim the Sphere of Light and return peace to the land. But even having a story at all, with characters and plot points conveyed through the game itself, put it far past other games of the time. Besides, the first game didn't have to knock it out of the park. Now that Horii had established these gameplay systems, he could use them to tell all sorts of new stories in the future, yet another quality taken from tabletop RPGs. Players act out countless stories in their Dungeons & Dragons campaigns, but the underlying rules remain the same. The same is true for *Dragon Quest* and its stand-alone sequels, for JRPG franchises in general.

Dragon Quest's story, with its medieval knights praying at vaguely Christian churches for wisdom, on paper sounds more European than Japanese. This trend goes beyond video games and probably traces back to Western art's aesthetic influence on manga, starting with Osamu Tezuka's Disney-inspired *Astro Boy* in 1952. Still, we can't talk about *Dragon Quest* specifically without mentioning its extremely anime-inspired artwork drawn by Akira Toriyama, the creator of global manga mega-franchise Dragon Ball. As with the story, the character and monster designs needed to be so cool you wouldn't even care that you didn't imagine them yourself. No one draws cooler characters than Goku's dad. *Dragon Quest*'s blue smiling slimes, its most basic enemies, are absolute icons.

The first *Dragon Quest* didn't quite catch on in the United States, despite receiving the more aggressive title *Dragon Warrior*. Nintendo had to give copies away with *Nintendo Power* magazine. However, in Japan, *Dragon Quest* is a wildly famous, incredibly popular, absolute phenomenon. A semi-true urban legend says that new *Dragon Quest* games can only launch on weekends in its home country; otherwise too many people will skip school and work to pick them up.

With this success, Yuji Horii's streamlined, console-friendly, tabletop RPG/video game/visual novel cocktail created a new genre. The greatest JRPGs paint sprawling worlds with gripping narratives in ways only literature can do. They stir such passion in fans that players will spend fifty, sixty, seventy hours tackling these adventures, finishing every side quest, and maxing out their stats. Without *Dragon Quest*, you don't get *Final Fantasy*, *Pokémon*, *Chrono Trigger*, *Shin Megami Tensei*, and the list goes on. "Japanese role-playing game" outlived its usefulness as a title years ago. Today, plenty of American games clearly model themselves off the genre, too. But whatever you want to call it, *Dragon Quest* gave us a thoughtful but action-packed form of interactive storytelling that exists only in video games.

DIE, CASTLEVANIA, YOU DON'T BELONG IN THIS WORLD

Dare to step into the monster mash that is Konami's *Castlevania*. In this spooky sidescroller, players pick up a whip and lash their way through a castle full of mummies, werewolves, Frankenstein's monsters, and more. Only once Simon Belmont slays Dracula himself will the nightmare end.

Early games in the series put players through brutal gauntlets. However, as producer Koji Igarashi exerted more influence over the series, it began incorporating more JRPG ideas, like leveling up. *Castlevania: Symphony of the Night*, the most acclaimed game in the franchise, features an elaborate and interconnected castle to explore. Like a vampire fiend, *Castlevania* lies dormant before springing back to life. Nothing this diabolical will truly die.

FINAL FANTASY TACTICS (1997)

Before *Game of Thrones* lit hearts on fire, *Final Fantasy Tactics* brought together the classic iconography of the *Final Fantasy* series and the historical in-fighting of the Wars of the Roses. Alongside this meaty narrative, a deep job system and the vast amount of units that can make up your squad combine to give you a great deal of flexibility in how you approach strategic encounters. Every time I return to *Final Fantasy Tactics*, there's a new way to tackle every fight. The ability to leave a unique tactical fingerprint is why it has such longevity twenty-five years later.

—MIKE WILLIAMS,
staff writer at Fanbyte

CASTLEVANIA: SYMPHONY OF THE NIGHT (1997)

I earned my first paycheck in 1998. I immediately blew it on *Castlevania: Symphony of the Night* and two *South Park* T-shirts. The T-shirts have long since disintegrated in the wash, but *Symphony of the Night* is timeless.

The journey of Dracula's tormented son, Alucard, emphasizes exploration over *Castlevania*'s usual whipping and platforming. Gothic beauty takes the place of grimy dungeons. And wherever you go, you're accompanied by an angelic soundtrack that validates the "symphony" in the game's title

Castlevania games were never the same. Hell, action-adventure games were never the same. Nearly every 2D adventure game aspires to be *Symphony of the Night*, and only a scant few have succeeded in touching it. It's like trying to grab a handful of moonlit mist.

—NADIA OXFORD,
cohost of the *Axe of the Blood God* RPG podcast

DIABLO II (2000)

I first experienced *Diablo II* through an animated trailer that debuted at E3, back when E3 was the only way to see if a new game was coming out. I remember sitting in front of my three-foot-tall CRT television, legs crossed, mouth agape. After we begged and pleaded with my father for months to let us play, he finally gave in and got the game for me and my four brothers.

We had a small setup in the basement: old, repurposed cubicles with separate computers for each of us. This allowed for a small bit of privacy while playing, but also kept us close enough to coordinate co-op fights. As the only girl of five children, and the eldest, I got to use my father's machine.

From the command center, I strategically determined the best way to take down Blood Raven, one of the first bosses in Act 1. Three of my brothers used the Necromancer's Raise Skeleton power to keep aggro; I used the Sorceress's Ice Bolt to keep her slowed and crowd controlled to hell until my other brother could finish her off as the Amazon. Upon her death, each of our characters spoke a special voice line, as if to reward our efforts. We also scooped up the loot, the other reward. Today, so much of gaming is competitive; one player must fight against another. *Diablo II* showed me how people can bond through games.

—DAPURPLESHARPIE,
streamer, host, fighting game community organizer

1987

THE ADVENTURE OF THE YEAR

EXPLORE THE LAND OF HYRULE AS COURAGEOUS
HERO LINK. SOLVE PUZZLES, CONQUER DUNGEONS,
AND DEFEAT THE EVIL GANON TO RECLAIM THE
MYSTICAL TRIFORCE AND SAVE PRINCESS ZELDA.

PRESS START

There are too many amazing games released each year to highlight in a single volume. Hard cuts must be made. Spoiler: There is no chapter dedicated entirely to **The Legend of Zelda: Breath of the Wild**. Blame **Fortnite**. A masterpiece that launched alongside the Nintendo Switch in 2017, **Breath of the Wild** is considered by many to be the greatest video game of all time. It's certainly in the conversation. Its wide-eyed sense of wonder, its mysterious and melancholy minimalism, and its perfect union of modern open-world design with old-school Nintendo craft is gush-worthy. It gifts players with an unparalleled sense of freedom and exploration that speaks from the deepest parts of gaming's adventurous heart. But that heart first began beating with 1987's **The Legend of Zelda**, the game that conjured mythical magic right from the start.

THE HERO OF TIME

Shigeru Miyamoto sees the fun all around us. Miyamoto's games amplify unacknowledged joys that already exist in the real world, and in his own life. Mario didn't jump through some abstract void, but across the rolling green hills Japanese commuters saw scroll by them through their train windows. After taking up gardening, he produced a strategy game about controlling ant-sized plant creatures called *Pikmin*. Like every dog owner, he knew the love these pets provide, so why not give that to players with *Nintendogs*? Miyamoto's hobbies inform his next projects so directly, Nintendo placed him under a gag order in 2008 forbidding him from discussing what he does in his free time, lest he accidentally leak upcoming plans. So what inspired *The Legend of Zelda*, the crown jewel of Nintendo franchises? Miyamoto wanted to create a game that captured what he felt while exploring forests and caves as a child. He wanted players to see new sites, discover new mysteries, and experience the simple freedom of going out into the world to do whatever you want. What a beautifully pure feeling to adapt into a video game.

It's remarkable, outrageous even, how well *The Legend of Zelda* pulled off the ambitious-bordering-on-impossible goal it set for itself as an NES game in 1987. It was the first video game cartridge where players could save their progress with battery-powered backup, because the journey is too huge for a single sitting. When you begin your quest, you can head off in any direction you like, with no one telling you what to do or where to go. Of course, what you should do is go through the door and get the sword from the old man. As he says, "It's dangerous to go alone," and you'll need something to fight the monsters waiting for you off-screen. But the game doesn't explicitly force you down this road. This initial encounter sets the tone for the entirety of the game.

Eventually, you'll learn the lay of Hyrule's land, creating a mental map of the overworld and acquiring actual maps for the discrete dungeons you can enter. Each dungeon is like a little game unto itself as you fight enemies, solve puzzles, defeat a boss, and reclaim a useful item alongside a piece of the Triforce relic. These designed dungeons make up the bulk of *Zelda*'s more bespoke gameplay, and completing them advances its larger story about saving the kingdom from the evil pig-man Ganon. Weapons you acquire from dungeons, like the boomerang and bow, make later challenges significantly easier. Meanwhile, items like the raft and stepladder are necessary for accessing distant parts of the overworld. There is a loose order in which you should finish the game, along with its postgame Second Quest.

However, *The Legend of Zelda* goes out of its way to make sure you never consciously sense this order, that you never feel constricted. It empowers you to forge your own path through Hyrule and find its secrets organically. Every key you find might open a hidden door. Every wall might be an invisible passage if you put a bomb next to it. Don't wait for someone to hold your hand like a child (even if you are one). Trust your instincts and follow your destiny to wherever it may take you. *Zelda* promises you'll go somewhere fun. *Zelda* shares some traits with RPGs like *Dragon Quest*, from the exploration to the overhead map to the fantasy theme. But the game is very much not an RPG. It's all about the action and adventure, not the numbers. This philosophy is how *The Legend of Zelda* imprinted itself on a generation of players like no other game before it, and cemented itself as Nintendo's original epic.

POWER, WISDOM, COURAGE

The Legend of Zelda on NES sired one of the most acclaimed series in gaming. *Zelda* games dominate many "best video games of all time" lists. The franchise is an embarrassment of riches. Take your pick! *A Link to the Past* supercharged the NES formula for the 16-bit Super Nintendo. *Ocarina of Time* brought the legend into 3D, while *Majora's Mask* remixed it into a time-loop horror game. Stay tuned for the whole chapter devoted to *Wind Waker*'s nautical left swerve. Even the less-beloved recent entries like *Twilight Princess* and *Skyward Sword* still exhibit more baseline quality than numerous other contemporary games.

As beloved as all these games are, though, some fans insist that they don't quite live up to the original. These games sent Link to stunning locations throughout the history of Hyrule, and challenged players to solve even more ingenious dungeon puzzles, like soaring through a sea of clouds on your giant bird before rearranging an entire temple to shift where its water flows. But these later *Zelda* games also doubled down on plot and linear solutions in a way that shifted their design away from the original's focus on open-ended exploration. This isn't an inherently bad thing. Sometimes the only way to guarantee players get the best experience is to take away some of their freedom. And it's not like the original *Zelda* didn't also subtly guide players toward making the choices the game wanted them to make at certain times. There are some hyperbolic claims that these excellent *Zelda* games are some betrayal of the original, and arguments can be made illustrating how they drifted away from the spirit of adventure players found so appealing in that first game.

Regardless of where you stand on this topic, it's clear *Breath of the Wild* was the course correction we didn't know we needed so badly. On one hand, the game seems to borrow shamelessly from other modern open-world games like *Grand Theft Auto*, *Skyrim*, and *The Witcher*. But on the other hand, much of what makes *Breath of the Wild* so magnificent traces back to the NES original. *Breath of the Wild* takes its ancestor's uncompromising dedication to mystery and lack of player restraint, and masterfully updates that ethos with massive 3D scope. No matter what direction you head off in, you're bound to find some incredible secret. On your expedition, maybe you won't succeed at first. A powerful enemy might kill you or you could fall down a mountain. Don't get discouraged, don't be afraid. Try again and you will create your own victory. Because you did it yourself, you'll feel that accomplishment right in your soul. That's *Breath of the Wild*, that's *The Legend of Zelda* on NES, that's what it's like to stumble into caves as a child. It's all the same grand adventure.

With *The Legend of Zelda*, Nintendo wrote gaming's most enduring foundational myth. Like a folktale, it constantly repeats, some details changing while themes remain constant. It's a call to action beckoning us into the enticing unknown. Answering that call, forging your own path, isn't just fun—it makes you a hero. *The Legend of Zelda* pushes players to view video games as singularly powerful portals to adventures, to legends, of their very own.

MIKE TYSON'S PUNCH-OUT!! IS THE REAL CHAMP

With *Mike Tyson's Punch-Out!!*, Nintendo turned Little Mac's championship Bronx boxing matches into epic battles. When video games take place in a more constrained space, developers can pack in much more detail without taxing the hardware. Only with its modest scope could this game achieve its greatest trick. Inside the ropes, *Punch-Out!!*'s developers dedicate basically the entire screen to the wonderfully wacky cast of cartoon boxers that loom large as your opponents.

From pathetic Glass Joe to towering King Hippo, *Punch-Out!!* characters form a master class in 8-bit sprite art and animation. This is one of the few NES games that still holds up visually today. The boxers are so detailed that you can recognize how one of them is a real athlete, Mike Tyson himself. Beyond looking pretty, the animation powers the game's fighting system. To beat *Punch-Out!!* boxers, you must analyze their patterns and rhythms, and strike when they're vulnerable. These bosses are one big puzzle. Bald Bull rushing toward you? Punch him in the stomach with expert timing to stop him in his tracks. Mike Tyson just wink at you? Get the heck out of the way.

Before it was an NES game, *Punch-Out!!* debuted in arcades, without Mike Tyson. Nintendo also removed Tyson from later versions of the game, replacing him with the generic Mr. Dream. Given Tyson's controversies, we'll probably never see him return, and getting any new *Punch-Out!!* game seems unlikely. The 2009 Wii remake was fantastic, but that twenty-first-century, Obama-era game made it really hard not to notice how all the boxers were really just gross ethnic stereotypes. That game didn't even include offenders like the Italian Pizza Pasta or the Russian Vodka Drunkenski. Squeaky-clean modern Nintendo most likely doesn't want to deal with this potential headache. Still, *Punch-Out!!* on NES will always be there ready for you to get in the ring.

THE LEGEND OF ZELDA: LINK'S AWAKENING (1993)

Link is an adventurer, like any video game protagonist. Shipwrecked, he washes up on the island home of a powerful dreamer and is told if he wants to go home, he must wake him up.

Like most dreams, the island is strange but familiar. Characters from other games appear in places they do not belong, faces you recognize are given names you do not. When you're young, none of this will have significance. Then one day, as an adult, you will wake up, having glimpsed the dream again, ever so briefly. You will wonder what you lost. You will try and dream again.

—JOSHUA RIVERA,
entertainment writer at Polygon

THE LEGEND OF ZELDA: OCARINA OF TIME (1998)

The Legend of Zelda: Ocarina of Time is a true love letter to nature. From the frozen depths of Zora's Domain to the fiery peaks of Death Mountain, every part of the sprawling map is an unforgettable sight.

The puzzled-packed temples were nestled among dense forests, desert landscapes, and enormous lakes, resulting in a deeply immersive experience. There were plenty of poignant plot twists, too, involving Link's connection to the Great Deku Tree and the wildlife of Hyrule.

When I played it as a fifteen-year-old, it was the first time I'd seen the natural world depicted so joyously in a video game. After all these years, no game has even come close to balancing the forces of darkness and light as majestically as *Ocarina of Time*.

—TOLA ONANUGA,
senior editor at *Business Insider*

1988

THE SEQUEL OF THE YEAR

RUN AND JUMP THROUGH IMAGINATIVE MECHANICAL
LEVELS AND SQUARE OFF AGAINST THE DEADLY
ROBOT MASTERS TO GAIN THEIR SIGNATURE WEAPONS.

PRESS START

eplayability, the ability to replay a game again and still have a great time, is highly valued in video games. After you watch a movie, read a book, or listen to a song once, you'll always know exactly how it goes. But your second, sixth, or hundredth playthrough of a video game can be a unique experience, even if only slightly. It's like theater. If you love a game, though, eventually you'll want something new. You'll want a sequel.

Like any sequels, video game sequels must walk the fine line between giving the audience what they already like and introducing them to fresher, and hopefully better, ideas. Video games have an especially wide variety of options for threading this needle, since the question of what defines a game has so many different and fascinating potential answers. What can change? What has to stay the same? Will fans accept a whole new genre? Should we ditch the main character? Can we just stick to the formula? There's no one-size-fits-all solution. Creators making a game sequel have to decide what's right for their game and their franchise. If you're looking for a sturdy sequel template, the ideal follow-up, look no further than Mega Man 2.

VIDEO GAME 2: ELECTRIC BOOGALOO

After the NES got its first wave of big hits, developers got to work making the sequels. By 1988, we already had *Castlevania II: Simon's Quest*, *Super Mario Bros. 2*, and *Zelda II: The Adventure of Link*. Fans of these franchises couldn't wait to dive back into their favorite game worlds. However, with these three examples in particular, what you thought you were getting probably didn't line up with reality.

In *Castlevania II*, you still whip monsters and try to stop Dracula once and for all. But instead of traveling through a single punishing castle, you travel the whole countryside, complete with tedious backtracking and nonsensical clues told to you by villagers. *Super Mario Bros. 2* isn't really a sequel to *Super Mario Bros*. The game is actually *Doki Doki Panic*, an unrelated Nintendo game about Japanese television mascots who yank vegetables from the ground. When Nintendo brought the game to North America, it slapped Mario characters in and literally made the entire thing a dream. *Zelda II: The Adventure of Link* ditches the overhead view for a sidescrolling perspective and more elaborate combat and magic systems.

When you look back, it rules how radically different these sequels are. Their new ideas genuinely changed their series for the better. Still, you couldn't blame anyone who played the original games for feeling perplexed by these genre-hopping follow-ups. These games feature the same characters, stories, and general aesthetics as their predecessors, but games are also their gameplay. Gameplay is often what makes us invested in those other elements, so maybe you don't need to throw the baby out with the bathwater. *Mega Man 2*'s makers at Capcom already knew they had a powerful weapon, a Mega Buster, they just needed to upgrade it.

ROCK AND ROLL

Released in 1987, the first *Mega Man* is a stone-cold NES classic. Not only did players need to jump past tight, tricky obstacles, they also had to keep up their offense and shoot at the enemies shooting back at them. Balancing these challenges gave the game a steep but sublime learning curve. The NES controller gives you two buttons and a D-pad, perfect for moving, jumping, and shooting. *Mega Man* took that simple, elegant set of commands to new heights.

Mega Man's formula was already a phenomenal starting point. The level design was genius. Letting players decide which order to tackle the Robot Master bosses gave some appreciated freedom. Using a defeated boss's gun felt incredibly empowering, and realizing that each boss was weak to another boss's gun added a meta strategy layer of trying to figure out the correct order. Freeze the fearsome Fire Man with Ice Man's Ice Slasher gun, then use your new Fire Storm gun to blow up Bomb Man.

Even *Mega Man*'s universe felt like home right away. Sure, it's pretty much just *Astro Boy* (so pretty much robot *Pinocchio*), but that's fine! You play as a robot child with a gun arm working with good grandpa scientist Dr. Light to stop bad grandpa scientist Dr. Wily. Artist Keiji Inafune drew up awesome and adorable mascot-worthy 1980s anime character designs, way better than the hideous box art Americans got stuck with. Plus, in Japan Mega Man is named Rock Man, and his sister is named Roll. Speaking of music, *Mega Man* also set the standard for unbelievably catchy NES chiptune music. People rejoiced when Capcom added *Mega Man* music to Spotify. Fill up multiple MP3 players with *Mega Man* fan remixes. *Mega Man* rocks.

IT AIN'T BROKE

Mega Man 2 acknowledges that *Mega Man* rocks. The original already had a lot of great stuff going for it, and it didn't need to be completely reimagined. A sequel just needs to be bigger and better, and that's exactly what *Mega Man 2* is. Pitting you against eight iconic Robot Masters instead of six, including colorful fan favorites like Metal Man and Crash Man, and featuring levels with even more inventive themes and layouts, the sequel further challenges your trusty running and gunning skills.

Hop on platforms before the wind blows you out of the sky. Shoot your way through a forest of deadly robot animals. Mega Man can use new Energy Tank health items to give him an edge in battle. While *Mega Man 2* is similar to *Mega Man*, don't think you're getting ripped off. This is a new game with entirely new stages. It's the game you thought a *Mega Man* sequel should be, and when you played it, you were happy you were right.

The first *Mega Man* didn't sell that well, but *Mega Man 2* was a smash hit, commercially and critically. *Mega Man 2* is still considered the best entry in the classic series, a vital part of the NES canon. When people think of video game sequels that top the original in virtually every way, *Mega Man 2* tops that list. The music? Even catchier.

Emboldened by this mandate, Capcom pumped out four more *Mega Man* games in this exact style on NES, and while the quality varies, overall there's little to complain about. As hardware improved, *Mega Man* evolved in various directions. Some, like shooter/platformers *Mega Man X* and *Mega Man ZX*, felt like natural extensions of the NES formula, just substantially upgraded for modern machines. Others, like the 3D action-adventure *Mega Man Legends* and RPG *Mega Man Battle Network*, were the kind of radical reinventions the original sequels definitely were not. In the late 2000s, Capcom even went back and made a pair of brand-new 8-bit throwback *Mega Man* games, *Mega Man 9* and *10*. Nostalgia aside, they're just genuinely awesome NES-style *Mega Man* sequels. *Mega Man 2* proved that it's okay to just make more awesome *Mega Man* sequels.

JOHN MADDEN PRESENTS FOOTBALL

Football dominates the American sports landscape. It's one of the most popular sports, and sports are just games but in real life, so it stands to reason that sooner or later football would also become a popular video game. NES players may have nostalgia for *Tecmo Bowl*, but football's true path to gaming gridiron glory began with *John Madden Football* in 1988.

Although the late coach/broadcaster John Madden and his larger-than-life endorsement were here from the start, the first *Madden* didn't even have the NFL license. Players also all looked white until producer Gordon Bellamy got Black athletes in the game and on the cover in 1995. Regardless, this PC game prided itself on being a simulation of the sport so realistic you could call it educational. Yes, *Madden* had a simple Quick Mode, but the real game revolved around stats and determining the proper plays and accounting for weather conditions. Unlike the more accessible arcade sports genre, simulation sports games re-create as much of the real sport as accurately as possible. With a game as mechanically dense as football, you really need to pay attention to keep up.

From there, *Madden* built a Super Bowl–worthy sports game dynasty. The game's designer, Trip Hawkins, also founded Electronics Arts. EA then became one of the most powerful publishers in the business thanks to the massive success of *Madden* and other sports games like hockey, golf, and soccer with its broad international appeal. In the early days, *Madden* wasn't even licensed by the NFL. Now, *only Madden* can use the NFL license, thanks to an exclusivity deal. NCAA football games (including the HBCU-themed *Black College Football: The Xperience*) used to provide some kind of alternative, but with college player licensing rights so tricky, *Madden* is pretty much the only football game in town.

Some players complain that annual sports games like *Madden* don't change enough. All they do is update the roster and charge another $60. Those people aren't always wrong. Recent *Madden* games included impressive cinematic story modes that play out like dramatic sports movies, but those experiments are not the norm. However, as far as game sequels go, sports games face a fascinating dilemma. Aside from minor rule tweaks, football as a sport doesn't change from year to year, so why should the game? *Madden* aims to represent the NFL football experience the best it can, and considering the millions of *Madden* fans who show up every season like clockwork, the games must be doing something right. Touchdown?

ASSASSIN'S CREED: BROTHERHOOD (2010)

Ezio Auditore da Firenze is the GOAT. Ubisoft's *Assassin's Creed* franchise leveled way up when they introduced him in *Assassin's Creed II*, but the iconic Templar-killing Italian stallion didn't reach his full potential as a video game protagonist until series highlight *Assassin's Creed: Brotherhood*.

Brotherhood is the gold standard for what a game sequel should be. It starts with an operatic opening act that literally blows Ezio's world to hell and immediately launches into even better iterations of the things people loved about *II* (Thrilling action! Engaging characters! Roger Craig Smith purring into the microphone!). Accompanying Ezio as he rebuilds the Assassin guild in Rome brings the player into the fold as a keeper of secrets, a leader of rebels, and a maker of history—all things that make the *Assassin's Creed* games great. *Brotherhood* is one of the greatest.

—ALEXIS NEDD,
author of *Don't Hate the Player*

1989

SIMCITY

THE UTOPIA OF THE YEAR

BECOME AN URBAN PLANNING GOD AS YOU STRIVE
TO CREATE THE PERFECT TOWN. PLACE BUILDINGS,
PAVE ROADS, SURVIVE A NATURAL DISASTER OR TWO.
THE ONLY THING HOLDING YOU BACK IS YOUR
IMAGINATION . . . AND CITY BUDGET.

PRESS START

Fantasies don't have to be fantastical. Sure, sometimes you want to do something impossible, like fight aliens or travel through time or learn magic. But there are plenty of exciting things you can technically do today, right here on planet Earth, they're just so dangerous or expensive or inconvenient that they might as well be impossible. Fortunately, video games don't discriminate when it comes to making dreams come true. There's no real-world task too boring, weird, or niche to turn into an endlessly enjoyable game. Video games can be the real world, but better. With SimCity, you construct that better world yourself.

INFRASTRUCTURE WEEK

The 1980s PC gaming market hummed along as its own distinct slice of the video game industry, with an energy all its own compared to its arcade or console counterparts. In the UK, young gamers flocked to personal 8-bit home computers, like the ZX Spectrum and Commodore 64, instead of the NES. American designer Will Wright began a long and fruitful relationship with PC gaming when he released his first game, *Raid on Bungeling Bay*, on the Commodore 64 in 1984. This top-down shooter, where players controlled aircraft to bomb enemy factories, received strong reviews and earned Wright enough cash and clout to make something new.

Unlike most gamers, Wright didn't care too much about the shooting in his own game. What captured his imagination were all the overhead maps he created as levels. These island fortresses were rudimentary communities; they shared supplies and expanded over time. If Wright enjoyed making these environments more than bombing them to bits, would players feel the same? For his follow-up project, Wright expanded his level editor into a full-on town-building experience called *SimCity*.

WE BUILT THIS CITY

The "Sim" in *SimCity* stands for simulation. In gaming, a simulation game is any game that simulates some aspect of the real world. *SimCity* simulates the act of building a city. You can begin with a scenario based on an existing location, like Detroit in the 1970s or Boston in the far-off future of 2010. You can also start with a totally empty map. Either way, you get to make your own metropolis. Make sure to include the essentials. Cities need power plants to function. Design a fluid and logical highway system, so your traffic doesn't get jammed. Along with logistics, there are social factors to consider, too—some hospitals, schools, and residential areas might be nice. *SimCity* at times serves as an anthropological experiment on how urban planning (an interest of Wright's) shapes a population's views on crime, leisure, and even religion. Plus, any worthwhile town needs a plan for how to survive a sudden tornado or giant monster.

Making cities takes hard work, in real life and in *SimCity*. Broderbund, Wright's publisher for *Raid on Bungeling Bay*, had concerns Wright's new game was too boring to be successful. Players want to shoot things, not manage construction budgets and zoning laws. There's no real way to win or lose *SimCity*. If you plan poorly, the worst that can happen is your budget runs dry. While that's a very PC-esque approach to game design, console players typically value fast fun over brainy long-term satisfaction, so when Nintendo helped Wright bring *SimCity* to the Super Nintendo in 1991, the game received a lot more game-y features like swanky mansion and casino rewards for a job well done. But fundamentally *SimCity* asks you to put in the work for work's sake.

What some see as boring work, though, others see as the ultimate power trip. A god game is a type of simulation game where players have absolute control over artificial life and guide it toward a successful existence. *SimCity* doesn't go quite that far (for that you'd have to wait a year for *SimEarth: The Living Planet*), but you do hold the fate of an entire town in your hands. In an outside world full of chaos, *SimCity*'s great responsibility provides totally satisfying total control. Click all the pieces together into a perfect clockwork machine, a utopia. Or don't! There's nothing stopping you from building a chaotic, dysfunctional, nightmare town that no human being could possibly live in. Build bridges to nowhere or let police stations crumble into ruin. You can't hurt anybody in a simulation.

It's easy to see why a publisher might be skeptical of *SimCity*. Wright had to create his own company, Maxis, to publish the game. But it turns out Wright's hunch was correct. *SimCity* launched incredibly well and kept on selling for years and years as it got ported to new platforms. PC and console players alike couldn't get enough of the city-building sandbox. As Wright, and other developers eager to emulate Wright's accomplishment, planned their next moves, they all asked themselves, "What else can we simulate?"

IT'S ALL SIMLISH TO ME

SimCity's smash success spawned an entire empire of sim PC games from Maxis and others. Turn any wacky hobby into a new PC game by sticking the word "sim" in front of it. Raise an ant colony in *SimAnt*. Run your own *SimFarm*. Navigate the US health-care system with *SimHealth*. These are all real. Build theme parks or perform surgery with purposefully awkward comedy physics. If you want to simulate managing a football team, running a video game development studio, or spraying dirty houses with a high-powered hose, there's a game for you. Meanwhile, *SimCity* received all sorts of sequels and expansion packs adding new content. 2013's *SimCity* reboot may have been a big disappointment, thanks to buggy servers and a pointless persistent online connection requirement, but it did reveal that countless players cared enough about *SimCity* to be excited in the first place after all these years.

Then there's *The Sims*. In 2000, Will Wright and Maxis took *SimCity*'s omniscient overhead camera and zoomed it in a little closer. Instead of a game about houses, Wright made a game about the people who lived inside those homes. *The Sims* is a digital dollhouse. You create and take control of a virtual person, a Sim, and guide them through the game of life. Care for not just their bodily needs but their emotional ones, as well. You may not understand their Simlish language, but you'll still feel pride when your Sim falls in love or starts a family or gets a job. Sims can die, introducing personal stakes *SimCity* largely lacks. But if things get too real, buy a wacky expansion pack to turn your Sim into a werewolf or whatever. Hang out in the city with *The Urbz*. Visit an uncannily accurate recreation of Disney's *Star Wars*: Galaxy's Edge theme park courtesy of smart brand synergy.

As popular as *SimCity* was, *The Sims* utterly eclipsed it. The franchise has sold nearly 200 million copies to a largely gender-balanced audience. It reaches mainstream players outside of "traditional" hard-core gamer guy demographics. Through no fault of their own, some people just have a hard time connecting with the nerdier aspects inherent to certain popular video games. But life is the realest thing there is; it's something everyone goes through and understands. The idea of creating and molding a (simulated) living person reaches right into the core of your humanity, and therefore your wallet.

Video game power fantasies can do more than just put a virtual gun in your hand. Games can take something as complex and serious and overwhelming as planning a city, and transform it into something that you can do, something you can't wait to do. Sure, even the most complicated sim games simplify their tasks immensely in order to make games that are even playable, let alone fun and satisfying. Video games, ultimately, can't substitute for the real world. But we're all in the real world whether we like it or not. So let's fire up *SimCity* and try to dream up a better place to live. We can't do any worse than Robert Moses.

RIVER CITY RANSOM PLAYS HOOKY

Asking players to simulate a life adds depth to even the shallowest game genre. *River City Ransom*'s delinquent kids taught us that lesson in 1989. In the late eighties and early nineties, lots of games drew inspiration from the grimy urban vigilante aesthetic. *Double Dragon*, *Final Fight*, and *Streets of Rage* set players loose in apocalyptic, gang-filled streets straight out of *Escape from New York*. The only way to win these beat-'em-ups was to punch and kick everyone around you, walk to the next screen, and do it all again. On paper, Technōs Japan's *River City Ransom* is another one of these games. However, there's more going on than just urban anarchy.

You spend a lot of time in *River City Ransom* walking around town and getting into combat encounters, but your life doesn't stop once the fight finishes. You also have a lot of downtime where you can explore what's actually a nonlinear open world, just presented as a sidescroller. Buy food, go to the spa, read books. This feeds into the game's RPG system, allowing you to increase your stats for later battles. *River City Ransom*'s gameplay also pairs perfectly with its 1950s street gangster teen melodrama. Of course "hot-blooded tough guy" Kunio is the kind of kid from a tough home who gets into random fights and

flunks out of class. It's like a video game version of *West Side Story* or *The Outsiders*.

Even if there was no gameplay reason to perform these side tasks, though, they still create a unique, compelling, and worthwhile rhythm because they mirror real life. With only a handful of tweaks, the indie game *The Friends of Ringo Ishikawa*, by developer Yeo, turns the *River City Ransom* formula into an art game about the futile but oddly poetic aimlessness of teen violence. Before *Grand Theft Auto* on PlayStation, *River City Ransom* let us act out our open-world urban crime dramas on the NES.

KILLER7 (2005)

Goichi Suda's *Killer7* is an art house game if there ever was one. From the second I saw the trailers, I had no idea what I was looking at, but I wanted it because the art just oozed personality. The emphasis on pushing style above everything else was a risky one, but the unwavering style is why the game still feels timeless. The gameplay is simple enough (a first-person adventure game with light-gun-esque shoot-the-core gun combat), but as we all know, gameplay can never be removed from aesthetics. *Killer7* is slathered under so much style that it didn't really need to be anything more, and it benefits from being exactly what it is.

The style is hard to explain. *Killer7* represents the peak of experimental graphic design in every fiber of its being: from the box art to the UI to the fonts used in the written dialogue to the T-shirts that a certain ghost assassin wears. It's part anime, part techno rave party. It's a middle finger to the game conventions of the time, and nearly twenty years later it's as captivating as ever. *Killer7* features samurai tales, angel assassins, a game of Russian roulette for the presidency of the United States, and a centuries-long battle between good and evil. And that's just the first level. *Killer7* is a game that truly cannot be summed up.

—SHAWN ALEXANDER ALLEN,
artist, writer, and game designer

1990

THE SECRET OF
MONKEY ISLAND™

THE GEORGE LUCAS GAME
OF THE YEAR

EXPLORE THE ENVIRONMENT, TALK TO OTHER
CHARACTERS, AND SOLVE PUZZLES TO FULFILL
YOUR SEAFARING DREAMS IN THIS COMEDIC
POINT-AND-CLICK ADVENTURE PIRATE YARN.

PRESS START

galaxy as vast and imaginative as **Star Wars** obviously inspired plenty of great video games. Want to pilot an iconic spaceship? Play **Star Wars: TIE Fighter**. Want to act out adventures that predate the original trilogy by centuries? Take up a role in **Star Wars: Knights of the Old Republic**. With not only a game but also a novel and toys, **Star Wars: Shadows of the Empire** was a multimedia event that aimed to be a movie without a movie. **Star Wars** secured its place in video game history as firmly as it secured its place in the rest of entertainment history.

George Lucas's legacy, however, was always bigger and cooler than even his most famous creation. There was a time when Lucas stood for quality video games that had absolutely nothing to do with Skywalkers and evil empires. If you want to celebrate George Lucas's real impact on video games, celebrate the classic, innovative, and hilarious adventure games Disney has all but erased. Ditch space piracy and pick up good old-fashioned regular piracy in **The Secret of Monkey Island**. Forget lightsaber battles. May Insult Sword Fighting be with you.

ADVENTURE A POINT
AND CLICK AWAY

To make *Star Wars* a reality, George Lucas and his various orbiting teams invented new types of technology-driven filmmaking. Following *Star Wars'* overwhelming success, those teams blossomed into their own separate divisions so they could apply their expertise to new challenges. The visual effects group became Industrial Light & Magic, the go-to studio for bringing impossible images to life on-screen. The graphics group became Pixar and revolutionized animation with its beloved CGI cartoons, and then joined the Disney family years before the rest of Lucasfilm did. The games group became LucasArts, fulfilling Lucas's desire to explore areas of entertainment beyond movies.

Ironically, even if LucasArts wanted to start making games based on its most famous property, it couldn't. In 1979, Atari had the rights to make *Star Wars* games, and although Atari and LucasArts worked together, LucasArts would have to make different adventures. But being forced to make different adventures is what gave us *Star Wars* in the first place and not some *Flash Gordon* fan film, so maybe this was for the best. For its first game, LucasArts did adapt a Lucasfilm property, the 1986 David Bowie/Jim Henson dark fantasy musical fever dream *Labyrinth*. However, just one year later, LucasArts showed the gaming world what it was really capable of with its original adventure game *Maniac Mansion*.

For such a broad-sounding genre, "adventure game" as a label actually refers to something fairly specific. *Zelda* is a game about adventure, but it isn't, strictly speaking, an "adventure" game. In an adventure game, you don't progress by jumping, shooting, fighting, or doing anything you might describe as "action." Instead, you move the story along by exploring your surroundings, collecting items, solving puzzles, and talking to characters. In early adventure games, your environment was usually an expansive and unmoving illustrated image with people and objects laid out

before you. Clicking on something let you interact with it in various ways, and moving to a new screen gave you new things to potentially interact with. They call these adventure games—the adventure games LucasArts excelled at—point-and-click adventures, because that's what you spent most of your time doing.

From the late eighties into the early nineties, LucasArts found itself locked in a bitter rivalry with another company for adventure game supremacy. Sierra On-Line fostered a passionate fan base with adventure franchises like the majestic *King's Quest* and the sleazy *Leisure Suit Larry*. These are important games in their own right, the first text adventures with graphics, vital parts of PC gaming history. Sierra's cofounder Roberta Williams is one of gaming's most celebrated female auteurs.

Between the two, though, I give LucasArts' adventure games the slight edge. This is already a somewhat niche genre, but LucasArts games lean more into its strengths while smoothing some of its inaccessible rough patches. For starters, you can't die in most LucasArts games, freeing you up to experiment and poke around without worry. Adventure games are also so text heavy, so story driven, that they're basically visual novels. LucasArts games push the genre's full storytelling potential with imaginative premises and hilarious writing. While these games may not always have a ton of animation, LucasArts adventure games also have gorgeous pixel art and cutscenes, as sprawling, colorful, and detailed as a matte painting from an eighties blockbuster movie. If you want to experience everything that makes a LucasArts game a LucasArts game, look no further than *The Secret of Monkey Island*, the pirate gold standard.

A CUTTHROAT COMEDY

By 1990, LucasArts had already cranked out multiple games with its SCUMM (Script Creation Utility for Maniac Mansion) engine, the tools it developed to make adventure games. For *The Secret of Monkey Island*, the team introduced various quality of life changes that are now standard for the genre, like dialogue trees and the ability to highlight objects with a mouse instead of typing them into a text field to interact with them. With the gameplay as intuitive as possible, players could more easily become engrossed in the story.

As for what that story was, the team drew inspiration from swashbuckling sources like Disney's Pirates of the Caribbean (the theme park ride, not the movie) and the Tim Powers novel *On Stranger Tides*. While George Lucas pushed his company to get into gaming, he wasn't the one writing any of these games or managing them from day to day. *The Secret of Monkey Island* was chiefly designed by Ron Gilbert, Dave Grossman, and Tim Schafer, all of whom ascended to the status of adventure game legends thanks to their work with LucasArts. Their boundless creativity was on full display in this game's story and world.

You play as young aspiring pirate Guybrush Threepwood as he seeks to prove his worth on Mêlée Island. As you explore the island, you pick up various pirate quests like uncovering buried treasure and calming down a cannibal village. Along the way, you'll strike up a romance with Governor Elaine Marley and contend with the dangerous Ghost Pirate LeChuck.

Adventure games can easily become tedious. You get stuck trying to solve a puzzle because you missed clicking on a small but crucial icon. Or maybe the solution only makes sense according to the game's logic, and not natural human logic. It grows frustrating, and makes victories feel more arbitrary than satisfying, the end of a long farce. But in a comedy like *The Secret of Monkey Island*, this gameplay weakness becomes a storytelling strength. Reading repeated dialogue becomes revisiting favorite jokes. Absurd puzzle answers become punch lines. Even when things go wrong, they always entertain.

Who knew Guybrush could find so many uses for an item as dumb as a rubber chicken with a pulley in the middle? Vanquish a voodoo curse with a bottle of root beer. Using the new dialogue system, you take part in Insult Sword Fighting, vicious rap-battle-style duels where players trade cutting remarks instead of sword slashes. Your opponent says, "You fight like a dairy farmer!" You respond with, "How appropriate. You fight like a cow!" Not just a top-tier comedy writing showcase, it's a genius, gut-busting way to spice up the pirate action without betraying what adventure games stand for. Honestly, if someone told me I was a "contemptible sneak," I would also react as if I'd just gotten stabbed.

LucasArts has a tremendously rich adventure game back catalog beyond *The Secret of Monkey Island*, from *Full Throttle*'s biker gangs to *Grim Fandango*'s world of the dead. Despite this, the developer doesn't make original games anymore. Now known as Lucasfilm Games, the company licenses Lucasfilm properties to other publishers and developers on Disney's behalf. And by Lucasfilm properties, I mean *Star Wars*. Lucasfilm Games exists to manage *Star Wars* games. However, 2022 saw the miraculous reveal of a brand-new *Monkey Island* game, *Return to Monkey Island*, from original creators Ron Gilbert and Dave Grossman. Here's hoping Disney continues to unbury the huge treasure trove that is George Lucas's contribution to interactive entertainment. Everyone, pirate or otherwise, should have a chance to solve *The Secret of Monkey Island* for themselves.

PRINCE OF PERSIA, PRINCE OF PANTOMIME

No game in 1990 felt as cinematic as Jordan Mechner's *Prince of Persia*. This Apple II home computer game played like any other platformer—you jumped past obstacles and fought enemies. However, the stunningly smooth and detailed animation added a layer of never-before-seen realism. The way the Prince waved his arms as he leaped into the air, scrambled his feet as he slowed to a stop, and gathered momentum for his next run looked exactly like a real person, just made of pixels.

In a way, the Prince was a real person. Mechner achieved this effect by recording his younger brother doing various moves and tracing over them while drawing the animations. Cartoonists have used this rotoscoping technique since the beginning of animation itself, but no video game, including *Dragon's Lair*, had used it so effectively before. Mechner used motion capture before motion capture, the 1989 equivalent of gluing Ping-Pong balls to your digital actors. *Prince of Persia* inspired a whole new subgenre of cinematic platformers like *Another World*, *Flashback*, and *Oddworld*.

After a few bad sequels, *Prince of Persia* got a second chance at life when Mechner teamed up with Ubisoft to reboot the franchise in 2003. *Prince of Persia: The Sands of Time* blew players away with its brilliant 3D platforming and loopy time-rewinding powers. You can draw a direct line from *Prince of Persia*'s crackerjack climbing to the historical parkour playgrounds that define Ubisoft's *Assassin's Creed* mega-franchise. So the next time you film your little sibling taking a tumble, hold on to that footage. You might just create the next great Jake Gyllenhaal movie.

JIGSAW (1995)

Plenty of mid-nineties computer games make use of your Macintosh Performa's ability to display thousands of colors, but you mostly find yourself using Z-machine emulators to play through Infocom's back catalog of black-and-white text adventures, words-only puzzlers that insist on addressing you directly in the second person. There's a whole cadre of early Internet denizens who love interactive fiction, too, and keep writing new stuff. Graham Nelson went so far as to write his own programming language to make his text games run on the Z-machine, and in 1995, he released *Jigsaw*.

You are the protagonist, White, time traveling through the twentieth century to foil the antagonist Black's attempts to "fix" history, silently making note each time the two of you are close enough to touch. Nelson—casually, effortlessly, seamlessly—refuses to ascribe a gender to either one of you, and so you the player, a bookish twelve-year-old who will realize in twenty-five years or so that your own gender lies somewhere in between the binary, see yourself for the first time in a video game.

—SARA CLEMENS,
vice publisher of Unwinnable

1991

SONIC ™

THE HEDGEHOG

THE RIVAL OF THE YEAR

BOUNCE INTO ENEMIES, RACE THROUGH LOOPING LEVELS,
AND SAVE CAPTURED ANIMALS WITH STYLE AND SPEED.

PRESS START

hen Sega came for Nintendo, it came for the king. It couldn't afford to miss. Thanks to the NES, Nintendo became the new Atari, the one name that stood for all video games. There were plenty of great third-party games, so Nintendo's first-party catalog wasn't the only reason to buy the system, but Nintendo ruled the industry with an iron fist and dictated strict terms. The Nintendo Seal of Quality may have protected gamers from another E.T. catastrophe, but it also forced publishers to play by Nintendo's conservative rules if they wanted to get just one of their games on the NES. What choice did they have?

It's not enough to have a variety of games. A healthy video game industry needs a variety of hardware, equally viable hardware, to prevent power from becoming too concentrated. One name shouldn't stand for all video games, and in 1991 a new name sped into the market to give gamers a choice, Nintendo . . . or Sega? The modern, multipolar games industry began with the Nintendo/Sega console war. To lead its army, Sega needed not just a game, but a symbol fans could all rally around, a mascot so fast we would follow him into the future. Enter Sonic the Hedgehog.

GENESIS DOES

In the early 1990s, no one thought about video games in terms of console generations that began and ended. When parents learned that they needed to buy a pricey new box every few years so their kids could play the latest games, they were pissed. It was bad enough these Nintendo games wouldn't fit inside the trusty Atari 2600, but what the heck is a Super Nintendo and why can't we play its games on the regular Nintendo? What a rip-off! Video games are technology, though, and technology either upgrades or gets left behind.

Sega's entire strategy revolved around convincing players to leave Nintendo behind. The Sega Genesis launched in 1989, two years before the Super Nintendo. So the public didn't see a battle between two comparable 16-bit systems. We saw a console far more powerful than Nintendo's creaky 8-bit NES. Sega arrived from nowhere to take us into the next generation (as long as we politely forgot about its failed 8-bit Master System).

The Super Nintendo put Nintendo on roughly equal footing when it came to raw horsepower, but Sega cultivated a radically different image compared to its rival. Sega aggressively called out Nintendo for being boring and old and slow. "Genesis Does What Nintendon't." It's a classic marketing strategy for any hungry upstart looking to take down the beloved, established leader. Be cooler. Pepsi is cooler than Coke. Burger King is cooler than McDonald's. Macs are cooler than PCs. Sega is cooler than Nintendo.

Some of this, a lot of it, was empty nineties marketing. However, Sega backed up its bold claims with legitimately forward-looking hardware and software. We still debate whether or not Blast Processing, a custom technique the Genesis allegedly used to run games faster, actually existed. Regardless, the Genesis is a capable 16-bit Japanese machine. To this day folks love the distinct synthesized tunes from its sound chip. Meanwhile, Sega's American branch, led by Tom Kalinske, used its shocking amount of autonomy to bring must-own games exclusively to Genesis. Sports games like *Joe Montana Football*! Musical experiments like *ToeJam & Earl*! Celebrity tie-ins like *Michael Jackson's Moonwalker*! Sequels to *OutRun*, *Space Harrier*, and ports of other awesome Sega arcade games! Old-school Nintendo forced Midway to censor *Mortal Kombat* when the smash-hit arcade game came to SNES, but on Genesis you could fight with all the blood and guts Scorpion and Sub-Zero intended. Sega is cooler than Nintendo!

To top it all off, Sega needed a flagship game, a youth icon of its own, to overthrow Nintendo's Mario as the cool new nineties face of video games. Imagine Mickey Mouse meets Kurt Cobain. If that doesn't sell you on *Sonic the Hedgehog*, nothing will.

IN THE ZONE, THE GREEN HILL ZONE

Sonic the Hedgehog came into this world already a winner. Artist Naoto Ohshima and programmer Yuji Naka won an internal Sega contest to determine who the company's Mario killer would be. Initial *Sonic* prototypes dazzled execs with their fast and fluid platforming, a perfect fit for the Genesis's slick self-image. Sonic's character design fulfilled both gameplay purposes (hedgehogs can turn into maneuverable balls) and aesthetic purposes (his attitude drew inspiration from sneaker culture, pop music, and Bill Clinton). This superfast, spiky rodent oozed cool. He tapped his foot impatiently when you stopped playing. He headlined Saturday morning cartoons, voiced by Jaleel "Steve Urkel" White (one of a few reasons why Sonic is also low-key Black, but y'all ain't ready for that conversation). He made Mario look like a musty old plumber for grandparents. You took one look at this guy and you understood immediately that, yes, Genesis does what Nintendon't.

Fortunately, even divorced from the fleeting console wars nonsense that created it, *Sonic the Hedgehog* is a genuinely great and innovative 2D platformer. Beneath the marketing flash lies real substance. If you tried to play *Sonic* like a *Mario* game you would probably die. Sonic's slippery controls don't mesh well with precise balletic jumps. But Sonic isn't Mario; he's Sonic. He's the Flash but also your adorable pet. Sonic has got to go fast, and so do you. *Sonic* games dare you to never stop running and trust that the exhilarating level design will keep you on track. Every time this blue blur speeds up a looping mountain and back down again, like a roller coaster crossed with a pinball table, players get chills. Enemies are less threats and more tools to maintain your energy and momentum as you bump into them. If you do have to stop, charge up your Spin Dash and you're off to the races once again. Processing so much thrilling information so quickly means you'll often fail to react in time on your first run. But the game never feels like it's holding you back. Thanks to the forgiving health system—if you collect and hang on to even one gold ring—you'll survive. You'll keep moving forward.

Sega couldn't just count on a cool character and cool gameplay to endear its mascot to the public. Every aspect of *Sonic the Hedgehog* had to be cool, and it is. The entire game features a funky and fleshed-out sense of style, wholly unique from what you saw in Nintendo games. According to the game's story, the villainous Doctor Robotnik/Eggman (who looks like a crude Mario caricature) terrorizes Sonic's forest by turning its animals into robots. All throughout the game you'll see this theme of technology intruding on nature. Green hills covered in artificial checkerboard patterns. Mushroom-filled landscapes that give way to industrial chemical plants and neon casino zones. Even something as simple as calling each level an act raises the drama. *Super Mario World* on the Super Nintendo is, unquestionably, still the superior game. But *Sonic* has a vibe that *Mario* simply does not. Michael Jackson wrote uncredited *Sonic* music!

Sonic the Hedgehog was the total package, exactly the game Sega needed it to be for the Genesis to give Nintendo its first serious competition ever. Sorry, TurboGrafx-16 fans, but *Bonk's Adventure* was no *Sonic the Hedgehog*. Bundled with Genesis hardware, *Sonic the Hedgehog* sold more than fifteen million copies. At the height of Sonic's success, it really did feel like Sega would achieve its goal of replacing Nintendo

as the market leader. Sonic made Mario sweat. Sonic makes the impossible look easy.

Console wars will never again reach the heated heights of the Super Nintendo versus the Sega Genesis. Today's consoles are a lot more interchangeable, and swearing loyalty to a brand is a lot less cute. Yes, Sega did technically lose. The SNES ultimately outsold the Genesis, and Sega's subsequent consoles performed much worse. But all of these consoles hosted so many amazing games that you won no matter which one you owned.

Sonic faced his own troubles following his Genesis glory days. He starred in some truly awful 3D games, got saddled with a widely hated cast of superfluous supporting characters, kissed a human woman, and headlined a live-action movie that needed a fan campaign to fix its hideous character designs. The best modern Sonic game, *Sonic Mania*, is a retro throwback literally made by fans with Sega's blessing.

Still, if there's anyone who knows how to keep running forward no matter what, it's gaming legend Sonic the Hedgehog. Every radical animal gaming mascot afterward, from Crash of PlayStation's *Crash Bandicoot* to Blinx of Xbox's *Blinx: The Time Sweeper*, owes a debt to Sonic. Sonic the Hedgehog, the nineties character to end all nineties characters, is timeless. He's the only video game character who knows how to be funny on Twitter.

SID MEIER'S CIVILIZATION, THE FOREVER GAME

Players willing to slow down could experience countless generations across the grand sweep of human history with *Sid Meier's Civilization*. Meier's previous work had already cultivated a passionate fan base, which is why publishers used his name in marketing, but those games weren't as titanic as *Civilization*. This epic strategy game pulled off the wildly ambitious feat of simulating, well, running a civilization. From guiding your people as they emerge from their caves to planting your flag in outer space, *Civilization* challenges you to win the greatest prize of all: unchallenged world domination.

Civilization brings together multiple gameplay styles in its patchwork approach toward simulating . . . everything. On your PC, the map looks like an evolving board game as rival civilizations compete to spread their reach across the world. You play as real-world ancient nation-states, from Egypt to Rome to the Aztec Empire, and control historical leaders as your avatar. Nobody messes with Mahatma Gandhi. Battles play out as turn-based tactical skirmishes. However, violence doesn't always equal victory. Win the long game through shrewd diplomacy or exerting your soft (cultural) power.

We call these 4X games because players must balance exploring, expanding, exploiting, and exterminating. Deep into the game, you'll have so many options to choose from that smart players spend hours or even days finishing a single turn.

Civilization reflects the real world almost too closely. You may accidentally end up thinking like an insidious colonizer or fail to deal with calamitous climate change. The game is so complex that one player stumbled into an unending, postapocalyptic loop against an AI opponent. A hilarious glitch or a horrifying prophecy?

FINAL FANTASY IV (1991)

Full disclosure, I didn't actually play *Final Fantasy IV* (or *Final Fantasy II*, as it was initially known in North America) until it was an Android mobile game back in 2013. I was too engrossed with the likes of *Super Ghouls 'n Ghosts*, *Battletoads*, and *Sonic the Hedgehog* to give *FFIV* any play. But looking back, eleven-year-old Sherri couldn't have grasped everything going on in the game.

Final Fantasy IV is a great redemption story. You play as Cecil, who at the start of the game is wreaking havoc on a neighboring kingdom as a dark knight on a mission to steal a legendary crystal for his king. By the middle of the game, he's renounced his past deeds and fights to become a paladin, a warrior for the light, in order to fight against an extraterrestrial force.

Along the way, Cecil meets many who would aid him in his journey, but not without some making the ultimate sacrifice against evil. My heart nearly broke when Palom and Porom were petrified. Not to mention the constant betrayal at the hands of Cecil's best friend, Kain. Throw in the different job classes, spells, and equipment and you had an angsty, drama-filled jaunt that the thirty-three-year-old me couldn't deny. The lessons of forgiveness, redemption, and self-acceptance taught by *Final Fantasy IV* stay with me to this day.

—SHERRI L. SMITH,
editor in chief of Laptop Mag

GUNSTAR HEROES (1993)

Sometimes you experience something so great, it makes you want to make things, too: a great film that makes you want to be a director, a great song that makes you want to be a musician. More than any other game, *Gunstar Heroes* made me want to make games. The visuals were vibrant, filled with variety and technical wizardry. The gameplay was a total blast, and I'd repeatedly play from start to finish. If you could peek into the souls of my games, you'd find *Gunstar Heroes* and a bunch of other games by Treasure. To me they are the most perfect game company, and *Gunstar Heroes* was the most perfect game.

—TOM FULP,
founder of Newgrounds and
cofounder of the Behemoth

video game of the year

1992

THE SHOOTER OF THE YEAR

SHOOT YOUR WAY THROUGH NAZI STRONGHOLDS
AS ONE-MAN ARMY B. J. BLAZKOWICZ BEFORE COMING
FACE-TO-FACE WITH ADOLF HITLER HIMSELF.

PRESS START

Close your eyes and imagine a video game. Back in the day, maybe you'd picture a bunch of pixels. But now, chances are you're staring down the sights of a virtual gun. You see **Battlefield**, **Call of Duty**, or **Halo**. You're thinking of a first-person shooter (FPS). 2D games work best by giving players a character to control, like a spunky little mascot. But when games moved into 3D, suddenly they could show us an entire world around us, seen through our own eyes, with nothing separating us from the action. Just give us a gun and show us what to shoot. For better or worse, first-person shooters dominate modern gaming. **Wolfenstein 3D**, the game of the year that introduced the FPS genre to the masses, won the war before it even started.

LONE WOLF

As early 3D graphics tech became increasingly viable, developers tried applying first-person perspectives to all sorts of genres to see the results. *Battlezone* put players inside a vector graphics tank. *Ultima Underworld* gave adventurers even more immersive dungeons to crawl through. After cutting its teeth turning unofficial *Super Mario Bros. 3* PC ports into *Commander Keen* platformers, the team at upstart studio Id Software tried its hand at 3D first-person action games. *Hovertank 3D* in 1991 offered more vehicular combat, while *Catacomb 3-D* sent players down dank dungeons of its own later that same year. Primitive computers at the time could only barely keep up while processing 3D graphics. But that didn't stop these technical and creative wizards from pushing the boundaries of what was possible. The anarchic young group (John Carmack, John Romero, Tom Hall, and Adrian Carmack) had what it took to shape this chaotic and cutting-edge raw energy into a fully formed new genre. With *Wolfenstein 3D*, they put a gun in your hand, and video games were never the same.

Wolfenstein 3D took the general premise of *Castle Wolfenstein*, Silas Warner's 1981 Apple II computer stealth game, but let you see the world through a radical and expansive first-person perspective instead of a flat 2D sidescrolling perspective. Id Software's FPS wanted you to hunt Nazis, not hide from them. As unstoppable force of freedom B.J. Blazkowicz, you use pistols, machine guns, and chain guns to singlehandedly blast your way through the treacherous Nazi castle. Scrounge for ammo. Knife a goose-stepping guard if you have to. Being able to move in any direction added entire new dimensions of depth to thrilling shoot-outs. After you put these Nazis in the grave where they belong, you'll confront gaming's most diabolical final boss: a cyborg version of Adolf Hitler known as Mecha-Hitler. When *Wolfenstein* told you to "Get Psyched," you got psyched.

We already know that gamers love shooting. So of course a game featuring the most realistic and exciting action-packed shooting ever was a huge hit. By taking advantage of the shareware model, Id Software spread copies of *Wolfenstein*'s first few levels for free. It became a viral hit before the Internet existed. Even kids who never wound up buying the full game got their minds blown when they "accidentally" played the demo covertly installed on school computers by cool kids who smoked cigarettes in the bathroom.

I can't stress enough how many Nazis you shoot in *Wolfenstein*, and shooting Nazis is something we're all on board with. Why is the Greatest Generation so great? They shot a bunch of Nazis. First-person shooters use World War II as a setting so much it became a cliché, but it makes sense. Not only is the era rich in history, but mowing down the Third Reich is morally correct. However, the FPS genre couldn't be contained to one relatively uncontroversial time period. Real guns are dangerous, and soon after *Wolfenstein*'s revolution, we learned that video game guns were dangerous, too.

MASTERS OF DOOM

Not every FPS had to be violent. *Chex Quest* and *Super 3D Noah's Ark* used Id Tech, the free open-source engine powering *Wolfenstein 3D* and other subsequent Id shooters, to create a playable cereal commercial and an interactive Bible lesson, respectively. But those were the exceptions. Shooters soon became the terrifying poster child for everything wrong with video games. Every scared parent feared that games weren't just a waste of time but a gateway to dangerous delinquency or worse. Meanwhile, any attempts at actual gun control, as usual, went nowhere.

It didn't help that the guys at Id Software, the rebels they were, actively courted controversy. After *Wolfenstein 3D*, the team unleashed *Doom* onto the world. In this heavy metal FPS masterpiece, you slaughter waves of demons pouring out of hell portals into a space station on a Mars-like planet. It was bolder, bloodier, and even more brutal. Weapons, like the signature shotgun, tore through foes with orgasmic impact. Your ultimate tool of destruction was the BFG, or Big F***ing Gun. In the live-action *Doom* movie, the camera literally goes inside Karl Urban's head to turn the movie itself into an FPS. That's pretty hilarious (even if *Rampage* remains the superior video game movie featuring Dwayne "The Rock" Johnson).

We now recognize *Doom* as a pivotal game for the genre and the industry. But at the time it was a scandalous rock-and-roll album, a comic book to be burned lest it pollute young minds. Concerns over video game violence had simmered for years. The 1976 arcade game *Death Race* caused a firestorm by rewarding players for running over pixelated pedestrians. But the issue exploded into the mainstream in the 1990s. *Wolfenstein*, *Doom*, or even shooters in general weren't the only target. A 1993 congressional hearing infamously brought up *Night Trap*, a truly hilarious FMV game about saving Dana Plato from vampires invading her teen girl slumber party. Still, in a country already plagued with shameful amounts of real gun violence, including school shootings, you can understand why some folks might have a problem with their kids treating guns as fun toys, even if the guns aren't real.

To stave off government oversight and censorship, in 1994 the video game industry Entertainment Software Association created the Entertainment Software Rating Board, or ESRB, a self-regulating organization to determine which games were appropriate for which ages, similar to the MPAA in the film business. That's a fair compromise, even if ratings boards aren't immune to certain cultural biases like extreme sex getting penalized more than extreme violence. By all means, put a little "Rated M for Mature" logo on the box to tell parents *Wolfenstein* isn't for kids. Just don't scrub an entire genre, an entire art form, from existence. Ultimately, these are video games, not murder simulators.

Many years, and a Supreme Court free speech ruling, later the FPS genre still persists, stronger than ever. Today we have crazy action-movie-style shooters, historical military shooters, fantastical sci-fi shooters, and shooters with deep stories and RPG elements. A decade after the government's video game violence debate, the United States Army launched its own official FPS franchise. Make of that what you will. Id Software doesn't quite dominate the genre like it used to, but the demonic 2016 *Doom* reboot, with its blistering speed and spine-ripping combat, set a new shooter standard as one of the finest games of the decade.

After seeing the endless parade of shooters that followed, it's wild to go back and play something as quaint as *Wolfenstein 3D*. You'll never believe that anyone ever thought this game could be mind-blowingly awesome or dangerously transgressive. *Wolfenstein* even managed to find new relevance in today's crowded FPS market. The new *Wolfenstein* games (*The New Order* and *The New Colossus*), are chock-full of *Inglourious Basterds*–style grindhouse gore. They're also shockingly thoughtful. Set in an alternate timeline where the Nazis won WWII with forbidden superscience, you still play as B.J. Blazkowicz. But now you get to see him build a family in a hostile fascist world, explore his Jewish identity, and listen to his weirdly beautiful and poetic corn-fed inner monologue. This franchise has maybe the most tasteful sex scenes in a major video game. The narrative examines the uncomfortable but extremely relevant overlap between Nazi ideology and deep-rooted American white supremacist ideology (modern right-wing gamers, take note). There's a scene where a senile Hitler kills young actor Ronald Reagan on Venus. *Wolfenstein* still rules.

MORTAL KOMBAT FINISHES US

You can't talk about video game violence in the early nineties without talking about the kung fu king of kontroversy: *Mortal Kombat*. As a pure fighting game, Midway's *Mortal Kombat* was always just okay. Aside from some nifty special moves, every character just uses the same uppercut and leg sweep, but *Mortal Kombat* became a legendary arcade experience thanks to its violent visuals. By scanning real actors to make the sprites, creators Ed Boon and John Tobias put players in control of an interactive live-action martial arts movie, an R-rated martial arts movie. Skilled players sealed their victories with Fatalities, special moves gorier than anything anyone had ever seen in a game before. Literally eye-popping levels of violence.

Mortal Kombat garnered a lot of attention, to say the least. If you're a kid and you see a game where fake Bruce Lee gets his head pulled off by a thunder god, or a fire-breathing skeleton ninja from hell burns a lady named Sonya Blade to a crisp, that's going to stick in your brain. You'll pay millions of dollars' worth of quarters to see Johnny Cage punch a dude in the nuts a few more times. Before we could use the Internet to quickly look up cheat codes or separate fact from fiction, schoolyards became hotbeds of *Mortal Kombat* rumors and urban legends. Fatalities became almost mythical, forbidden knowledge, the perfect metagame for energizing the naturally social arcade community.

Mortal Kombat remains as violent as ever. With today's realistic graphics, even the developers report having nightmares after working on the game too long. But the franchise wouldn't have stuck around this long if violence was all it offered. While people want to chop off arms and drown fighters in their own blood, they also care about the cheesy lore with its extradimensional tournaments and four-armed Goro puppet monsters and Cary-Hiroyuki Tagawa's evil wizard Shang Tsung saying, "Your soul is mine!" We're honestly invested in Scorpion and Sub-Zero's dumb colorful ninja drama. The fighting itself has also gotten drastically better, good enough for serious high-stakes competition. The cinematic story modes run circles around other games in the genre; it's not even close. *Mortal Kombat* has its cold, dripping hands around our still-beating hearts and won't let go, no matter how hard we struggle.

DOOM II (1994)

When *Doom II* came to Macintosh in the summer of 1995, I was still swimming in amniotic fluid. By the year's end, my dad and I were whiling away the late nights slaying demons and saving Earth. With him on controls, and me still fusing my skull, this ultraviolent first-person shooter was my first foray into games. I don't remember much, but revisiting *Doom II* in my teen years began my love affair with the franchise. Its first sequel is especially good, crystallizing what *Doom* does really well: killer songs, spectacular set pieces, and hellishly hard levels. Good luck, soldier.

—ALISON FOREMAN,
entertainment journalist and editor at IndieWire, seen on the A.V. Club, Mashable, and CNN

1993

THE SLAM DUNK OF THE YEAR

FLAMING BASKETBALLS, OVER-THE-TOP ANNOUNCERS, AND BONKERS SECRET CHARACTERS MAKE THIS TWO-ON-TWO BASKETBALL GAME FEATURING REAL PLAYERS PERFORMING UNREAL STUNTS THE QUINTESSENTIAL ARCADE SPORT EXPERIENCE.

PRESS START

Squash any dumb beef between nerds and jocks. Electronic entertainment and physical sports go together perfectly; they're all just games. The most popular sports video games strive to re-create these real-world activities with as much technical accuracy as possible. **Madden** simulates football, **FIFA** simulates soccer, and **NBA 2K** simulates basketball. They feature real players, real leagues, and gameplay that converts human athleticism into button presses as realistically as it can. As all good sports dramas teach us, though, the joy of sports comes from our emotions more than our reality. The most memorable matches ensnare us, ratchet up the tension, threaten us with crushing defeats, and launch our victorious spirits through the roof. What if a sports game ignored realism in favor of making that feeling, that hype, as potent as possible for as many players as possible? That game, **NBA Jam**, would set the world on fire.

COME ON AND SLAM, AND WELCOME TO THE JAM

Gamers lost something, a little bit of our shared social culture, when we lost the arcade. There was no better place to hang out with your nerdy friends, meet new ones, and publicly show everyone watching just how much better at games you were than them. The games that shined brightest were the competitive ones that knew how to turn arcades into a real Thunderdome, as publisher Midway learned with its fighting game phenomenon *Mortal Kombat*. You didn't just beat your buddy's high score or defeat them in a friendly bout. You literally ripped their head off as the crowd cheered.

Arcades welcomed many players, but they also alienated others. Gaming spaces in general assume a collective knowledge that not everyone has. Not just specific tips and cheats, but the ability to walk up to a *Mortal Kombat* machine and generally know what you should be doing. Yup, you should block the blue ninja's Ice Ball so he doesn't freeze you, crouch to avoid his overhead swing, and punish him with an uppercut. Got it? This reflexive insularity is a problem that keeps gaming from expanding its audience, but how do you fix it? Sorry, nerds, but here comes sports to the rescue.

Midway may have had great success with *Mortal Kombat*'s ultraviolence, but the publisher's similarly gory shooter *Total Carnage* didn't do nearly as well. So for his next arcade project, Midway designer Mark Turmell proposed a game with mass appeal, a game everyone would instantly understand, a game based on a sport already watched and beloved by millions of people. Midway had previously developed a basketball game called *Arch Rivals* in 1989, but for this new project the company went straight to the NBA for some official prestige. The league needed some convincing, and Midway's bold pitch included more than a few impossible promises, but the team got the license to make a branded NBA product. Similar to how *Mortal Kombat* digitized live-action actors to make its realistic graphics, this game scanned real-world basketball

footage and slapped famous faces from the 1992–93 season onto the bodies (make sure to turn on Big Head Mode). *NBA Jam* was the real deal. Except it wasn't. It was better than real.

ALTITUDE WITH AN ATTITUDE

NBA Jam is many things, but it is first and foremost a basketball game. You want your team to score more points than your opponent. Mix up strategies by knowing when to pass, when to take it to the hole, and when to go for a three-pointer. The shot clock forces you to actually play instead of stalling forever, and you can't interfere with shots already in or near the basket (goaltending). This is all basic basketball stuff, and in *NBA Jam* it plays far simpler than today's complex basketball sims. It's accessible to casual fans. This is the immediate familiarity Turmell hoped would lure in nongamers if they caught a glimpse of an *NBA Jam* cabinet.

When you played *NBA Jam*, though, you quickly discovered that this was basketball like you'd never seen it before. If streetball is basketball with fewer rules and more flash, then *NBA Jam*'s arcade-style basketball is no rules and all flash. Each team only has two players, but each player runs so fast they can move up and down the whole court dozens of times in a few seconds. Feel free to push and shove and throw elbows all you want because you'll never get fouled for it.

Real-life NBA stars jump like nobody else, but in *NBA Jam* these gravity-defying cartoon characters slam dunk and alley-oop like their lives depend on it. When you score the normal way, you'll feel like a Harlem Globetrotter who didn't get the memo. Each team has unique strengths and weaknesses, but unlike in sim sports games where real players actually get offended over low stats, everyone here is so exaggerated and ridiculously powerful it doesn't matter. The one gloriously petty exception is that Turmell programmed the game so that his beloved Detroit Pistons would always have an advantage over the Chicago Bulls, despite Midway being a Chicago-based company.

Finally, there's *NBA Jam*'s signature fiery feature. Score three baskets in a row and your team becomes "on fire." Not only will you run faster and shoot more accurately, but the ball will literally catch on fire in your hands. It explodes as it shatters the backboard and swishes through the net. Satisfying and empowering, getting on fire is *NBA Jam*'s stylish and family-friendly equivalent to ripping your opponent's head off while the crowd cheers.

Chaos reigns on the court in *NBA Jam*, and the game's atmosphere raises hype levels even higher. The repeated screaming of "He's on fire!" "From downtown!" and "Kaboom!" is infectious. When voice actor Tim Kitzrow shouted these catchphrases and others as the game's deliriously energetic announcer, he became an arcade gaming legend in his own right. He puts you in the exact right mood to slam the ball so hard you'll punch a hole in the center of the Earth. Don't get any lava on your sneakers. *NBA Jam*'s antics strike the perfect balance between hilarious and the most awesome thing in the universe, hip-hop culture's braggadocious grandiosity in game form. Nothing captures that better than a grown man bellowing "oomshakalaka!" at you through an arcade cabinet.

There's also a specificity to this madness that's worth remembering. From the Chicago Bulls to the 16-bit graphics to the fact that President Bill Clinton is a secret character, *NBA Jam* is another extremely nineties video game. It comes from the same nationwide basketball fever that gave us the Looney Tunes/NBA crossover *Space Jam* just a few years later. My name is Jordan and I was born in 1991, a time when everyone was obsessed with Michael Jordan. Funny enough, Michael Jordan isn't actually in *NBA Jam*, except for one special version of the game he commissioned just for himself. Only *NBA Jam* is worthy enough to be the GOTY for the GOAT. *NBA Jam* hit the public at the exact right moment, the hoop dreams zeitgeist. It made millions of dollars, more money than any movie in theaters, and cemented Midway as the new decade-defining publisher for the American arcade industry. Nothing but net profits.

Many other arcade sports games followed in *NBA Jam*'s wake, from Midway and others. There's *NFL Blitz*, *NHL Hitz*, and even a fantastic *NBA Jam* reboot from EA in 2010. In M-rated football game *Blitz: The League*, you can inject players with steroids as a power-up. But these days sports games are either ultrarealistic sims, like *NBA 2K*, *FIFA*, and *Madden*, or arcade sports games totally removed from anything in the real world, like the Mario sports games, *Windjammers*' high-flying battle discs, or *Rocket League*'s phenomenal go-kart soccer. Maybe sports fans want their games to be all business, and maybe people who want wackier games couldn't care less about actual athletes. We can and should have both, and *NBA Jam* agrees.

MYST CLEARS OUR BRAIN FOG

Some games used the freedom of technology to create interactive experiences that can hardly be called games at all. Games like *Myst* go beyond mere mortal labels.

After reading a mysterious book, *Myst* drops you onto an even more mysterious open island, an illusion made up of twenty-five hundred photorealistic static images strung together. From your first-person view you must figure out where you are and what's even happening. You piece together the truth by collecting objects, looking at your surroundings, and absorbing other bits of nonverbal storytelling. As you find yourself transported to various Ages, realms beyond the island, you'll encounter *Myst*'s most traditional gameplay: its various adventure-game-esque puzzles. The total immersion and confident refusal to hold your hand make *Myst* a brilliant and bewildering brainteaser. With no enemies or time limits, *Myst* challenges you more than enough all by itself.

Myst's creators, brothers Rand and Robyn Miller, wanted to make a game for adults. *Myst* isn't violent or crude, it's sophisticated. The gambit paid off, and *Myst* became the best-selling PC game of all time, an honor it held until *The Sims* found an even bigger adult audience. Even now *Myst*'s game design feels unbelievably forward-looking. Today's most avant-garde independent games ask players to wander unknown spaces and solve simple puzzles while the narrative happens around them, just like *Myst*. Games like *That Dragon, Cancer*, and *What Remains of Edith Finch* are gaming's answer to independent, award-winning film festival fare. After setting off a new indie game renaissance with time-traveling platformer *Braid*, Jonathan Blow made what might as well be an unofficial *Myst* remake called *The Witness*. More closed-minded gamers derisively call these games walking simulators because they don't accept the genre's gameplay as meaningful (and they resent these games' tendencies toward progressive politics). But when an experience impacts you as much as *Myst* does, who cares what you call it?

NBA STREET VOL. 2 (2003)

The greatest fighting games are almost never about fighting. *NBA Street Vol. 2*, EA Sports Big's 2003 take on arcade basketball, is the best example of that. It abstracts the head-to-head battling of a fighter through a pristine layer of basketball mechanics.

NBA Street Vol. 2 works because it is a video game first but also still a love letter to the look and feel of its real-world sporting counterpart. By dropping the baggage of simulation, *NBA Street* is able to represent a deeper truth about basketball. One about the physical relationship between the players, the ball, gravity, and the rim. And then it colorfully fills in the spaces between those pillars with strong combo mechanics, RPG-style character development, and aesthetic customizations.

By the time you get through the campaign, you have a maxed-out character that is ready to battle your friends and their ballers. And nothing feels better than humiliating them with a kick pass into an alley-oop that ricochets off the backboard. This is basketball as ballet, only you do the dance to the music of Nate Dogg and Just Blaze instead of Tchaikovsky.

—JEFF GRUBB,
   video producer at Giant Bomb

1994

THE NEXT ROUND OF THE YEAR

PICK A FIGHTER AND USE THEIR UNIQUE BLEND OF
OFFENSIVE, DEFENSIVE, AND SPECIAL MOVES TO DEFEAT
YOUR OPPONENT BEFORE THEY DEFEAT YOU IN THIS
TURBOCHARGED UPDATE FEATURING BONUS CHARACTERS,
NEW MOVES, AND FASTER SPEED OPTIONS.

PRESS START

Gamers form communities, and some games are entire communities unto themselves. For a genre all about beating your opponent senseless, nothing brings people together like fighting games. Invite aspiring world warriors to your arcade tournament, and watch them tear each other apart, out of love. For the competition to stay compelling, it needs to evolve and change and keep pace as players get better and smarter. The game needs to be just as alive as its most dedicated fans. Street Fighter II could have rested on its laurels, content in the knowledge that it created the fighting game genre as we know it. Instead, like a dedicated athlete, it kept training, kept growing stronger, and kept surpassing every challenge. Super Street Fighter II Turbo is the next step on the journey.

A NEW CHALLENGER

Street Fighter never got it right on the first try. There's a reason why, when we talk about this franchise, we start with *Street Fighter II*. Granted, Capcom's original *Street Fighter*, released to arcades in 1987, featured the first sparks of what we would eventually call fighting games. It had a stick for movement and six buttons for three different kinds of punches and kicks. Players could pull off special moves with specific command inputs. The main characters, stoic martial artist Ryu and his cocky blond American rival Ken, have remained the faces of the franchise ever since. However, fighting games above all else need to feel fun to play. You need to enjoy doing the moves because that's basically all there is. No one had fun playing the first *Street Fighter.*

Street Fighter II, on the other hand, feels incredible to play. Released in 1991, the expanded international roster now included characters with distinct playstyles, courtesy of codesigners Akira Nishitani and Akira Yasuda. Not only could you launch Hadouken fireballs and perform Shoryuken uppercuts with Ryu, but now you could knock heads with Chun-Li's Spinning Bird Kicks, barrage foes with E. Honda's Hundred Hand Slap, or grapple opponents into submission with Zangief's Spinning Piledriver. During development, producer Noritaka Funamizu discovered a glitch where players with precise timing could link together multiple moves for combo attacks. Originally a hidden hard-core Easter egg, today the entire competitive fighting game community revolves around discovering and effectively using combos. What a fantastic, beautiful mechanic.

Even with diverse characters and flashy combos, *Street Fighter II*'s true brilliance comes from its sublime balance. Everything feels fair, every character and every tactic feels viable. It's as honest a test of skill as you'll find in a video game. Each head-to-head skirmish on the flat plane is a careful dance of offense and defense. Use your long-range projectiles to control space before moving in with hard-hitting close-up strikes. Grab and toss opponents who block too much. If an attack misses, the character usually has to wait

a few milliseconds before they can do anything else. During this vulnerable time a smart player will punish their enemy's mistake. Every action has a possible reaction, every gambit has a counter. Just think of fighting games as Rock Paper Scissors with dozens more choices and each round lasting a second before you're on to the next one. Fighting game players count individual frames of animation to determine which attacks are superior to others. *Street Fighter II*'s flawless fisticuff philosophy formed the foundation for the entire fighting game genre.

Advanced fighting game inputs might even be too complex for their own good. To perform *Street Fighter II*'s most powerful moves, you need to quickly roll and jerk the stick around in various directions while pressing the right buttons in a way that mirrors the physical challenge of properly training your body for real martial arts. All that remains then, in *Street Fighter* and in real fighting, is the high-level meta strategies of anticipating your opponent's every move, conditioning them to make mistakes, and defeating their mind before their body. Fighting game players call this mind games, and it's the best-feeling mechanic of all.

Street Fighter II defeated all challengers. The game's multibillion-dollar sales ushered in fighting games as the hot new genre for arcades. Its characters became gaming legends, inspiring cartoons, fake character April Fools' jokes in *Electronic Gaming Monthly* magazine, and a live-action movie starring Jean-Claude Van Damme and the late Raul Julia in his final role. As big as *Street Fighter II* got, and it did get absolutely huge, the fighting game community that formed up and spread out around it got even bigger.

EVOLUTION

Before corporations realized they could cash in on gamer competition through esports, those competitors took it upon themselves to form their own grassroots communities celebrating the games they loved. The fighting game community (FGC) is one of gaming's most vibrant and inspiring subcultures. Having emerged organically from arcade culture, particularly in big cities where everyone on the block would get in on *Street Fighter* action, the FGC values authenticity in a world full of phonies. It also values diversity. Black and brown people love to play all types of video games, but head to Las Vegas for the Evolution Championship Series tournament (Evo, aka the FGC Olympics) and you'll see an audience that reflects the real world better than any all-white gaming event. Granted, most of those players will unfortunately be dudes. The FGC's problems with sexism range from annoying microaggressions to serious assault. But the FGC is also a place where Dominique "SonicFox" McLean, a queer, Black nonbinary furry, can be a world champion while wearing their big, fuzzy cartoon fox costume onstage.

The FGC's raw strength has forged a fascinating symbiotic relationship between fighting game players and developers. The FGC can keep a game alive long after it's been abandoned by its original publisher, but publishers and players alike realize it's in everyone's best interest to keep one another happy. Like the world's best testers, fighting game players offer valuable feedback on how well a game is balanced, which broken moves need to be fixed, and which characters are too weak to be worth playing. Developers observe tournaments like Evo, where the best of the best push these games to the limit, to determine future adjustments. These days, fighting games get tweaked after the fact through online updates. Thanks to the Internet, you can even buy new characters for existing games. But in the offline arcade days of *Street Fighter II*, if you wanted to improve your old game, you basically had to make a new one.

Between 1991 and 1994, Capcom released four updated versions of *Street Fighter II*, wholly new arcade machines that replaced outdated models. These revisions added more characters, like playable versions of the boss characters. Did you know that in Japan M. Bison is the boxer's name, but in the United States it's the dictator's name because Capcom didn't want to offend Mike Tyson? Existing characters also received extra moves, some inspired by features in bootleg, hacked arcade machines that became urban legends in FGC's early days. *Super Street Fighter II Turbo*

marked the end of the original *Street Fighter II* series. The apex of the lineage, its faster game speed provided the ultimate challenge for anyone who had stuck with Ryu and the gang all this time. More than twenty-five years later, the game's competitive scene rages on like Akuma's Raging Demon attack.

Nearly every fighting game franchise follows this path and releases regular updates. *Street Fighter III* and *Street Fighter IV* (the game that revived the FGC after a lengthy hiatus) all got multiple revisions. *The King of Fighters* series slaps the current year onto the game's title, like *The King of Fighters '95* or *The King of Fighters 2003*. Whenever an arcade game gets ported to consoles, like *Tekken 7: Fated Retribution* or *Virtua Fighter 5 Ultimate Showdown* or *Tatsunoko vs. Capcom: Ultimate All-Stars*, it usually comes with additional enhancements. Today, it's much harder to convince players to buy the same game over again just for one or two perks when you can simply sell it as individual DLC (downloadable content). However, after developers release enough DLC, they'll typically package it all together as a definitive version of the existing game like *Mortal Kombat 11 Ultimate*.

Even *Street Fighter II* saw new life in the new millennium with 2008's *Super Street Fighter II Turbo HD Remix*, which redrew everything with striking illustrated HD artwork, and 2017's *Ultra Street Fighter II: The Final Challengers*, which added gimmicky minigames alongside Evil Ryu and Violent Ken. For fighting games, release dates are just the start. We will see another *Street Fighter II* in our lifetimes.

Video games don't exist without people playing them. We pour our lives into games, and they become living organisms in response. The path that brought us to *Super Street Fighter II Turbo*, and the fighting game community that uplifts it, shows us that to keep on fighting is to prove you're still alive.

SUPER METROID 'S
CAPTIVE AUDIENCE

Super Metroid isolates you. On the Super Nintendo, the game perfected the *Metroid* formula by stranding players on an unknown alien planet with a twisting, interconnected map to uncover. The queen of the Metroidvania subgenre, the game tasks you and you alone with finding the right path by using the right tools and weapons. It's a single-player campaign through and through. Fans get legitimately upset whenever the main character, intergalactic bounty hunter Samus Aran, breaks her stoic exterior and tries to connect with other people. *Super Metroid* is a game for loners about a loner.

And yet, *Super Metroid* also has a thriving competitive community, just not one the creators may have anticipated. *Super Metroid* gives you some choices for how to proceed, but there's generally one way to finish the game. However, after years of playing, rebels have discovered ways to use glitches and exploits to break the game's sequence, get powers early, and finish the mission way faster. Just jump off walls to get the Power Bombs and kill Kraid before getting the Spazer Beam. Competitive *Super Metroid* consists of races to see who can finish the game in the shortest time, using both their knowledge of the game and their talent for rapidly pressing the right buttons.

A most unique competitive community, speedrunners twist all sorts of games inside out to finish them as fast as possible, from open-world epics like *The Legend of Zelda: Breath of the Wild* to random kids' games like *SpongeBob SquarePants: Battle for Bikini Bottom*. Only someone who loves a game so much can break it like a speedrunner can, and the results are mesmerizing to watch, like seeing someone tear open a wormhole and slide right through it. Is this the right way to play? All that matters is that you're having fun. No matter how fast you play it, with an audience or all by yourself, *Super Metroid* is a masterpiece.

STREET FIGHTER II (1991)

Street Fighter II isn't the first video game I ever played, but it's the first one I distinctly remember being obsessed with. When I wasn't spamming Hadouken fireballs to finally vanquish M. Bison or trying to sneak some games in with the cool older kids in my basement, I would simply let the attract screen idly play, taking note of Chun-Li's birthday or Ryu's blood type as I clutched my *Street Fighter* action figures, which were really just poorly reskinned G.I. Joes.

This obsession would snowball into a deep love for competitive fighting games that brought me to tournaments and trade shows around the country, and inspired me to start creating the type of content that I now do for a career. But most importantly, *Street Fighter II* is as playable today as it was decades ago, and every time I spot a cabinet in the wild and place my hand over those familiar six buttons, I become that same wide-eyed kid all over again.

—MIKE ANDRONICO,
senior writer at CNN Underscored

1995

THE ILLUSION OF THE YEAR

CONTROL AGILE CHIMP DIDDY KONG AND HIS
HIGH-FLYING PARTNER, DIXIE KONG, AS THEY RUN,
SWING, JUMP, AND BARREL BLAST THROUGH FAUX-3D
SIDESCROLLING LEVELS TRYING TO RESCUE DONKEY KONG.

PRESS START

Graphics aren't everything. Games need to be good, not just look good. Still, awesome visuals can make a game much better. Who doesn't like to look at cool stuff? We don't just begrudgingly accept expensive upgraded next-gen consoles, we eagerly anticipate them because they give us games more beautiful than ever before. As we shifted away from 16-bit machines toward consoles capable of truly 3D experiences, games were about to sport their greatest graphics yet, a leap forward so seismic that no other generational transition can compare. However, before Nintendo pulled the trigger, the company reminded us why it's the best at finding creative solutions for old technology, not riding the bleeding edge of new technology. Donkey Kong Country 2: Diddy's Kong Quest proved you could still teach an old ape new tricks.

STUBBORN APE

The original *Donkey Kong* arcade game may have kick-started modern Nintendo as we know it, but the gorilla's comeback tour began at a totally different company in another part of the world. While Japan and North America may dominate global game development, the robust British game dev scene is also a force to be reckoned with, and Rare Limited stood tall as one of Britain's most prolific game studios. Founded in 1985 by brothers Chris and Tim Stamper, Rare pulled off the seemingly impossible feat of reverse engineering the NES. Astonished, Nintendo gave Rare an unlimited budget to officially release an unbelievable amount of games for the console in a very short time. In 1989 alone, sixteen Rare games launched on the NES, from a *Marble Madness* port to a *Sesame Street* educational title to a game about shooting sea monsters on a speedboat called *Cobra Triangle*. Rare pushed its tech, and itself, to the limit. When the next generation began in the early nineties, Rare prepared to pull off its most ambitious stunt yet.

Rare shifted from making lots of games to investing its resources into making the single most groundbreaking game the UK, and the world, had ever seen. The company purchased pricey Silicon Graphics workstations. Using these advanced computers, Rare could generate 3D models, like *Toy Story* characters. None of the home consoles on the market could render these characters in real time, constantly drawing and redrawing them as players controlled their movements, because they weren't powerful enough. However, Rare devised a technique for taking those models and reverse engineering them, flattening them into 2D sprites that could easily run on an SNES. Sure, they lost some detail, but just as grainy digitized characters in *Mortal Kombat* and *NBA Jam* still look like real people to your brain, these Silicon Graphics visuals look like 3D models instead of flat images. When the illusion is this compelling, who cares that it's smoke and mirrors?

Nintendo certainly didn't. The company was looking for a graphical showpiece that could compete with Disney's recent *Aladdin* game, which featured gorgeous graphics drawn by actual Disney animators. Meanwhile, because Nintendo was too arrogant to strike a deal with Sony for revolutionary CD-ROM tech, Sony developed its own competing console. The Sony PlayStation, with its full 3D graphics, was on track to arrive in 1994. This was well before Nintendo's own 3D console, the Silicon Graphics–powered Nintendo 64, so having a game that at least *looked* 3D would hopefully keep the aging SNES from looking too obsolete. Rare had already shown impressive technical skill and great loyalty to Nintendo in the NES days, so Nintendo decided to buy 49 percent of the company and lock down this promising Silicon Graphics tech. All we needed now was a game to show off these technical marvels. It was time for Donkey Kong to get back in the swing of things.

JUNGLE HIJINKS

Most of what follows ultimately applies to all three games in the *Donkey Kong Country* trilogy released from 1994 through 1996, but in the spirit of graphics not being everything, let's highlight the best *playing* game in this bunch. *Donkey Kong Country 2*'s nimble controls and creative levels make it a 2D platformer worth playing no matter how it looks. Mario would play this game and feel proud at how far his original enemy has come.

The visuals are also quite special. The *Donkey Kong Country* series looks absolutely incredible. Blurry nineties CRT TVs do retro games a wonderful favor by smoothing out their jagged edges, something developers took knowing advantage of at the time since there were no alternatives. *Donkey Kong Country* characters honestly look like Pixar cartoons hopping around on the screen. Even if you didn't know all the computer wizardry happening behind the scenes, you looked at *Donkey Kong Country* and you could see something futuristic, something with depth and volume, something from the real world. The game's lush, moody jungles come alive with more atmosphere than the pleasant but plastic Mario universe. David Wise's legendary soundtrack brings you into a dreamy trance state you didn't think was possible in a Donkey Kong game. *DKC2*'s hypnotic "Stickerbrush Symphony" track should be classified as a controlled substance.

Donkey Kong Country boldly reinvents what a Donkey Kong game even means. Alongside DK's sidekick, Diddy Kong, and Diddy's female counterpart, Dixie Kong, the game introduces a wide cast of Kong characters like DK's girlfriend, Candy Kong, and the blissed-out pilot/arms dealer Funky Kong. It expands the existing Donkey Kong lore, too. Technically, the Donkey Kong you play as, the gorilla wearing a tie with his own initials on it, is supposed to be Donkey Kong Jr. from the arcade era. Your crotchety grandpa Cranky Kong is the original Donkey Kong who tussled with Mario back in the day and won't let you forget it. Instead of battling plumbers, though, the DK crew now tosses barrels at crocodile-like enemies called Kremlings and their leader, King K. Rool. In *Donkey Kong Country 2*, he rechristens himself Kaptain K. Rool, and some of the game's best set piece moments come from clambering around his pirate ship lair. While Donkey Kong is a Nintendo character through and through, Rare left its own distinct authorial stamp thanks to a very cheeky and very British sense of humor. The game's instruction manual makes fun of you to your face, a playful edginess that very much feels like Nintendo's response to Sega and *Sonic*.

As 2D platformers, the *Donkey Kong Country* games have more going on than just stunning visuals, especially *Donkey Kong Country 2*. Swap between two different Kongs to gain access to their unique skills. Dixie Kong's Helicopter Spin hair twirl is an absolute lifesaver. You'll frequently hop into floating barrels to blast yourself around at high speed. Unlike Mario, who only rides his trusty dinosaur steed, Yoshi, the DK crew can hop on all sorts of animal buddies like charging rhinos, swimming swordfish, and hopping frogs.

Those graphics, though, put *Donkey Kong Country* over the top. The games combined sold more than seventeen million copies on the Super Nintendo, just behind *Super Mario World*, and successfully extended the system's life. Nintendo used the extra time for more tech experiments like *Star Fox*'s Super FX chip–

powered polygons. The *Country* games blew up the Donkey Kong brand like never before, it was Nintendo's star franchise once again. *Donkey Kong Country* may have started as a cutting-edge computer graphics tech demo, but when you inspire your own horrifyingly low-budget CGI Saturday morning cartoon, that's when you've really made it. The games were everywhere. My most vivid, formative SNES memories by far come from *Donkey Kong Country*, and I'm not alone.

Donkey Kong himself became a bit of a second banana following his greatest adventures. After making legendary Nintendo games like 3D platformer *Banjo-Kazooie*, pioneering James Bond shooter *GoldenEye 007*, and unbelievably vulgar mascot parody *Conker's Bad Fur Day*, Rare got acquired by Microsoft in 2002 and never quite regained its same strength. And while I adore the offbeat *Donkey Kong Jungle Beat*, which gives you a pair of actual bongo drum controllers to beat on as you guide DK through a rhythmic platforming world, *Donkey Kong Country* didn't truly return until 2010's *Donkey Kong Country Returns* by Retro Studios.

Donkey Kong Country 2 went above and beyond its original purpose. It delivered a great game with fake 3D visuals on your SNES so amazing you'd ignore the real 3D visuals on the PlayStation. All these years later, *Donkey Kong Country 2* remains beautiful inside and out.

EARTHBOUND STINKS, AND WE LOVE IT

Nintendo games have the most dedicated fans in all of gaming, it's not even close. Only Disney grips childhoods tighter. Even the most obscure Nintendo franchises still have countless people who can't get enough of them. However, no Nintendo franchise buries its way deep into your very soul the way *EarthBound* does.

EarthBound takes the traditional turn-based Japanese role-playing game formula but replaces the fantasy trappings with a heartwarming parody of childhood in US suburbia. As young boy Ness, you'll team up with fellow youths to beat cultists with baseball bats, vanquish neighborhood zombies with psychic powers, and save your progress by talking to your absentee dad on the phone. The game's director, Shigesato Itoi, is more famous in Japan for writing essays and acting in Studio Ghibli movies and being an *Iron Chef* judge than making video games. You get the strong sense that a video game just happened to be the venue where Itoi wanted to explore his Japanese outsider perspective on Western culture. A lot of songs on the soundtrack sound suspiciously close to Beatles music.

EarthBound is hilarious and bizarre. Toward the end you wander around nude in a pink dreamscape. But it's also very earnest and emotional, leaning into the novel idea of an RPG that takes place in basically the real world. Unfortunately, Nintendo's marketing failed to respect *EarthBound*'s dignity when the game launched in the United States, focusing only on the comedy with scratch-and-sniff cards that literally said the game stank. No wonder no one bought it!

While it wasn't a commercial success, *EarthBound* became the cult classic to end all cult classics. *EarthBound* is actually the second game in Itoi's *Mother* franchise, and to this day fans passionately campaign for Nintendo to give the even more emotional *Mother 3* a chance in North America. Like any proper underappreciated gem, *EarthBound* inspired plenty of imitators. Countless twee indie games, most notably Toby Fox's *Undertale*, put their own spin on *EarthBound*'s unique vibe. *EarthBound* does not, in fact, stink.

SUIKODEN II (1999)

The odds were against *Suikoden II* from the start. It was a 2D game in an age of burgeoning 3D graphics. It came out just a week before *Final Fantasy VIII*, a competitor with far more pedigree and eye-popping visuals. It was poorly localized in English. And then there was that terrible, unpronounceable title. (It's SWEE-koh-den.)

But if you walked into a Toys"R"Us one day in the fall of 1999 and that beautiful white box cover caught your eye, you were in for the experience of a generation—a game that today might be best described as "*Game of Thrones* meets *Pokémon*." You'd run your own castle and go around the world finding recruits to join you, from eccentric soldiers to lethargic wizards. You'd fight in sprawling army battles across a fantasy world full of magic and mystery. And you'd unravel a story that was simultaneously epic and intimate, capturing both the brutality of war and the tenacity of friendship. The game was hilarious, astounding, and truly moving.

Suikoden II was underappreciated during its time—how could it not have been? But today, it's rightfully remembered as one of the greatest games ever made, a game where you get to save the world from evil . . . and pretend to be on *Iron Chef*.

—**JASON SCHREIER,** *New York Times*–bestselling author of **Press Reset** and **Blood, Sweat, and Pixels**

1996

THE THIRD DIMENSION OF THE YEAR

RUN AND JUMP IN EVERY DIRECTION TO
EXPLORE DENSE, DIORAMA-STYLE WORLDS FULL OF
CHALLENGES TO COMPLETE AND STARS TO COLLECT
IN MARIO'S FIRST 3D ADVENTURE.

PRESS START

To perceive new dimensions, you must either expand your consciousness or break your brain. Even though we all exist in 3D space, playing a 3D video game might be the biggest challenge you can ask a newcomer to attempt. Most people can wrap their heads around moving up and down and left and right on a 2D plane. But adding depth, that dreaded z-axis, makes everything exponentially more complicated in virtual space. To paraphrase **The Matrix**, it bakes your noodle.

After two generations of 2D machines, headlined by effortlessly intuitive Mario sidescrollers, Nintendo's developers had their work cut out for them with Mario's inevitable 3D reinvention. To create the first definitive 3D platformer, Miyamoto's team once again had to make a game that totally redefined what a video game could be and change the game industry forever. Familiar Mario philosophies required complete overhauls. The game needed new, entertaining ways to explain itself to players. It would either expand consciousness or break brains. The first 3D Mario game couldn't be just another great game; it had to be a potential contender for the greatest game of all time, a game all games afterward would learn from if 3D really was the future. What game could possibly do all this? **Super Mario 64**.

X, Y, AND Z?

What makes 3D so tricky? The biggest culprit has to be the camera. Aside from cowardly enemies and cheap obstacles hiding off-screen, in 2D games you see pretty much everything you need to see immediately all around you. You can focus on moving your character. However, in 3D games, not only do you need to move your character, but you also need to fiddle with the very lens through which you see the world. If you can't see something, it'll probably kill you, and that's no fun. Even with today's intelligent, preprogrammed cameras, games constantly ask you to adjust the camera to get the right angle to set yourself up for success. Bad cameras ruin even the greatest games—just ask *Ninja Gaiden* fans.

3D camera control also created a huge complication for game controllers. You could technically use a trusty D-pad, which is all the first PlayStation controller had, but only moving in four directions suddenly becomes restrictive in a world that should have 360 degrees of freedom. So when you bought your new Nintendo 64 to play *Super Mario 64* in 1996, you got to rest your thumb on something called an analog stick. Move it in a full circle. Push it softly or smash it from side to side. The analog stick solved the 3D character-control problem so well that every controller adopted the feature, including PlayStation's later DualShock controllers. In fact, PlayStation did Nintendo one better by adding a second analog stick: one for moving the character and one for aiming the camera, since camera controls call for similarly fluid movement.

So what's the problem? Manipulating both the character and camera independently of each other in 3D space, while logical, is not a simple task for anyone who doesn't regularly play games. Even with its one analog stick, the N64 controller is a huge, confusing, nightmare trident to hold. With two analog sticks, sensitive devices that register the slightest inputs, it becomes all too easy to spin yourself around, walk your character off a cliff you can't see, and wind up completely disoriented or even scared. Dual analog stick control schemes, especially when it comes to the camera, might be the single biggest modern hurdle for getting casual players into more complex games. They don't know the grammar. If only we all had a teacher as thoughtful as Mario.

JUMP FOR JOY

You must understand just how difficult the transition to 3D game design was because when you play *Super Mario 64*, when you see how the game made it all so effortless from the start as a Nintendo 64 launch title, the magnitude of its achievement becomes all the more breathtaking. *Super Mario 64*'s first bit of utter brilliance comes in the first few seconds as the game explains its camera system. In 1996, no one understood 3D camera control, hard-core gamers and casual players alike. So to introduce this fundamental gameplay shift to puzzled players, Nintendo personified the abstract concept into a friendly helper. You didn't just control the camera, you controlled a floating turtle in a cloud who followed Mario's every move with a camera like a documentarian. That metaphor, while basic, made the whole idea so much easier to accept. Nintendo's "turn confusing gameplay mechanics into in-game buddies" idea worked so well, it also appeared in another grand 3D reimagining on N64: *The Legend of Zelda: Ocarina of Time*. In that stone-cold classic, developed concurrently with *Super Mario 64* by much of the same staff, the Z-targeting 3D aiming system becomes your helpful fairy guide Navi.

Now that you could see where you were going, *Super Mario 64* next blew your mind by demonstrating how you were going to get there. Before any action starts, the game simply asks you to walk up to Princess Peach's castle to eat a cake. As you start walking, you'll experience your first tantalizing taste of Mario's pitch-perfect movement controls. Smoothly transition from tiptoeing to walking to sprinting. Before you used Mario's momentum to extend your jumps, but now you could long jump, somersault, backflip, ground pound, slide, triple jump, and wall jump to put Mario precisely where you wanted him. He became a pure expression of your platforming will. His prominent shadow helped you gauge your jumps as you judged depth. Or forget jumping, now Mario throws a punch! With no enemies or obstacles, the castle courtyard provided a satisfying sandbox to teach yourself just what Mario was capable of now that the 2D shackles were off. *Super Mario 64* controls better and feels less dated than 3D platformers that were released decades later. It's no coincidence that *Super Mario 64* marks the first major appearance of Mario's voice actor, Charles Martinet. With this much freedom, Mario could finally speak all the Italian gibberish he wanted.

Camera control and character movement arguably presented the toughest obstacles when making *Super Mario 64*. The team spent months ensuring these two aspects were up to snuff before moving to full production. The Nintendo 64 itself got delayed to accommodate Miyamoto's request for extra time since "a delayed game is eventually good, but a rushed game is forever bad." That quote may be misattributed, but it's still true. Miyamoto's own son struggled playing early prototypes so much, Miyamoto worried about his boy's intelligence. That's how tough 3D design was to crack.

With a framework this outstanding in place, the pressure was now on the team to develop levels that did it justice, that made players never want to go back to the claustrophobic 2D games of old. To do this, *Super Mario 64* radically rethinks how to structure a Mario level from the ground up. Instead of linear obstacle courses, stages like Bob-omb Battlefield are huge and filled with secrets. Like the castle grounds, they're sandboxes for you to experience the joy of Mario's movement, only now with enemies and obstacles getting in the way. While 2D Mario levels reward you for making it to the end, *Super Mario 64* rewards your curiosity and willingness to approach each stage from different angles. As you run off in every direction, you'll find different self-contained challenges. Collect all the red coins. Defeat King Bob-omb at the top of the mountain. Shoot yourself from a cannon onto a sky island.

Completing each challenge rewards you with a star. You use stars to unlock more parts of the castle's interior to explore, and find more paintings that serve as portals to new worlds, so you can confront Bowser and rescue Peach. This gives you more freedom for how and when you tackle each level. This also lets developers remix levels into fresh challenges. Sure, you can make it to the top of the mountain for a boss fight, but can you beat Koopa the Quick in a footrace to the summit? 3D didn't just open up Mario's field of movement, it unleashed Nintendo's imagination. You run and jump, but you also sled with penguins, chase rabbits, lure sea monsters out of their caves, and straight-up soar through the sky with the Wing Cap.

Super Mario 64's journey into the third dimension felt like an adventure, at long last a thrilling paradigm shift we hadn't seen since *Super Mario Bros.* on the NES. It set the standard for adapting games from 2D to 3D, changing everything practical that needs changing while honoring the spirit of what works. Games would never evolve if they didn't tackle complicated challenges. If there were any doubts that Nintendo's premier franchise could keep leading gaming into the future no matter what changes that future held, Mario squashed them under his shiny 3D boot.

MARIO KART 64
REVS OUR ENGINES

The original *Super Mario Kart* sent Mario off to the races on the Super Nintendo, using the console's Mode 7 graphics to produce pseudo-3D racetracks. However, *Mario Kart 64* showed how these go-karts and power-ups made way more sense in true 3D, even if the characters themselves were still rotating 2D sprites.

Courses such as the idyllic Koopa Troopa Beach or congested Toad's Turnpike came alive like never before. When you got hit by shells and banana peels, during a race or in the chaotic battle mode, you really felt it. *Mario Kart 64* introduced the Blue Shell, the friendship-ending weapon that targets the player in first place. It's the epitome of Nintendo's sadistic, gleeful, *Harrison Bergeron*-esque willingness to sabotage skilled players who succeed to guarantee everyone else enjoys themselves equally. The Nintendo 64 had four controller slots instead of two, and *Mario Kart 64* served as the perfect showcase for local multiplayer with even more buddies.

If you look at sales numbers, *Mario Kart* might be even more important to Nintendo than regular Mario games. *Mario Kart* is the king of Mario spin-offs and allows Nintendo to take chances on other experiments, like Mario sports games and Mario RPGs. Whether it's shifting to 3D or entering an entirely new genre, Mario can do anything as long as the game is fun. Like a true plumber, Mario gets the job done no matter what. Like a true racer, he leaves the competition in the dust.

VIRTUAL PRO WRESTLING 2 (2000)

More than twenty years removed from their heyday, there are still no greater wrestling games than the best-in-class games produced by Japanese developer AKI for the Nintendo 64, and there is no greater game among those than *Virtual Pro Wrestling 2*. You might be familiar with AKI's US-licensed efforts like *WCW/nWo Revenge* and *WWF No Mercy*, but chances are that unless you were heavily into the N64 import scene around the turn of the millennium, you never got a chance to check out *VPW2*.

Including a licensed roster of All Japan Pro Wrestling's then-incredibly stacked roster, as well as dozens of just-different-enough-looking-to-not-get-us-sued representations of wrestlers from New Japan, FMW, Michinoku Pro, and the like, *VPW2* runs the gamut of different wrestling styles, and even throws in some straight-up MMA fighting to boot. And if you happened to have a stack of N64 memory cards lying around, you could re-create plenty of other famous fighters using what was easily the best create-a-wrestler mode in any game of that bygone era.

Pro-wrestling games may not be an obvious pick for a game of the year, especially given how far the genre has fallen in the ensuing decades, but for my money there is no more significant game from the year 2000. Let me put it this way: I still have an N64 plugged in right now, and it's not to screw around in *Super Mario 64* or *Ocarina of Time*. *Virtual Pro Wrestling 2* is the game of the year, if not the game of the decade, the century, and possibly even the millennium!

—ALEX NAVARRO,
cofounder of Nextlander

1997

FINAL FANTASY.VII

THE CHANGE OF THE YEAR

CONTROL CLOUD AND HIS BAND OF PLUCKY FREEDOM
FIGHTERS AS THEY ATTEMPT TO SAVE THE PLANET
FROM THE MALEVOLENT SEPHIROTH IN THIS TURN-BASED
JRPG SET IN A DYSTOPIAN SCI-FI WORLD.

PRESS START

If your game franchise gets to entry number seven, you did something right. You figured out a formula players can't get enough of and will return to again and again. Once the Roman numerals in your title start getting some *V*s in them, though, it may be time for a change. Existing fans that stuck with you this far will be ready for a bold reinvention, and nothing attracts potential newcomers like the promise of a fresh start. Final Fantasy VII struck gaming like the meteor that graces its box art. It brought radical change to its own series and genre, while shifting the balance of power at its publisher and in the industry at large. If you've ever been curious about "One-Winged Angel," or wanted to know why some people cry at the mere mention of Aerith, it all comes back to Final Fantasy VII.

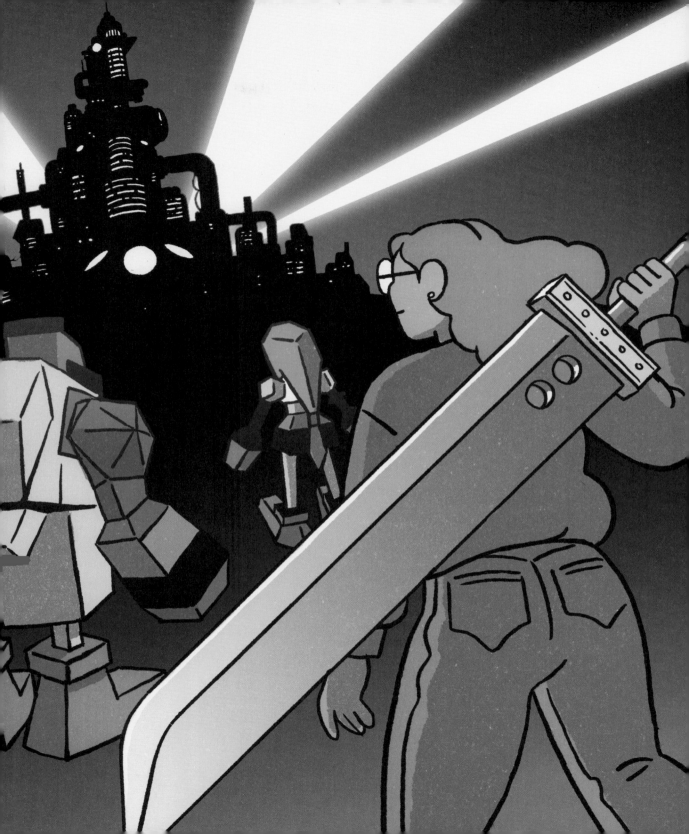

FINAL FANTASY VII CHANGED FINAL FANTASY

Enix's *Dragon Quest* may have invented the Japanese role-playing game and gathered a massive fan base in Japan, but Square's *Final Fantasy* series became the genre's gold standard worldwide when *Final Fantasy* launched in 1987 for the NES. That's why once these two companies merged into Square Enix, they had the entire genre on lock. Designed by Hironobu Sakaguchi, *Final Fantasy* introduced several innovations, like multiple party members appearing on-screen during a battle, or a job system where characters learned different abilities depending on their class, like sturdy fighters or magical black mages. The Active Time Battle system gave players only a few moments to take their turn before enemies would respond, adding exciting time pressure to the cerebral menu-based combat. Throughout the first six entries, the series grew increasingly ambitious with its storytelling, finding new ways to wring drama and emotion out of medieval and primitive industrial 16-bit game worlds. *Final Fantasy VI*, the other *Final Fantasy* game that definitely deserved a chapter, famously asks players to act out an opera scene. Like other JRPG franchises, each *Final Fantasy* game stood on its own, with only a few common elements like crystal motifs, rideable ostrich-like yellow birds called Chocobos, and a character named Cid. Even still, no one could've predicted just how drastically *Final Fantasy VII* would depart from convention.

The most immediate change? *Final Fantasy VII* abandoned the classic sword-and-sorcery fantasy for a cyberpunk sci-fi future like *Akira* or *Blade Runner*. Enemy soldiers chase after you in helicopters. The evil Shinra Electric Power Company literally sucks the life from the planet. In the bleak and bustling city of Midgar, your first mission with ecoterrorist group Avalanche has you battling giant robots with arm-mounted machine guns. Party members include corporate spies, experimental monsters, and a big, buff Black guy named Barret. More traditional fantasy aesthetics eventually emerge, but from the opening hours the game sets a completely distinct visual atmosphere, and not just because it's the first entry with 3D graphics. This blending of magic and technology has stuck with the series ever since.

Final Fantasy VII uses its setting to introduce the most beloved cast of characters in the franchise by far. From amnesiac and guilt-ridden hero Cloud Strife to his driven, diabolical, angelic nemesis Sephiroth, there's so much more to these characters than their giant swords. Aerith and Tifa aren't just Betty or Veronica, good girl and bad girl choices, but real people with their own warm (and tragic) relationships with the rest of the cast. Max Eddy of PCMag once described *FFVII* as "*The Catcher in the Rye* of video games" because, while it is very good, it also has a sulky, juvenile quality that attracts sad teenagers. But sad teenagers buy a lot of video games, and their love turned *Final Fantasy VII* into a franchise unto itself. Under its *Compilation of Final Fantasy VII* initiative, Square Enix created spin-off games, CGI movies, snowboarding cell phone mini-games, and more ways to dive back into this story and world we couldn't resist.

Underneath all this was still a role-playing game, one that didn't feel that different from past *Final Fantasy* games. You still level up, cast spells, and summon powerful deities to aid you. The Materia system gives you more flexibility in customizing gear to suit your playstyle, but compared to other game genres, in RPGs the gameplay itself is sometimes just a means to an end. The real purpose is delivering a narrative to live inside of. Familiar gameplay didn't change the fact that *Final Fantasy VII* took you somewhere you never even could have imagined before.

FINAL FANTASY VII
CHANGED THE CONSOLE WARS

It's almost Shakespearean how Nintendo, fresh off of barely defeating Sega, created its own worst enemy by stubbornly, publicly refusing to partner with Sony (in favor of the Philips CD-i debacle that's not even worth discussing). Instead of adding its CD-ROM technology to the newest Nintendo console, Sony shook off this betrayal and went and made its own console. The PlayStation easily muscled its way into the new market. Developers eagerly ditched the Nintendo 64's expensive, limited cartridges (and Nintendo's seemingly tyrannical attitude) for Sony's affordable discs with so much room for extra data. High-quality audio, expansive worlds, cinematic cutscenes, and more suddenly became possible. *Final Fantasy VII* needed the PlayStation's power, and ending the franchise's Nintendo exclusivity once again showed how this game felt no need to stay beholden to the past.

Final Fantasy's shocking jump to PlayStation anointed Sony's machine as the next big thing in gaming, the next brand to stand for gaming as a whole. The game looks and feels like the future. *FFVII* features prerendered environments, which means that while the characters are 3D models you can move around, the backgrounds are static images like matte paintings in a movie. Combined with carefully selected camera angles, this grants the game an unprecedented level of rich detail. The dark, sophisticated mood reflects a more mature game, a game you can only enjoy on your grown-up PlayStation console.

Final Fantasy VII sold more than 10 million copies, selling more than any prior entry. The PlayStation sold more than 100 million units, more than any other video game console in history at the time. Sony became one of gaming's most powerful leaders and holds on to that position to this day through closely cemented alliances, with games like *Final Fantasy XVI* still exclusive to its consoles.

FINAL FANTASY VII
CHANGED SQUARE ENIX

For all its shifts, *Final Fantasy VII*'s core creative team consisted of the same folks who had shepherded the series since the beginning, from director Hironobu Sakaguchi to unparalleled video game composer Nobuo Uematsu. However, the game's success turned a lesser-known face, a debugger-turned-character-artist named Tetsuya Nomura, into the defining creative voice at the defining JRPG company for the next two decades.

Previous *Final Fantasy* games sported delicate, intricate watercolor illustrations from Yoshitaka Amano, who still designs each game's trademark logo. This style worked fine for the 2D games, where no one expected the sprites to look exactly like the art. *FFVII*'s 3D character designs required a different approach, simplified designs that could translate to blocky polygonal characters. Enter Nomura. His art style featured big eyes, bigger weapons, and the spikiest nineties anime hair this side of *Dragon Ball Z*. He covered characters in belts and zippers and other nonsensical yet extremely cool fashion choices. His sharp, angular silhouettes not only seamlessly turned into 3D models, but felt more of the moment.

When *FFVII* catapulted the series to new heights, Square Enix went all in on Nomura and his aesthetic as the future for its output. Nomura himself became a director and producer on high-profile titles, including multiple *Final Fantasy* games. As popular as Nomura's style is, it has arguably hurt Square Enix as much as it has helped it. Sometimes we get the legitimately stylish Shibuya streetwear nightmare *The World Ends with You*. Other times, after years languishing in finicky development hell, we get the garishly overdesigned *Final Fantasy XIII* trilogy. Even the best aesthetics can't help but become parodies of themselves after so long. Regardless, you can't talk about *FFVII*'s massive influence without discussing how it led to Nomura's ascent.

By fearlessly embracing change, *Final Fantasy VII* reshaped its series, its genre, its publisher, its industry, and even itself. It leaves a long and lasting legacy whose ending, miraculously, has yet to be written.

INTERPLAY'S RPGS BRING EVEN MORE CHANGE

Video game RPGs always owed a debt to their table-top forebear Dungeons & Dragons. *Baldur's Gate*, published by Interplay, made this connection explicit by setting its campaign in the popular world of Forgotten Realms. Developer BioWare later honed its RPG exper-tise to make not just more DnD games but original franchises like *Dragon Age* and *Mass Effect*.

Fallout, also published by Interplay, turned postapocalyptic USA into an irradiated playground for role-playing adventures. Robust character customization and meaningful choices emphasize the "role" in "role-playing." War may never change, but your playstyle sure can.

FINAL FANTASY VII (1997)

Unlikely heroes, memorable villains, double agents, a high-stakes plot, a sweeping musical score, and a gray ending make *Final Fantasy VII* one of the best games of all time, and certainly the best game of 1997.

Final Fantasy VII still holds up as one of the great stories of our time thanks to its main baddie, Sephiroth. He's utterly mad but also incredibly sympathetic. How would you react if you found out you were a science experiment? Burning a small mountain hamlet seems excessive, but Sephiroth isn't one to do things by halves.

Final Fantasy VII touches on all the things I hold dear: friendship, the role of capitalism in the planet's even-tual destruction, talking stuffed cats, the fear of never really knowing your friends, plucky teen ninjas, and the list goes on.

If you can't handle the blocky nineties graphics, try the remake. *Final Fantasy VII* is a beautiful story rendered in video game form, and I'm happy that it's still a part of my life.

—**KIM KEY,**
analyst at PCMag

FINAL FANTASY VII REMAKE (2020)

If I had to pick a video game that had an incredible impact on the year it came out, I'd choose *Final Fantasy VII Remake*. For so many people 2020 was a dark year, one where most of us were forced to stay indoors, in some cases with our own demons. Just like heroes do, *Final Fantasy VII Remake* serendip-itously showed up in that time of need. I'm sure I'm not alone when I say the hype leading up to the release (and the hype after beating the game) made that year substantially more bearable.

Beyond that, the original *Final Fantasy VII* is just so meaningful to so many video game fans. Playing the remake, seeing how that universe we first experienced as kids had grown, made us reflect on how much we have grown as well in between 1997 and 2020. For many of us this game worked as a reunion between our adult selves and our inner children. It did so with an outstanding technical quality, and a reimagining both loyal to the original in so many details but mind-shattering and new in other ways at the same time.

FFVII Remake is a brave game done with a lot of heart, and one that brought a lot of light into the world. That's quite fitting since the entire *Final Fantasy* brand started with the legend of the Warriors of Light.

—**ALEX MOUKALA,**
composer and YouTuber

1998

TACTICAL ESPIONAGE ACTION

METAL GEAR™
SOLID

THE HIDEO KOJIMA GAME
OF THE YEAR

SNEAK AROUND THE SHADOW MOSES ISLAND
COMPOUND AS SPECIAL AGENT SOLID SNAKE TAKING
OUT ENEMY GUARDS WITH STEALTH RATHER THAN
BRUTE FORCE. ALONG THE WAY, YOU`LL UNRAVEL
A VAST MILITARY CONSPIRACY THAT WILL LEAVE
YOU QUESTIONING YOUR OWN EXISTENCE.

PRESS START

Gaming's jump to 3D graphics, a massive move toward visual realism, reignited the medium's desire to be seen and respected as a mature storytelling art form to rival films. Auteur theory, a popular critical lens through which to view films as art, analyzes works as the unique visions of singular artists and the partners they frequently choose to collaborate with. You trace their common themes, motifs, and obsessions. When you watch a Wes Anderson or Spike Lee movie, you'll know to expect symmetrical compositions or a dolly shot. While some dedicated individual developers have created indie games all by themselves, video games, like movies, are typically group efforts. Plenty of talented people worked on Metal Gear Solid and deserve credit, but when you experience this work of stealth game art from writer/producer/director Hideo Kojima, whether playing it or just watching, you know precisely who authored it. No other video game auteur leaves a stamp this proud and obvious.

OPERATION INTRUDE N313

Hideo Kojima's fascination with gaming's storytelling potential goes back to the beginning of his career. Kojima cites *The Portopia Serial Murder Case*, the 1983 adventure game Yuji Horii developed before elevating game narratives even more with *Dragon Quest*, as the reason why he entered the industry. Before that, he just wanted to make movies. After landing a game development job at publisher Konami, he didn't create sprawling epics. He worked on sequels to penguin platformers for the MSX, a home computer that was quickly overshadowed by the NES. Eventually, he directed, wrote, and designed a pair of story-driven adventure games of his own, very much influenced by popular prestige films. 1988's *Snatcher* drew from cyberpunk sources like *Akira* and *Blade Runner* years before *Final Fantasy VII*, while 1994's *Policenauts* married hard sci-fi and social issues with American buddy cop tropes.

On his Twitter profile, Kojima says, "70% of my body is made of movies," and that cinephile spirit appears in everything he touches. He's friends with Guillermo del Toro and geeked out when he met Robert De Niro at the Tribeca Film Festival. His latest game, *Death Stranding*, stars Norman Reedus, Mads Mikkelsen, a de-aged Lindsay "The Bionic Woman" Wagner, director Nicolas Winding Refn, and del Toro himself.

Text-heavy adventure games may be perfect for delivering raw narratives, but they've never been the most mainstream genre in the world. For Kojima to reach the masses, he needed to deliver his vision through a type of game most players could get into. He (and his team) needed to make *Metal Gear*. Released for the MSX2, NES, and other platforms in 1987, *Metal Gear* is the original game in the saga. As hard-bitten action hero Solid Snake, whose box art appearance is literally Michael Biehn in *The Terminator*, players infiltrate a rogue military base named Outer Heaven to shut down a mysterious weapon called Metal Gear.

Metal Gear's gruff military aesthetic instantly appealed to any red-blooded gamer who saw it. After all, Konami also published the classic run-and-gun military shooter *Contra*. *Metal Gear*'s "Gear Up" promotional flyer showed rocket launchers, land mines, and other destructive toys. But *Metal Gear* was sneaky, in more ways than one. Despite the shared military themes, *Metal Gear*'s gameplay couldn't be more different from *Contra*'s. *Metal Gear* brought the stealth game genre to consoles for the first time. In stealth games, from military espionage in *Tom Clancy's Splinter Cell* to *Tenchu*'s ninja shadow assassinations, you don't want to loudly murder every enemy you see. You want to quietly and patiently sneak around them, skillfully observe their movement patterns, and know when to move, strike, or stand still. Your gun is a desperate last resort, something you use only when things go sideways. Even then, later games rewarded you for using nonlethal tranquilizer guns instead of bullets. In *Metal Gear*, a room with two smart enemies is more tense and challenging than an arena full of brainless fodder.

The stealth genre's methodical pace also gave Kojima plenty of room to weave his intricate narrative, primarily delivered through text conversations between Snake and his handlers. *Metal Gear* kicked off a dense and delirious odyssey of geopolitical intrigue, government conspiracies, and legendary soldiers leading their own nation-states. A Metal Gear itself is a tank capable of launching nuclear missiles from anywhere . . . because it walks on two legs. Between the first *Metal Gear* and its sequel *Metal Gear 2: Solid Snake*, Snake had already discovered his mentor Big Boss's treachery and defeated him twice. The franchise spawned more than enough lore to spare, but Kojima's ambitions clearly called for a bigger canvas.

WAR HAS CHANGED

The original two *Metal Gear* games were commercial and critical successes, but they were also warm-ups for the main event that was *Metal Gear Solid*, released for the PlayStation in 1998. *MGS*'s underlying stealth gameplay remains largely similar to that of its predecessors: 1990's *Metal Gear 2* didn't release in North America until it was included in compilations years later, but some fans who played both it and *MGS* say that *Solid* is virtually a remake. You still sneak around a hostile military base, this time a remote Alaskan facility called Shadow Moses Island. You still monitor guards and find safe routes, this time using an intuitive radar system. The games even share boss fights, like a duel with a ninja or a battle against a helicopter. If you look past the presentation, the similarities are uncanny.

Presentation, though, makes up the heart of visual storytelling. As a film lover, Kojima intimately understood this. So he used the PlayStation's 3D CD-ROM power to present the most cinematic experience one could still confidently call a video game. Carefully chosen color palettes create a world-weary espionage atmosphere that also happens to gracefully hide hardware limitations. Artful camera angles and thrilling choreography turn the puppetlike character models into full-blown action heroes. People criticize Kojima for egotistically taking too much credit, but *MGS*'s opening also highlights its star, voice actor David Hayter. *MGS* wouldn't work nearly as well without Snake's iconic gravelly voice interacting with other stellar performances, like Debi Mae West's Meryl Silverburgh or Paul Eiding's Colonel Campbell, both in lengthy cutscenes and codec conversations. Celebrating your actors is another very auteur move.

With all these enhanced storytelling techniques at his disposal, Kojima continued to explore the themes that have since defined the franchise. Snake must not only stop another Metal Gear mech but also grapple with the fact that he is one of several disgruntled clone sons of the villainous yet misunderstood Big Boss. For a game with so much firearm fetishism, *MGS* is always staunchly anti-war, dreaming of a world without nuclear weapons. Characters go into winding monologues about their tragic backstories in brutal war zones, muse on post-Soviet Russian politics, and spout dialogue like, "Do you think love can bloom even on a battlefield?" It has the conflicted tension you'd expect from a Japanese creator who loves American action movies. It's a G.I. Joe anime, confusing and pretentious but also profound.

It's also very funny! In between all the somber violence, *MGS* constantly cracks silly jokes. Characters have absurd code names like Revolver Ocelot and Liquid Snake. At one point, your nerdy sidekick, Hal, pisses himself out of fright. Snake hides in a cardboard box to escape danger. Wild tonal shifts became yet another Kojima hallmark.

For as much as *MGS* wants you to think of it as a movie, the real reason it can get away with this much (extremely entertaining) self-indulgence is because *MGS* is an excellent video game. *MGS*'s gameplay, its "Tactical Espionage Action" according to the box art, would feel just as fun and satisfying even with a more conventional story. The stealth challenges, from manipulating enemy behavior to attempting nonlethal takedowns with close-quarters combat, force you to fully consider your surroundings. Balancing being careful with being confident gives the action a cerebral edge. It's a thinking person's action game. Because you are very much not invincible, Snake himself has a fallibility that makes him even more heroic, like John McClane in *Die Hard*.

That's not to say the gameplay doesn't occasionally get as esoteric as the plot. To defeat one psychic boss you must physically plug your controller into a separate port, a borderline-unfair puzzle mechanic but a brilliant way of conveying story meaning through gameplay. The sheer amount of story also gives the game very untraditional pacing for the time. Still, considering future *Metal Gear* games have multiple hourlong cutscenes with no interactivity whatsoever, the first *MGS* finds the right ratio between watching a game and playing it.

Many talented creators made *MGS* a reality. When I close my eyes and think of this series, I see Yoji Shinkawa's entrancing watercolor artwork. And not everyone is fully on board with what Kojima likes to do. He edits trailers that intentionally mislead the audience about character appearances or hide the fact that they even are *Metal Gear* trailers. *Metal Gear Solid V: The Phantom Pain* has a painfully stupid and arguably offensive "explanation" for why its sexy female character wears no clothes.

But without Hideo Kojima, what's the point? When Konami unceremoniously parted ways with Kojima after *MGSV*, the publisher put out one last soulless spin-off game before shelving the franchise. *Metal Gear Solid* shows how Hollywood doesn't have the monopoly on big-budget yet deeply personal works from cherished auteurs with distinct voices.

STARCRAFT ZERG RUSHES IN

Chess packs so much tactical depth into a handful of pieces arranged on a board, it's clear why intellectuals have spent hundreds of years mastering its possibilities. The only video game that gives chess a run for its money is Blizzard's ingenious, enduring PC strategy game, *StarCraft*.

StarCraft is a real-time strategy game, meaning all actions happen in real time instead of during discrete turns—a genre Blizzard had proven its mastery of with the original *Warcraft* games years earlier. Starting with a handful of workers, you gather resources to build structures and raise armies to fight other players or computer-controlled armies in the campaign. You must maintain a strong economy as you expand across the map while also quickly building defenses and scouting enemy territory to determine how best to strike.

StarCraft's sci-fi universe features three factions: Terrans (human space truckers), Zergs (xenomorphs with their evil sexy alien queen, Sarah Kerrigan), and Protoss (religious predators with a thing for pyramids). These factions have unique units, all with strengths and weaknesses to consider. If you rush in with a Zergling army, you can wipe out your foe before the game even starts. However, Zerglings are so weak, just a handful of mighty Protoss warriors can carve through a whole swarm. Exquisite balance and polish mean infinite tactics are viable.

In high-level play, you'll perform hundreds of actions per minute. That's a lot of mouse clicking, but it's all worth it, because nothing makes you feel more like an absolute genius than successfully executing a plan in *StarCraft*. You can even get vicarious thrills watching matches from the thriving competitive scene. In South Korea, it was so popular it was esports before we had that word. As a kid, my eyes always turned bloodshot while intensely playing a match. When my first late night with the long-awaited sequel *StarCraft II* left them teary, the pain felt almost nostalgic. *StarCraft* is my personal favorite game of all time.

METAL GEAR SOLID (1998)

I'd never heard of Gulf War syndrome or MUF before *Metal Gear Solid*, and neither had legendary mercenary Solid Snake. He's told of these things by an elderly weapons manufacturer after saving him from an elderly gunslinger (look, it's complicated). The game cut away from PlayStation polygons to show real-world footage of corroding oil drums and missile launches.

This stuff was eye-opening, scary. Link and Mario never brought up Pentagon black budgets or thermonuclear geopolitics. But this is not a miserable game. Enemy guards get diarrhea. Wolves pee on you. Dialogue is delivered by the 1990s cartoon voice actor hall of fame. (Want to hear a Ninja Turtle call J. Edgar Hoover a "well-known racist"?)

Though it sliced through my adolescent naivety, *MGS* remained a thrill, full of ideas and scenarios that would inspire the next generation—it was the birth of a new genre at the beginning of the twenty-first century. Yes, the world is a battlefield, full of dirty nukes and dirtier politicians. But as Snake learns, even while facing a cloudy and uncertain future, fun can bloom there, too.

—TIM TORRES, writer

METAL GEAR SOLID 3: SNAKE EATER (2004)

Metal Gear Solid 3: Snake Eater is arguably the franchise's finest hour and one of the finest games of 2004. Eschewing the man-made structures of its predecessors, *MGS3* tossed you into the middle of a Russian jungle filled with all manner of dangers. Soviet soldiers could kill you just as easily as an alligator. But as protagonist Naked Snake, you could use that very jungle to your advantage. Situational awareness was vital when dealing with the game's eccentric bosses, as every tree, rock, or marshy swamp could become a useful tool. The epic and tragic prequel story line, along with the sublime gameplay, made *MGS3* an instant classic.

—TONY POLANCO, computing writer at Tom's Guide

1999

system shock™

THE PREMONITION OF THE YEAR

STRANDED ON AN ABANDONED SPACESHIP IN A
FUTURE FULL OF PSYCHIC-POWERED SOLDIERS AND
MALEVOLENT AI, YOU MUST LEARN FROM YOUR
SURROUNDINGS AND TAKE ADVANTAGE OF EVERY TOOL
AT YOUR DISPOSAL IN ORDER TO ESCAPE AND SURVIVE.

PRESS START

From partying in 1999 to crossing into the year 2000, the new millennium excited everyone. It sounded like a leap forward into the future prior generations could only dream about. Or maybe it would all end. Y2K also scared people who didn't understand how computers actually worked into believing a few coding oversights could cause civilization to collapse. Considering how increasingly entrenched computers have become in our lives, we're still not out of the woods yet. In **System Shock 2**, a technological apocalypse actually comes to pass. An evil artificial intelligence threatens to wreak more havoc on humanity than even the wildest Y2K doomsday nightmare. **System Shock 2** did more than just predict the future, though. It established an entire school of video game design so forward-thinking that today's games still try to keep up.

THROUGH THE LOOKING GLASS

Gamers take for granted just how tricky game genres can be if you don't inherently know what they mean. A racing game or a sports game sounds pretty self-explanatory (if you don't make the distinction between arcade-style and sim-style) but not everything has such a clear and easily understandable real-world analog. "Roguelike" and "Metroidvania" only make sense when you know the specific games those titles reference. The genre we'll be discussing here, the immersive sim, isn't quite as inscrutable. But without built-in knowledge, it still requires explanation.

Immersive sims came about as an attempt to build on concepts Western PC designers found appealing in both early *Ultima*-style RPGs as well as first-person shooters. These genres used their primitive 3D environments to create authentic-feeling spaces for players to interact with, whether through number-crunching dice rolls or torrents of bullets. Immersive sims merged these ideas. For the game world recreations to feel truly realistic, they needed to offer players a variety of ways for them to engage with their systems. To tackle problems with multiple open-ended solutions, using your brain and taking action couldn't remain separate. Immersive sims have dice rolls *and* bullets. This genre saw realistic graphics and more powerful technology not as an excuse to make games more like movies, but as a way to make games the most intricate sandboxes and clockwork machines of all time. It's right in the name: immersive simulation.

SHODAN SHOWDOWN

Let's see how this all comes together in immersive sim standard-bearer *System Shock 2.* Before you find yourself trapped on the treacherous *Von Braun* spaceship, you pick your character's military career and which subjects they chose to focus on during years' worth of cryosleep. Like stats in an RPG, this strengthens you in some areas while weakening you in others, encouraging you to adopt certain playstyles. The choices you make therefore affect how you'll approach combat. For superior first-person gunplay, become a marine and increase your weapon skills. If you want to mess with physics and launch exploding barrels at psychic monkeys using only your mind, then dump more points into psionic abilities as you level up.

System Shock 2 constantly presents you with choices, both in the middle of the action and for long-term character growth. Scrounge for gear and health items off dead bodies to survive. Spend precious nanite currency to hack into security cameras or locked containers with better loot. The game features elements of first-person shooters, role-playing games, stealth games, and even survival horror games, but the overall experience is something unique. The specifics may change, but above all else immersive sims establish clear rules and then challenge players to manipulate those rules to their advantage. These games treat players as people with agency, not computer programs that can only perform set tasks.

Immersive sims also craft some of the richest narratives in gaming and deliver them in fascinating ways only games can. In the first *System Shock*, the hacker hero stopped an evil artificial intelligence named SHODAN (Sentient Hyper-Optimized Data Access Network) from conquering the human race. *System Shock 2* picks up decades later in a universe where corrupt companies attempt to regain power and new technology is kept in check. As you encounter a distinctly biological menace on the *Von Braun*, you'll nonetheless discover a disturbing link back to forbidden cyberspace.

As strange as that all sounds on paper, *System Shock 2* unfurls its story in an enticingly organic way. You don't watch cutscenes or read walls of text. You listen to audio messages left behind in the chaos or piece together what happened by walking through scenes from the aftermath. Your psychic powers allow you to hear ghosts of residual consciousness from victims moments before their deaths. You don't just passively observe the story. You actively live inside it. You're immersed in the simulation, and that motivates you to see it through to the end. It helps that SHODAN herself remains one of gaming's most legendary villains.

Designers like Warren Spector, Ken Levine, and Harvey Smith carried forward *System Shock 2*'s immersive sim ideas (and the 0451 passcode Easter egg) into games like *Deus Ex*, *BioShock*, and *Dishonored*. However, despite a recent resurgence, immersive sims seem to have peaked and begun to decline. The genre is just too niche. But even if the label goes away, immersive sims' spirit will haunt gaming for a long time. By focusing on intelligence, telling a thoughtful narrative while simulating a complex world for skeptical players to upend, there's no genre better suited to tackle the future. Immersive sims prepare us for the darkest outcomes; they train us for Y3K. As far as we know, this world we live in now is the most immersive simulation of all. If more people play *System Shock 2*, we may all finally choose to break free.

TONY HAWK'S PRO SKATER DOES A 900

Skateboarding culture blew up in the 1990s, and every kid wanted a piece of the action. Unfortunately, many suburban parents were afraid this "extreme sport" would crack their children's heads open, or worse, turn them into punks. Good thing game developer Neversoft was there to bring the magic of skateboarding to your safe TV screen.

Tony Hawk's Pro Skater is no pale imitation of the real sport. Initially, the arcade-style control scheme simplifies skating to the point where anyone can grasp it. Doing ollies, grinding on rails, and performing different flips and grabs required little more than a button press and holding the stick in a certain direction. However, only the most dedicated shredders can master the deceptive amount of depth. To earn the highest score in your two-minute run, you must intimately learn each level's every nook and cranny to maximize the amount of moves you can string together while staying on balance. That's how you go from rolling up and down a basic vert ramp to skating your way across Roswell, New Mexico.

Alongside its finely tuned gameplay, Tony Hawk's Pro Skater took care to honor the youth skater culture that birthed it. You could play as other pro skaters like Bob Burnquist and Kareem Campbell alongside Birdman himself. Later games even featured Darth Maul and Spider-Man as unlockable characters. The videotape collectibles and home movie aesthetic reflected skate culture's obsession with filming itself, as seen in stuff like Jackass. No video game franchise curates contemporary music as expertly as Tony Hawk's Pro Skater. Like skateboarding itself, Tony Hawk's Pro Skater is a serious athletic feat that knows when to not take itself too seriously.

INCREDIBLE CRISIS (1999)

Incredible Crisis is a party game for one player and one player only. Incredible Crisis distills the PlayStation era to its purest form: trying everything at once and seeing whatever worked. It's a comedy/drama about a family going through difficult times, including an affair on a Ferris wheel, an alien invasion, a kaiju teddy bear, and doing morning exercises at work. It's just truly bottom-of-the-soul weird. The gameplay itself is oddly timeless: namely that it's just as frustrating now as it was in 1999.

—MIKE DRUCKER, writer

TONY HAWK'S PRO SKATER 1 + 2 (2020)

You'd think I, as a person who is both bad at and generally disinterested in video games, have no place to say what makes for a good video game. Let me tell you this: you're wrong. It makes me more qualified than anyone. Here's the thing: if a video game can hold the attention of my brain, a brain ravaged by twenty-seven years of ADHD and three years of pandemic ADHD (they're different things), it is as great a testament as anything to its quality. The Last of Us? More like Tres Passed on Us. Death Stranding? If I want to walk around and pick up trash, I'll just go outside.

That's why the best game of 2020 was Tony Hawk's Pro Skater 1 + 2. Dropping in the dog days of Quar Summer (Part One), it provided the perfect pandemic video game vibe: you can turn off your brain and free skate. You can focus on repeating any number of courses, knocking off level goals one by one. You can make a custom skater with stupid hair and a dump-truck ass. It was impossible to have a bad time playing THPS in the early aughts, and it's impossible now. That game came at the perfect moment, and I look forward to letting my brain fade to fuzz as I go back and forth on a half-pipe hitting 900s for years to come.

—TRES DEAN,
author of We Ride Titans and For Your Consideration: Dwayne "The Rock" Johnson

2000

HλLF-LIFE®
COUNTER-STRIKE

THE MOD OF THE YEAR

TWO TEAMS COMPETE TO CARRY OUT VARIOUS
OBJECTIVES FROM PLANTING BOMBS TO RESCUING
HOSTAGES IN THIS MOD-TURNED-OFFICIAL MULTIPLAYER
FIRST-PERSON SHOOTER SPIN-OFF OF HALF-LIFE .

PRESS START

On consoles, first-party companies call the shots. Microsoft, Nintendo, and Sony run the show on their machines, while third-party companies and paying customers alike fall in line. The PC, though, is democratic. Computers already do more than play video games. Even when you do play games on your PC you have so much more freedom and technological flexibility, as long as you know what you're doing. Only one company comes close to being PC gaming's unofficial first-party developer: Valve. After all, Valve's founder Gabe Newell got an up-close-and-personal look at how to run a computer monolith while working at Microsoft during the height of Windows. Valve's tendrils into PC gaming number too great to count. What we need here is a vertical slice, a single cross section with a little bit of everything, an example that shows how Gaben and friends achieved this dominance. So strap in, defuse that bomb, and get ready to learn about **Half-Life: Counter-Strike**.

G-MEN

Before we get into *Half-Life: Counter-Strike*, we must start with the first part of the title: *Half-Life*. Released in 1998, *Half-Life* was Valve's first game, and few developers have had such a massively impactful debut. The late nineties in general saw a shift toward more cinematic storytelling, and *Half-Life* brought that energy to the first-person shooter genre. While Id games like *Doom* and *Quake* focused on fun but mindless slaughter, *Half-Life* took players on an expertly paced journey with enigmatic characters and thrilling set pieces. Playing as silent, bearded physicist Gordon Freeman, you used your trusty crowbar to beat back an interdimensional alien menace. What is Black Mesa really researching? Who is the G-Man? Instead of levels, you traveled through a continuous world that transitioned from one environment to the next with dramatic chapter cards. Even calling it a shooter, although accurate, downplays the game's scope and inventiveness.

Half-Life, its sequels, and its expansions developed by Valve's partners all excelled as single-player experiences. Being a single-player game also made *Half-Life* stand out in a shooter market dominated by multiplayer. But multiplayer dominated because that's what players wanted, and unlike console players, PC players know how to take what they want when companies won't give it to them. Just as PC gamers build and modify their own machines to optimize performance, a huge part of PC gaming culture revolves around players modifying existing games and tech into something new. *Half-Life* itself runs on a modded *Quake* engine. Mods can be jokes, like putting Thomas the Tank Engine into horror games, but mods can also be ambitious love letters from fans to their famous franchises. Valve gave its blessing to fans who successfully remade *Half-Life* in 2020 as *Black Mesa*.

And then there's *Counter-Strike*.

INSURGENTS

Counter-Strike began as a multiplayer *Half-Life* mod. Cocreators Minh "Gooseman" Le and Jess Cliffe used the game's GoldSrc engine to create not a lofty single-player sci-fi journey but a grounded and endlessly replayable competitive shooter game. However, something *Counter-Strike* did have in common with its parent game was a design much smarter than the rest of the market, even if those designs served very different shooter styles.

In *Counter-Strike*, two teams of five—one team of terrorists and one team of counterterrorists—compete to complete objectives where only one can emerge victorious. You either have to disarm a bomb or plant a bomb and guard it until it explodes. Rescue hostages or prevent them from being rescued. Assassinate someone or keep them alive. Win a round, or at least kill some enemies, and you get money to spend on better guns and equipment to take into the next round. Trade your basic knife and pistol for beefy assault rifles and C-4 explosives. By giving you larger tasks to think about beyond just shooting everyone in sight, *Counter-Strike* forces you to play with purpose. Being on a team encourages you to synergize, to talk to teammates on voice chat, as you come up with tactics.

Throughout 1999 and early 2000, Le and Cliffe put out various *Counter-Strike* betas. PC modders value community, and famous level makers contributed to the project as Le and Cliffe incorporated fan feedback. The game grew so popular that you could easily mistake it for an official Valve product. In 2000, Valve made it officially official when it bought *Counter-Strike* and hired Le and Cliffe to work on the project full-time, blurring the line between mod and full-blown game. *Counter-Strike* wished upon a star and became a real boy, and one of the most popular competitive shooters ever with millions of fans.

Hard-core gamers love *Half-Life*. It . . . probably should've gotten its own chapter. Valve's PC shooter mastery continued in *Half-Life*'s (still unresolved) episodic sequels as well as the brilliant, hilarious, physics-based first-person puzzle game *Portal*. Like a first-party company using its highest-quality games to sell consoles, Valve's games now primarily exist to make some other product or service seem more valuable, from the Steam digital marketplace to the Valve Index virtual reality headset. Valve and PC gaming stay joined at the hip.

Counter-Strike, however, represents Valve as a company better than we realize. Valve's other multiplayer shooters, the cooperative zombie survival shooter *Left 4 Dead* and the colorful class-based team shooter *Team Fortress*, became smash hits in their own right. It's not a shooter, but *Dota 2's* origins also come from a mod that Valve turned into an official game with staggering esports success.

The company savvy enough to see *Counter-Strike* and bring it into the fold is the company that has kept its finger on PC gaming's pulse for more than two decades. Valve is rich and private enough to do whatever it wants. What Valve wants to do is not release too many games but release smart, enduring games. No PC shooter has proven smarter or endured longer than *Half-Life: Counter-Strike*.

DYNASTY WARRIORS 2
CUTS ARMIES DOWN TO SIZE

Even the most passionate *Dynasty Warriors* fan would admit these games are pretty dumb. Whereas the first *Dynasty Warriors* game was a fighting game with an emphasis on weapons, *Dynasty Warriors 2* is where developer Omega Force shifted the series into its stupidly, gloriously over-the-top current form.

Dynasty Warriors 2 drops players into battles inspired by ancient Chinese wars. You play as actual historical figures of the Three Kingdoms like Guan Yu, Dian Wei, and Sun Shang Xiang. That's where the realism ends, though. *Dynasty Warriors 2* introduced the gargantuan 3D beat-'em-up action that would become the franchise's staple. As your lone hero roams the map, you'll encounter huge hordes of enemies. Instead of meeting them with an army of your own, you take them down personally, using your overpowered blade to slash through thousands of foes at once with simple but stylish combos. Opponents are so dumb they wait their turn to die.

To be fair, *Dynasty Warriors* does try to spice things up with mild strategy elements. When you defeat a fort full of enemies you take it over, allowing your troops to surge deeper into hostile territory.

But eventually the never-ending attacking, no matter how cathartic, turns repetitive. Also repetitive? The never-ending number of *Dynasty Warriors*-style games, or musou (unrivaled) games, Omega Force cranked out afterward. For a while, *Dynasty Warriors* served as the easiest punch line in gaming.

However, like a hardheaded hero staring down legions of opponents, *Dynasty Warriors* kept pushing forward. It found new life by grafting its formula onto other franchises and adapting its mechanics to new genres. Suddenly, button-mashing crowd combat became much easier to tolerate when paired with *Persona 5*'s beloved characters, beautiful aesthetic, and RPG elements. *Hyrule Warriors* injected a healthy dose of hard-hitting musou action into the otherwise modest *Legend of Zelda* adventures. *Dynasty Warriors* demonstrates that with enough time and clever thinking, every game can find its place, even the dumb ones.

GUJIAN 3 (2018)

Gujian 3 (古剑奇谭三) is a Chinese RPG about a free-spirited swordsman named Beiluo, whose life was thrown into upheaval when he inherited the throne from a dying king of a celestial race. But it's also a xianxia game—a Chinese fantasy genre that's rife with influences from Chinese folklore and Taoism. It's set in an unimaginably vast universe, composed of several realms where immortal warriors and demonic beings frequently clash with one another. Fight scenes are as complex as they are grand. At the same time, there are also plenty of detours to take; you can grow crops at a farm, decorate your home à la *Animal Crossing: New Horizons*, or play minigames as a talking gopher. *Gujian 3* may demand a lot of hours from its players, but the experience it delivers in return is worth several times more.

—KHEE HOON CHAN,
  game critic and journalist from Singapore, with bylines in Polygon, *Edge* magazine, and *PC Gamer*

2001

THE XBOX SAVIOR OF THE YEAR

FIGHT AN ALIEN MENACE AS THE HEROIC MASTER CHIEF
AND FIGHT YOUR FRIENDS IN INNOVATIVE MULTIPLAYER
MODES IN THIS SCI-FI FIRST-PERSON SHOOTER.

PRESS START

Launch games, games that release on the same day as a new console, don't have an easy job. Although developers get access to the hardware months in advance, they only barely have enough time to understand how it works, let alone make a good game. Launch games have to do more than just sell themselves—they have to sell the entire expensive new toy they're tethered to. Many times, launch games are forgettable garbage only early adopters pick up because they simply have nothing else to play. But sometimes we get killer apps that serve as playable thesis statements for their systems. Sometimes a launch game is so spectacular it single-handedly props up an entire system, an entirely new contender in the video game industry, for generations to come. Without Halo: Combat Evolved, kiss Microsoft's Xbox goodbye.

GATES'S GAMBIT

In 2001, Microsoft slid under a rapidly closing door to become the last major new player in the video game console market. Bill Gates couldn't have picked a better time. Microsoft already had plenty of gaming experience thanks to PC gaming on Windows machines, and with its first console, Microsoft wanted to marry PC gaming power with console convenience. Previously, Microsoft had worked with Sega to bring Windows to its 1999 Dreamcast console, but when that system died before its time, Sega gave up on making consoles in favor of making games for its former rivals, finally bringing *Sonic the Hedgehog* games to Nintendo systems. Prior to the Xbox, Microsoft had tried—and laughably failed—to buy Nintendo, which at the time was not doing much better than Sega. While the Game Boy had the portable market on lock, Sony's PlayStation absolutely dominated the console space. But if Sony could suddenly declare itself gaming's king, why couldn't Microsoft step in to snatch the crown? In an industry controlled by Japanese corporations, why shouldn't the United States of America get in on the action?

Enter the Xbox, because what else is a video game console but an extreme box? In truth, the *X* actually refers to DirectX, Microsoft's collection of programming tools. But the system itself, with its chunky black chassis and glowing Mountain Dew–green accents, looks like it can't wait to snowboard down the tallest mountain and crush some Taco Bell. The console infamously launched with a controller so huge, nicknamed the Duke, only professional wrestlers could comfortably hold it. Microsoft executives like J Allard came out onstage at press events wearing suit jackets with hoodies sewn into them. Xbox debuted with an edgy Sega-like image meant to set itself apart from lame established competition and balanced it out with a Sony-like strategy to appeal to grown-ups rather than little kids. Xbox just needed a launch game to solidify its street cred. Xbox needed big guns.

Before *Halo*, the developers at Bungie were already best known for big guns. The team's *Marathon* trilogy brought sci-fi first-person shooter action to Apple Macintosh computers in the mid-nineties. Going into the new millennium, Bungie pivoted away from shooters in favor of tactics games like *Myth: The Fallen Lords*. The team first envisioned *Halo* as a strategy game, too. However, by the time Steve Jobs himself unveiled *Halo* at Macworld 1999, it had become Bungie's next Mac shooter.

Then Microsoft got its hands on it. Any tech journalist can tell you there's no love lost between Microsoft and Apple. Any games journalist can tell you Apple has never maintained much serious interest in video games. So when Bungie was in need of serious financial assistance, Microsoft swooped in and bought the developer outright, a deal negotiated by Bungie cofounders Alex Seropian and *Halo* director Jason Jones. *Halo: Combat Evolved* then turned into the centerpiece of Xbox's launch lineup. *Halo* went from a Mac exclusive to a brand so intimately intertwined with Microsoft it's now impossible to separate them.

RISE OF REACH

Before *Halo*, few developers attempted to make first-person shooters on consoles. Aside from early *Doom* ports and *GoldenEye 007* on Nintendo 64, the genre just felt so much more natural on PC with superior visuals, smoother mouse-based aiming, and online multiplayer. So while there's no shortage of great shooters on consoles today (hello, *Call of Duty*), the fact that *Halo* wasn't just a functional console shooter but a fantastic one already made it, and the Xbox, something to pay attention to. Suddenly, this whole PC-meets-console pitch sounded much more appealing.

You still point a gun in first person to shoot at targets, but *Halo* tweaked the FPS formula just enough to feel intuitive on consoles instead of compromised. Dual analog stick controls let you freely move with one stick while aiming with the other. You couldn't sprint, you could only carry two weapons at a time, and instead of finding health packs you let your shield recharge by avoiding fire for a few seconds. Combined, these rules gave the game a heavy, more methodical pace that favored smart tactics over fast reaction times and the best keyboard shortcuts. Whether fighting fellow humans or surprisingly crafty artificial intelligence, *Halo* just felt right. Combat evolved, indeed.

Halo's finely crafted user experience made it a great launch game on Xbox (and eventually PC), but its content would make it a great game no matter what. *Halo* is chock-full of fun and fresh ideas, far more fascinating than the generic military sci-fi theme may imply. The Halo itself is a giant ring-shaped alien planet that serves as the main setting. Along with blasting through linear corridors, *Halo* lets you explore lush natural spaces, on foot or with rugged vehicles like four-wheeled Warthogs and flying Banshees. It's not a completely open world, but you have a lot of freedom in how you approach enemy encounters in a mission like the Silent Cartographer. Having only two guns also makes you carefully consider your attack plan. *Halo* offers a nice blend of conventional firearms, like pistols and shotguns, along with mysterious alien weaponry like the Needler, which peppers opponents with purple spikes until they explode.

The Halo may be the setting, but the hero is the true face of the franchise. In the single-player campaign you step into the hulking boots of Master Chief, an elite Spartan supersoldier defending Earth from a hostile alien coalition known as the Covenant. Chief's metallic military-green space armor is iconic, plausible yet cool. What gives him character, what keeps him from being just an empty shell, is his relationship with his AI companion, Cortana. Yes, it's kind of skeezy that as the games go by, Cortana's character goes from a fuzzy blue hologram to a straight-up naked blue woman with some circuit boards drawn on her. Still, her relationship with Chief genuinely works and is the closest thing the franchise has to an emotional through line. Microsoft named its Windows voice assistant Cortana for a reason.

Single-player campaigns, even the best ones, don't last forever. *Halo*'s multiplayer is eternal. Thanks to local multiplayer, friends on the same couch had a blast gunning each other down. Load up a map like Blood Gulch for a game of Slayer or Capture the Flag. As fun as this digital paintball was, though, 2004's *Halo 2* took console multiplayer to new heights, thanks to online play through Microsoft's revolutionary Xbox Live service. Blurring the line between console and PC even more, now you could play against people from all over the world. On the Internet, you can shout whatever anonymous insults you want over voice chat. Thanks! *Halo*'s connected multiplayer created a community and culture, inspiring fan-made games like Grifball. Through *Halo*, Rooster Teeth's *Red vs. Blue* series introduced the masses to machinima, the art of using in-game footage to make short films.

The original Xbox didn't come anywhere close to beating the PlayStation 2's sales numbers. However, *Halo: Combat Evolved* and *Halo 2* sold a very respectable 5 million and 8.5 million copies, respectively. More importantly, the *Halo* phenomenon set the stage for the next Xbox consoles. The Xbox 360 and its successors made the console wars much more competitive with more franchises, like *Gears of War* and *Forza*, and even more powerful online features, like the Netflix-esque Xbox Game Pass subscription. Microsoft did it. Xbox had arrived, and twenty years later it's still here.

ICO MAKES YOU FEEL

Not every game franchise drives console sales, but some bring a different kind of value to the brand. By supporting the gentle artistry of *Ico*, by Fumito Ueda and Team Ico, Sony made the PlayStation 2 look like an interactive independent theater, not just a fancy DVD player.

In the simplest terms, *Ico* is an action-adventure game. You control a little boy with horns guiding a little girl named Yorda out of a castle. Solve puzzles, avoid enemies, overcome obstacles, help Yorda when she needs it. Typical video game stuff. But that hardly describes what *Ico* is. The game uses its fairy-tale framework to subtract distracting clutter and leave a minimalist atmosphere that reaches into your soul. The world hums with a hazy history just beneath the surface, and the game feels no need to ruin the mystery by explaining itself. By not worrying about facts, *Ico* centers the emotions and relationships between the characters and you the player. *Ico* is art you absorb, not a product you consume.

JURASSIC PARK (1993)

The DOS release of Ocean's *Jurassic Park* game is, on first blush, a fairly rote top-down action game where you shoot at various dinosaurs on your way from objective to objective. At eight years old, though, I didn't mind. Dinosaurs count for an awful lot at that age. But what I would soon learn is that the game had a secret: its back half suddenly shifts genres, playing out as a first-person shooter.

In 1993, first-person games were still something of a rarity. The vast majority of game worlds were explored from the side or from a top-down view. So to go from an overhead view of the verdant fields and rocky canyons of Isla Nublar to being placed directly into the game's dark-blue steel corridors felt like a revelation. It was as if I could feel myself escaping from the humid jungle breezes to a too-quiet air-conditioned stillness. Before, the raptors were distant things, small sprites hunting paleontologist Alan Grant. Now, they were hunting me.

By today's standards the game's first-person sections are (charitably) quaint, but the impact they left at the time taught me a profound lesson about the power of perspective over players. More than that, though, it taught me about the importance of our own imaginations in bringing what's on-screen to life.

—**CHRIS FRANKLIN,**
video essayist at Errant Signal

SHADOW OF THE COLOSSUS (2005)

A game—a good game—is like a fishhook. You take it into your mouth willingly and, after struggling, are yanked forcibly out of your comfortable medium and into a new and often hostile atmosphere.

In Fumito Ueda's 2005 PlayStation 2 masterpiece *Shadow of the Colossus*, many of the trappings that gamers know and cherish are there. As young Wander, you explore a massive landscape and battle enormous beasts to the death to restore the life of your fallen love. But that's the shiny lure on the hook. The world doesn't burst with trinkets to collect and level-ups to grind. The majestic beasts are sometimes unnervingly passive, only fighting back as a last defense. And the heroic journey winds up in a cold, dark place.

I won't spoil the game's stark, minimal narrative for you, even if it's nearly twenty years later. But when you see Wander's quest through to the end, you'll gasp for air, like that miracle fish long ago who, instead of suffocating when pulled from the pond, learned to finally breathe.

—**K. THOR JENSEN,**
cartoonist and author

2002

THE CRIME OF THE CENTURY

AS NEWLY FREED MOBSTER TOMMY VERCETTI,
UNLEASH WHATEVER CHAOS YOU WANT IN THE OPEN
WORLD AND FORGE YOUR OWN CRIMINAL EMPIRE
THROUGH ANY MEANS NECESSARY IN THIS DRUG-FUELED
1980s CITY THAT DEFINITELY ISN`T MIAMI.

PRESS START

Shoot gangsters! Steal cars! Hire sex workers! No game courts nearly as much controversy as Grond Theft Auto. Parents hate it. Politicians from Hillary Clinton to Arnold Schwarzenegger have tried to ban it. Disbarred quack lawyer Jack Thompson made it the centerpiece of his crusade against gaming itself. No matter where you fall on the debate, GTA shocks you. However, shock value alone would not sustain the lasting, astronomical success GTA has enjoyed for two decades. GTA isn't just popular and contentious; it's a legitimately fantastic game franchise that revolutionized game design in ways that have nothing to do with its naughty content. For proof, look no further than the neon nightmare Grond Theft Auto: Vice City.

YOU WOULDN'T STEAL A CAR

It's fun to do bad things. It gives you a little thrill. In the real world, any fleeting excitement you may get from crime and violence quickly gets overwhelmed by serious consequences. By removing the consequences, violent video games just leave you with the fun. In *Body Harvest*, you slaughter alien invaders before they slaughter you. In *Lemmings*, you try to save dumb little animals before they throw themselves off a cliff. Violent? Maybe, but only in the way old anvil-loving cartoons are violent. No real pain, just goofs. Both of those games were developed by DMA Design, a British developer who had a strong relationship with the famously anti-violent company Nintendo. DMA Design almost made a *Kirby* game. The company's next game, however, was about as far away from a Nintendo game as a game could be.

Released for Windows and the PlayStation in 1997, the first *Grand Theft Auto* game envisioned a city full of crime and chaos and bravely said, "That'll make a fun game." You view the action from an overhead, top-down perspective, like looking at a moving road map with your character in the center. To advance, you need to earn a high score, pretty typical for a video game. But in *Grand Theft Auto* you earn points by shooting people, working for the mob, evading the police, and stealing lots and lots of cars. Choose between three barely disguised versions of real-world cities. Liberty City is fake New York, San Andreas is fake San Francisco, and Vice City is fake Miami. The satirical British perspective on American urban life provides the irreverent tone that holds the comedy and carnage together.

As fun as the first two *Grand Theft Auto* games were, though, the pulled-out camera created a sense of distance between you and the bloodbath before you. To fulfill its immersive potential, *GTA* needed to take a revolutionary, *Super Mario 64*–sized leap into the full third dimension. That's exactly what we got next.

I PLAY THE STREET LIFE

On paper, 2001's *Grand Theft Auto III* on the PlayStation 2 makes only one seemingly simple change. The camera now follows the players from behind on the ground, instead of up in the air. In practice, that massive change turned *Grand Theft Auto* into the template for the world's most popular games for years to come. Suddenly, you didn't just watch the action; you were in the action. Everything from gunfights to car races became so much more immediate and visceral, true to how we actually experience the world.

Most importantly, instead of staring at a map, *GTA III* invited us to live inside a breathing city and explore it however we like. *Grand Theft Auto III* is the gold standard for open-world video games. Rather than breaking up the game into different levels or environments, open-world games place players in one huge, interconnected space they can freely explore—in this case, Liberty City. No matter what direction you travel, you're bound to come across a mission in this sprawling, gritty, grown-up playground, whether it's part of the story, an optional side activity, or a diversion you invent yourself. What matters is that you choose what to do, where to go, and when to start some trouble. Deal with the dramatic fallout from your girlfriend's betrayal, park yourself on a highway and unload a machine gun at oncoming traffic for no reason, or take a joyride while listening to Top 40 hits on the radio. This masterpiece, anarchy as game design, set the template for so much more to come. It taps into the same spirit of adventure *The Legend of Zelda* tried to capture, albeit with drastically different subject matter.

So why is *Grand Theft Auto: Vice City* the game of the year? *Grand Theft Auto III* didn't start the franchise, and while it made the biggest leap forward in bringing *GTA* to where it needed to be, *Vice City* added the final missing pieces that created the franchise as we know it. DMA Design developed *GTA III*. For *Vice City*, the team adopted the appropriately punk name we all now know it by: Rockstar Games.

SUNSHINE STATE

Vice City refined the game mechanics *GTA III* established; it polished the controls and technical interface. You don't make something that bold and original without leaving behind some jank to clean up. *Vice City* also vastly improved the game's sense of place. While *GTA III* featured a passable modern-day fake New York, Vice City itself is an incredibly convincing, cocaine-fueled, neon-drenched, fake 1980s Miami. Despite how far the city stretches, each humid inch here feels carefully constructed. Whereas lesser, lazier open-world games blatantly copy and paste sections to artificially inflate their maps (looking at you, *Saints Row*) you see the human touch in every *Grand Theft Auto* city. Again, while their tones couldn't be more different, Rockstar's games display a very Nintendo-esque commitment to craft.

Vice City also fully embodies the swaggering sense of character we expect from *Grand Theft Auto*. Rockstar, particularly its cofounders, brothers Dan and Sam Houser, loves aping popular gangster movies when writing these crime epics. *Vice City* drips with bloody affection for sensational sleaze like *Miami Vice* and *Scarface*. No one remembers *GTA III*'s blank protagonist, Claude. No one can forget *Vice City*'s clever hothead antihero, Tommy Vercetti, voiced by none other than famous goodfella the late Ray Liotta.

At times, *GTA*'s rigid cinematic story feels at odds with its otherwise nonlinear gameplay. You get strange, discordant moments like characters going from a serious cutscene to a ridiculous player-controlled massacre or two. However, *GTA*'s narratives also give you some context to hold on to, a reason to push forward when formless violence grows stale. With their intoxicating mix of lurid thrills and genuine drama, gangster movies make up some of the most acclaimed films in the canon. Why should gangster video games be any different?

Success doesn't equal quality, but *Grand Theft Auto*'s unprecedented success (*GTA V* sold more than 170 million copies!) suggests its freeing, open-world gangster shenanigans connect with people in an undeniable way. Hard-core gamers, mainstream audiences, and everyone in between drop everything to play the new *Grand Theft Auto*. You don't need someone to tell you that *Grand Theft Auto* is the game of the year. You've already played it and know for yourself, even if you haven't told your parents. Don't worry, I won't snitch.

KINGDOM HEARTS IS ANYTHING BUT SIMPLE AND CLEAN

Before anyone knew what *Kingdom Hearts* was, it sold itself as a Disney adventure, with Mickey Mouse's best friends, Goofy and Donald Duck, right on the cover. The actual game, though . . . oh boy.

Flying high from the success of *Final Fantasy VII*, Tetsuya Nomura stepped into the director's chair for the first time to lead a Square Enix project that sounds like a parody. *Kingdom Hearts* merges *Final Fantasy* gameplay and legendary Walt Disney characters. Instead of a stuffy turn-based RPG, *Kingdom Hearts* is a bouncy action RPG where you jump around colorful Disney worlds fighting bad guys with your best animated pals like Goofy and Donald Duck.

At least, that's what you think *Kingdom Hearts* is. It quickly becomes apparent that Nomura is far more interested in weaving his own, original, absolutely bonkers story. For every few minutes of Mickey Mouse in a black trench coat, you'll sit through hours of conversations between very serious people talking about swords shaped like keys. The sequels triple down on endless doppelgängers, nonsensical subtitles, and anime shenanigans happening in the margins during a re-creation of *Frozen*'s "Let It Go."

It's astonishing that Disney executives even allow *Kingdom Hearts* to exist. However, the first game must've done something right because it got so many players so deeply invested in this inexplicable series. Their passion puts hard-core Disney fans to shame. Even I have to admit that the theme song, "Simple and Clean" by Hikaru Utada, is a genuine bop.

GRAND THEFT AUTO V (2013)

Grand Theft Auto V is special for many reasons. It's a game that I've played regularly over the last decade due to its ever-expanding online mode. Yet, beyond its growth and sustainability as an ongoing game, *GTA V* was a dream come true even in 2013.

As a kid, *Grand Theft Auto: San Andreas* was the game that opened my eyes to the scope, scale, and potential of open-world video games. Jump forward and *GTA V* answered my biggest wishes for the franchise by returning to Los Santos with new and improved graphics, up-to-date gameplay, and online multiplayer. Characters like Trevor and Lamar (the memes!) are memorable, and the story hits with great humor. *Grand Theft Auto V*'s Los Santos is purely a joy to exist in.

—BLESSING ADEOYE JR.,
   host and producer at Kinda Funny

KINGDOM HEARTS III (2019)

Kingdom Hearts III is a good video game in its own right. An evolution of the combat introduced in the second installment, it's the first game that truly gives the feeling of well-animated anime fights without resorting to quick-time events. The breadth of attack options, form changes, and character combos feels entirely unique to the series.

But what truly makes *Kingdom Hearts III* special is how it weaves in and closes off plot points and character stories made since the series started, while leaving some dangling threads for future entries. Games like *Assassin's Creed* and *Xenosaga* may try, but *Kingdom Hearts III* managed to continue one long story over not only multiple games but multiple console generations.

—TERENCE WIGGINS,
   @TheBlackNerd

2003

THE NINTENDO LEFT SWERVE OF THE YEAR

SOLVE PUZZLES, CONQUER DUNGEONS,
AND SAIL A VAST OCEAN IN A VIBRANT,
CARTOON-STYLED HYRULE.

PRESS START

intendo never regained the ironclad grip it once had over the entire video game industry. By the time the GameCube launched in 2001, it only continued the trend that saw Nintendo consoles losing more and more market share every generation. Pundits still love to declare that "Nintendo is doomed!" and that we'll see Mario on the PlayStation any day now. Nevertheless, even during the stormiest weather, Nintendo's ship keeps sailing. How?

Nintendo makes fantastic games, and the more time passes, the more nostalgia grows for those games among more people. Nintendo also always does the unexpected. The company fiercely commits to charting its own course compared to its rivals. Nintendo never misses an opportunity to confound fans by giving them not the games they want, but the games they didn't know they needed. Those games, games like **The Legend of Zelda: The Wind Waker**, prove why Nintendo is the one that keeps this industry exciting.

KING OF RED HERRINGS

The Legend of Zelda: Ocarina of Time, released in 1998, masterfully established how classic *Zelda* game design works in 3D. So for *Majora's Mask*, just two years later, Nintendo tried to flip the formula on its head and present a *Zelda* game no one saw coming. A *Zelda* game about apocalyptic, *Groundhog Day*–style time loops? Sure! But for all that game's mechanical weirdness, *Majora's Mask* still looked like a traditional *Zelda* game. It ran on *Ocarina*'s engine and used many of the same assets. Plus, the spookier atmosphere appealed to aging audiences who wanted to see the franchise grow up with them. Years of viciously hip marketing from Sega, PlayStation, and now Xbox had left many insecure Nintendo fans worrying if their console of choice really was for babies.

A new console meant a new opportunity for an even darker, grittier *Zelda* game, one that could go head-to-head with *Halo* and *Grand Theft Auto*. At its 2000 Space World trade show, Nintendo showed off a GameCube *Zelda* tech demo featuring a grueling sword battle between Link and the evil Ganondorf that looked straight out of a *Lord of the Rings* movie. People lost their minds. One year later, Nintendo fully unveiled the next-gen *Zelda* game, *The Legend of Zelda: The Wind Waker*, and people lost their minds again, but for a very different reason.

Wind Waker is not the mature *Zelda* fans wished for. Quite the opposite. The game looks like a living cartoon. Once again a little boy, Link wears a bright-green tunic and observes the world through expressive, cat-like eyes on his giant head. Exaggerated animations turn enemy encounters into adorable slapstick comedy instead of fights to the death. *Wind Waker* uses a technique called cel shading to achieve this aesthetic effect, and it's a stunning technical marvel. With cel shading, 3D objects take on a flat, hand-drawn appearance with a purposeful rejection of realism—you can practically see the brushstrokes on every puff of smoke and ocean wave.

Objectively, *Wind Waker*'s cel-shaded graphics on GameCube surpass anything the Nintendo 64 could pull off (even if the Dreamcast did it first with *Jet Set Radio*). That didn't stop fans from resenting what that graphical prowess was being used for, though. After being teased by the earlier, edgier demo, players felt lied to. They mockingly called *Wind Waker* "Celda." A cartoon *Zelda* confirmed all their fears that Nintendo's most important games would never grow up. They hated it . . . until they played it.

BEYOND THE SEA

Once players actually got their hands on *Wind Waker* in 2003, it soon became clear this was still very much a *Zelda* game, with the same high quality that pedigree implies. The mix of vast overworld and challenging dungeons hewed close to *Ocarina of Time*'s structure. You still solved puzzles, found items like the Boomerang and Hookshot and Master Sword, and had to learn about some mysterious wish-granting relic called the Triforce.

However, don't dismiss *Wind Waker*'s radical new presentation, either. All that familiar action now took place in a beautiful nautical world, incredible to look at in motion. Instead of riding a horse, you sailed the hypnotic seas with your majestic talking boat named *The King of Red Lions*. The Wind Waker itself is a baton you use to control the breeze and guide yourself to your next adventure. The ruins of Hyrule Castle rest at the bottom of the ocean. Set near the end of whatever the *Zelda* timeline is supposed to be, the game even offers longtime villain Ganondorf some deeper characterization. He expresses world-weary remorse before your cute yet surprisingly violent final duel.

If *Wind Waker* has any messages beyond "*Zelda* but with water," it's that players should view *The Legend of Zelda* as a myth that gets handed down, celebrated, and reinterpreted with each generation. We should expect to see ideas we remember reemerge in unexpected, revitalized forms. Tetra, your surly pirate companion, turns out to be none other than the reincarnation of Princess Zelda herself. We should both embrace tradition and welcome the possibility of change in our world and in our video games. Besides, if you want your gritty GameCube reinvention of a classic Nintendo series, go play the phenomenal FPS *Metroid Prime*.

The year after *Wind Waker* released, Nintendo announced the dark and moody *The Legend of Zelda: Twilight Princess*. Finally, the mature *Zelda* game everyone wanted. The game promised that "blades will bleed" and grown men literally cried in the audience when the trailer debuted. However, while that game is very good (no *Zelda* games are bad, some are just better than others), years later *Wind Waker* has the better reputation. Ironically, *Wind Waker*'s timeless, stylized cartoon visuals have aged far better than *Twilight Princess*'s dated attempts at realism. More importantly, by bravely following its own heart, *Wind Waker* resonates with a stronger sense of identity than a game that just wants to give you *Ocarina of Time* again.

There are times when you should listen to your fans and incorporate their feedback. *Wind Waker*'s HD rerelease in 2013 on Wii U removed many of the original game's tedious fetch quests that had been complained about for years. Ultimately, though, art improves when it sticks to the courage of its convictions. "Leave luck to heaven" may be a mistranslation of what the name Nintendo actually means, but it still fits. Nintendo stays confident even when everyone (players and shareholders) thinks it's crazy. Nintendo carved itself a permanent place in the industry by making weird and wonderful games exactly how it wants to make them. Wish upon the Triforce that this always stays true.

DOTA SCORES THE LAST HIT

Where to even begin with *DotA*? *Defense of the Ancients*, or *DotA*, is a fan-made mod for Blizzard's real-time strategy (RTS) game *Warcraft III*, based on an earlier *StarCraft* fan mod called Aeon of Strife. In *Warcraft III*, you could now play as special hero units against weak enemy hordes called Creeps that power you up when you defeat them. *DotA* turns those gimmicky new mechanics into a game unto itself.

As you may expect, this reverse engineering leads to some weird results. True to its RTS roots, you'll still do a lot of clicking as you move your hero across the map and unleash their special skills. But *DotA* plays more like a team sport than a war game. With your own Creep army at your back, you and your five-person squad must battle other players, take down their defense towers, and topple their base before they topple yours.

Little did those modders know that *DotA* would become the esport to end all esports. *DotA* spawned the MOBA genre, multiplayer online battle arena, which exploded in popularity. Think *League of Legends* and *Smite*. Even *Pokémon* has a MOBA now. IceFrog, one of *DotA*'s original lead designers, jumped ship to Valve to develop an official sequel in 2013 called *Dota 2*. Valve's biggest game is a sequel to a mod for another company's game, and it's far more successful than Blizzard's own more accessible take on the genre, *Heroes of the Storm*. Hilarious. Top *DotA* players earn millions of dollars competing in tournaments for this free game. MOBAs in general, and *DotA* specifically, are not going anywhere anytime soon. Truly, the biggest games arrive from the least likely, most humble places.

BEYOND GOOD & EVIL (2003)

There weren't many video games in the early 2000s that meshed my love for *Zelda*'s dungeon combat exploration with the female protagonists I was looking to play as. *Beyond Good & Evil*, in 2003, was a fantastic exception. You play as Jade, a photojournalist who is recruited to find evidence of a hostile alien takeover of the planet, all taking place under the guise of an authoritarian regime doing business as usual. The game's melee combat was incredibly fluid, the story was emotionally impactful, and the gameplay is surprisingly diverse. Simply put, *Beyond Good & Evil* is one of the greatest linear adventure games of its generation.

—**LAURA KATE DALE**,
freelancer for Polygon, IGN, Destructoid, Kotaku UK, and Vice

WARIOWARE, INC.: MEGA MICROGAMES! (2003)

2003 was an era before subscription services, instant downloads, and—since I was only in fifth grade—disposable income. When my parents were kind enough to take me to the store, the pressure was on for me to pick a game I would love for a long time—or at least learn to love.

Luckily, my choice in May '03 was *WarioWare, Inc.: Mega Microgames!* While his more famous archrival had found success with the hybrid board game/minigame series *Mario Party*, Nintendo's premiere garlic-loving plutomaniac aimed to capitalize on my generation's rapidly shortening attention span with seconds-long microgames that ranged from nostalgic (remixed versions of classics like *Metroid* and *Ice Climber*) to gross (one franchise favorite requires picking a series of noses). For months, my little brother and I fought for high scores on simple, silly games that involved things like flying paper airplanes past a series of treacherous walls or helping Wario eat an increasingly big hot dog. While the main game itself is a joyous, overwhelming blast, it was this semi-forced long-term engagement that makes *WarioWare* my game of the year.

—**JJ BERSCH**,
researcher for *Blank Check with Griffin and David*

2004

THE MATRIX OF THE YEAR

JOIN MILLIONS OF PLAYERS IN A SHARED,
ONLINE FANTASY WORLD FULL OF QUESTS TO COMPLETE,
ALLIANCES TO BUILD, AND GEAR TO COLLECT.

PRESS START

When you really enjoy a video game, you get sucked into it. You tune out the real world to live in the fantasy. Most games, even great games, can only keep their hooks in you for a few minutes or hours. Eventually, you move on to something else. But what if a game provided a fantasy so alluring, for you and your friends and everyone all over the world, that you would abandon the real world to live the fantasy forever? **World of Warcraft** is the game of the rest of your life.

THE BLUE PILL

Apple achieves success by polishing and refining existing consumer tech rather than inventing concepts from scratch, like turning awkward MP3 players into sleek iPods. Blizzard operates much the same way. There were real-time strategy games, class-based team shooters, and collectible card games before Blizzard. But games like *StarCraft*, *Overwatch*, and *Hearthstone* elevated those genres and turned millions of players into lifelong fans. Blizzard knows how to take dense, systems-heavy, PC-centric gameplay and make it more accessible while retaining its core appeal.

The MMO (massively multiplayer online) genre definitely has a strong core appeal. With most online multiplayer games, you'll play with maybe four to sixteen other players, perhaps a few more in a shooter with big maps like *Battlefield* or a hundred-player *Fortnite* battle royale. In an MMO, all players, millions of people, can interact within the same game world. We all exist in the same virtual space. Think *The Matrix*, but you know it's fake and you aren't trapped in a gooey pod . . . yet.

MMOs have a ludicrously large scope and face many technical hurdles to pull off this grand illusion of a unified alternate reality. Graphics tend to be mediocre, so the game can attract the widest audience even on weaker machines and ease the load on servers attempting to keep everyone linked up. To pay for pricey servers, MMOs typically charge a subscription fee, or at least try to extract money afterward from free players. The population fluctuates as the game grows more or less popular. MMOs also frequently separate players into smaller, more manageable groups residing in their own versions of the game called instances. As funny as it sounds, you don't want to wait in a line with thousands of people to talk to one quest giver. Instances prevent these annoying bottlenecks. Even with these quirks, few game genres have as much vast, untapped potential as MMOs. They're our best shot at transcending this mortal plane.

Blizzard didn't invent the MMO genre. Role-playing games like *The Realm Online* and *Ultima Online* built off of early experiments with online, text-based, multi-user dungeons, or MUDs. NCSOFT published MMOs in a variety of styles, from the superheroic *City of Heroes* to *Auto Assault*'s car combat. Linden Lab's *Second Life*, released in 2003, abandoned all pretenses of being a game and embraces the idea of MMOs as virtual worlds for people to live real fake lives in, even if it gets a little creepy.

World of Warcraft wasn't even the first fantasy MMO to capture the public's imagination. That happened five years earlier when Sony Online Entertainment's *EverQuest* launched in 1999. *EverQuest*'s huge success allowed SOE to develop MMOs based on hit properties like *Star Wars*, *Lord of the Rings*, and, yes, *The Matrix*. In fact, *World of Warcraft* set out to be the scrappy upstart going up against the *EverQuest* goliath. Suffice it to say, *World of Warcraft* became a lot more than just "the new *EverQuest*."

FOR THE HORDE

World of Warcraft, like Blizzard's best work, took something that already existed and polished it to a sheen. You couldn't ask for a stronger foundation. *Warcraft* was already a beloved franchise, going back to the original *Warcraft: Orcs & Humans* real-time strategy game from 1994. Players already wanted to live inside the land of Azeroth and meet familiar characters like Orc war chief Orgrim Doomhammer or King Varian Wrynn of Stormwind. When you create your character in *WoW*, you either join the noble Alliance or sinister Horde, a choice made much easier when you already know the lore and history of each race. *WoW*'s cartoony art style also helps the game perform better on a variety of computers without having to sacrifice much visual quality. Plus, whimsical graphics make it easier to accept the game's more fantastical fairy-tale aspects, like talking cows and panda people.

MMORPGs don't stray too far from Western role-playing game concepts. *WoW* is no different. You still explore new lands, take on quests, fight monsters, level up, outfit your character with powerful weapons and spells, and experience an unfolding story. You just now perform those tasks with more people. Team up with friends to tackle quick dungeons or join a guild with the best of the best to beat tough raids that last hours.

What *WoW* did was make all of this more accessible than it had ever been. *WoW* doesn't harshly penalize you for dying and reduces tedious grinding. Quickly talk to whoever can give you your next quest and see if the reward is actually worth it. Freely transition between hostile zones where players fight one another and zones where everyone just relaxes. Play enough and you'll earn a mount, like a gryphon or a wyvern, so you can just fly anywhere. *World of Warcraft* balances structure and freedom in a way that makes you feel like there's always something to do but that you can also choose what you want to do. Execute a meticulous battle plan with your teammates, or be like meme legend Leeroy Jenkins and shout your own name as you charge into the fray by yourself.

World of Warcraft's series of small but smart tweaks added up to something so much bigger. It unlocked the MMO genre for a critical mass of players, allowing it to gain the self-sustaining momentum vital for a social game. You can't stop playing *WoW*. You invite your friends, and soon they can't stop playing, either. And so on, and so on. Some describe *WoW* as "a chat room with pictures." While you do need to pay attention to the gameplay, especially during the grueling multiday raids depicted so well in that *South Park* episode, it's not so demanding that you also can't use *WoW* as an excuse to hang out and talk with buddies online. At the game's absolute peak in 2010, it had twelve million active subscribers. That's a lot of buddies.

World of Warcraft goes beyond being a video game and becomes a fascinating accidental model of mass human behavior. With so many players all coexisting, it really is a world, complete with its own observable social dynamics. *World of Warcraft* addiction is as real as gambling addiction, with, occasionally, similarly tragic results. So no matter how much you enjoy it, be sure to take breaks and get rest. *WoW* has a black market where people, including, per the *Washington Post*, former Trump stooge Steve Bannon, sell in-game items for real money in a practice called gold farming.

Here's a real doozy. In 2005, *WoW* added a new boss that afflicted players with a disease called Corrupted Blood. Players suffered for only a few seconds in the boss's lair, but a glitch allowed pets to spread the disease into the world itself. Blizzard unintentionally unleashed a pandemic. Many weaker players died, others set up quarantine zones, and densely populated cities dispersed. Some even took the drastic measure of . . . not playing the game. Ultimately, Blizzard had to reset the world to stop the spread (something we've now learned you can't do in a real pandemic), but the incident created so much potentially valuable data that real-life epidemiologists study it. This is when *World of Warcraft* simply becomes the world.

World of Warcraft is no longer quite the behemoth it once was. During its peak, the subscription revenue probably surpassed multiple countries' GDPs, whereas now *WoW* is free to start. Exciting new MMOs like *Final Fantasy XIV* also give *WoW* true competition it has never had before. One day, *World of Warcraft*, like all worlds, will come to an end.

But today is not that day. More than fifteen years later, *World of Warcraft*'s longevity still astonishes, from new expansions to recreations of *WoW*'s early days. *WoW*'s unparalleled success proved the promise of MMOs. It gave us more than a game to play, it gave us an entire existence we let wash over us, a waking dream where we could fully live as the Gnome Monk or Blood Elf Death Knight we always wanted to be. It's *Warcraft*'s world, we just live in it.

EVE ONLINE 'S AGONY AND ECSTASY

Eve Online sets spacefarers loose in a sci-fi world to do . . . literally whatever the hell they want. The unbelievable freedom leads to even more unbelievable results. An achievement more towering and impressive than some dumb pyramids, *Eve Online* is the next great wonder of the world.

When you start playing *Eve Online*, you're supposed to travel around the galaxy trying to make a living in your spaceship. Explore and mine for resources, become an independent pirate and fight other players, or join up with a private company. But because the game's developer, CCP, provides little regulation and oversight beyond technical support, players run everything in *Eve Online*, and I mean *everything*.

Enterprising capitalists create massive conglomerates from the ground up and hire other actual players to work for them in mundane desk jobs. Sometimes, those unassuming low-level employees turn out to be corporate spies and spend several real years waiting patiently before launching a backstabbing coup. Player coalitions amass sprawling starship armies as shows of strength. You convert actual money into in-game money to buy supplies, and veterans recall multiday *Eve* wars, like the Bloodbath of B-R5RB, that permanently destroyed more than $300,000 worth of in-game ships and resources. *Eve Online* might be the single most fascinating video game of all time, even if most people will, understandably, never take the time to experience what makes it so buck wild.

EVE ONLINE (2003)

Eve Online is not exactly fun. It's famously difficult to learn, punishingly brutal. Moments of joy in the bleak star cluster New Eden are few and far between.

Despite that, its community still logs in every day. Decades after release, miners still undock their rigs to prospect asteroids. Pirates still hunt them. Industrialists still buy the yield to build starships and ammunition. Fleet commanders still use them.

It's a single-server online world, which means every moment is written into the history of the community, live, as it occurs. Every person who logs in becomes entangled in the vast conspiracy that binds the community together. From the simple miner to the dictator who thinks they run the whole show.

You don't exactly play *Eve Online*. Closer to say you become part of it.

—ANDREW GROEN,
Author of *Empires of EVE: A History of the Great Wars of EVE Online*

FINAL FANTASY XIV: A REALM REBORN (2013)

"Remember . . . that we once lived . . ." It's the final request of a man who is both a monstrous despot and a sympathetic would-be "player one" hero finally acknowledging that he's lost. It's one of the most emotionally resonant lines in not just *Final Fantasy*, but gaming as a whole.

It also applies to the MMO genre as a whole and *FFXIV*'s history specifically. MMOs are built on the feats of a diverse many over the contrived spectacle of a single overpowered player one. But what really sells the moment is that *FFXIV* only exists because its developers, like the in-universe deity that sponsors the game's players and opposes the despot uttering this line, were willing to deconstruct its initial failed launch and start again.

The result was one of the most well-considered narratives in all of gaming. Like the characters in its story, *FFXIV* builds on the failures of its predecessor. Rather than wiping away the original 1.0 version of the game and pretending like it didn't happen, it's the integral lynchpin of the game's lore. And the resulting, living, here-and-now world is only stronger because it remembers where it came from, while not being bound by nostalgia.

—MICHELLE EHRHARDT,
deputy editor at Gizmodo

2005

THE NEW NIGHTMARE OF THE YEAR

ATTEMPT TO RESCUE THE PRESIDENT'S DAUGHTER
AS AGENT LEON S. KENNEDY AND SHOOT YOUR
WAY THROUGH A VILLAGE THICK WITH DREAD AND
SWARMING WITH INFECTED ENEMIES IN THIS
MASTERFUL MERGER OF HORROR AND ACTION.

PRESS START

Fear feeds on the unfamiliar. Nothing frightens us like the unknown. Horror needs to stay fresh to keep its bite. Just look at slasher movies. Freddy Krueger, Michael Myers, and Jason Voorhees started off as terrors we had never imagined. But once they became famous faces, once we learned their cheap tricks, they became kitschy jokes, nostalgic even. Capcom's **Resident Evil** is the most iconic video game horror series, but its iconic status also nearly turned it into a joke. It needed radical, horrifying, necessary change. It needed the spine-tingling, action-packed, immensely innovative **Resident Evil 4.**

ITCHY, TASTY

How do you make a video game scary? For starters, you fill it with scary things. *Resident Evil*'s 1996 debut drops players in a spooky mansion full of flesh-eating zombies, ladies with spiders for heads, and a giant snake for good measure. *Resident Evil*, known in Japan as *Biohazard*, took inspiration from classic monster movies as well as icky, squirmy, biological body horror. Zombified scientists left behind stomach-churning diaries detailing how "itchy" and "hungry" they were. The game even impressed *Night of the Living Dead* director and zombie master George A. Romero, who wanted to adapt it into a movie.

Making people look at scary things will probably scare them, but how do you bake fear into gameplay? Games have an advantage over movies in that they force you to play an active role in your own demise. You have to summon the courage to walk down that dark and dangerous hallway, not close your eyes when someone else makes that dumb decision on-screen. To ratchet up the terror, horror games usually disempower the player somehow. You aren't big and strong, but weak and vulnerable. We call them survival horror games because living is victory enough.

Resident Evil doesn't totally abandon you. Instead of hapless civilians, you play as well-trained special forces STARS agents, with awesome names like Jill Valentine, Chris Redfield, and the shady Albert Wesker. You're not superheroes, but you do know how to shoot. However, *Resident Evil* never makes you so powerful that enemies become trivial, and therefore not scary. Fiddly tank controls, with which you awkwardly adjust your character's direction and movement separately, mimic a feeling of panic when you can't control your own body. Fixed camera angles mean you can only see what the game wants you to see, and fret over what threats might lurk out of frame. To escape zombie dogs flying through the windows, you need to focus and act fast. You have limited space to manage healing items, and can only save the game by spending one of your precious few ink ribbons on a typewriter, so death becomes that much scarier when it also means losing hours of progress.

Although it hasn't always struck the perfect balance, from the beginning *Resident Evil* was never afraid to blend horror and action elements, even compared to other pure horror games. It features adventure-game-style puzzles, ideas pulled from Capcom's original 1989 horror game, *Sweet Home*, but also ends with a rocket launcher boss fight. *Resident Evil* leans more toward *Aliens* than *Alien*, and that gave the game just enough broad mainstream appeal to explode as the next big gaming juggernaut. The first three *Resident Evil* games sold nearly 15 million copies combined on the first PlayStation alone. Audiences may have feared these zombies, but Capcom's executives sure didn't.

After the original PlayStation era, *Resident Evil* clearly became overexposed. By 2005, we had not one but two schlocky live-action *Resident Evil* movies starring Milla Jovovich and directed by her husband, Paul W. S. Anderson ("best" known for the first *Mortal Kombat* film). Sorry, Romero. Between the ports and spin-offs and increasingly wacky storylines (*Resident Evil 3* ends with a nuke dropping on a small town), we knew the *Resident Evil* formula, so it couldn't scare us. The Umbrella Corporation, the sinister pharmaceutical company behind the franchise's zombie viruses, loves to experiment to find evil's next evolution. Shinji Mikami, the original *Resident Evil* director, did that same experimentation to find the next core game in the franchise, to remind us that these games will keep you up at night. In 2005, after testing multiple ideas during a lengthy development process, *Resident Evil 4* unleashed its plague upon the world.

LOS ILUMINADOS

Even before you pressed a single button, *Resident Evil 4* challenged your expectations. Whereas most previous games launched first on PlayStation, *Resident Evil 4* launched exclusively on the Nintendo GameCube as part of a limited Nintendo/Capcom deal, complete with a bloody chain saw controller. While heartthrob hero Leon S. Kennedy first debuted in *Resident Evil 2*, now he worked for the American government instead of the local police department. After a trilogy of games set in the undead-infested Raccoon City, Leon's promotion allowed the game to go international. His mission to rescue the president's kidnapped daughter, Ashley Graham, took him to an ominous European village. Whatever lurked here, it was an evil players had never encountered before because in the time between *Resident Evil 3* and *4*, the Umbrella Corporation finally collapsed.

When the descent into terror kicks off in earnest, at first you would be forgiven for not even thinking this was a *Resident Evil* game at all. The dreary, decaying wooded village evokes rustic dread, and as an American in rural Spain you felt like an outsider, especially with your stylish coat. These locals weren't zombies, just simple burlap-wearing peasants. You weren't locked in a mansion, you had plenty of room to move around. You were safe . . . right?

A church bell rings. A horde of formerly peaceful villagers converges on you, brandishing pitchforks, scythes, and, yes, chain saws. They moan the name of their enlightened lord, Saddler. You barricade yourself in a rickety shack with one of your only allies and fend off the invaders with your pistol. You shoot one target in the head, only to see writhing tentacles erupt from the fleshy stump as the body continues to shamble toward you. Yup, this is a *Resident Evil* game.

Resident Evil 4's completely original approach to the franchise gives the game a palpable sense of renewed vigor. It feels more alive than ever, even in a game all about death. These enemies, infested with parasites called Las Plagas, still retain much of their human intelligence, allowing them to attack you with

frighteningly coordinated tactics. The new location and in-game monster explanation gives the game a fascinating visual aesthetic. The village perverts old-world Catholic charm into a demonic fever dream. Insect legs erupt from would-be priests. One of your chief torturers in the Los Iluminados cult is the pint-size lord of a noble family castle. El Gigante lives up to his name as a fearsome giant who tosses boulders at you. In case you start to feel uncomfortable butchering all these Spanish speakers, you also have to contend with an all-American mercenary, your old buddy Jack Krauser, who's also up to no good. Even tranquil moments in *Resident Evil 4* unnerve you because the game trains you to never know what to expect next. That's scary!

DOUBLE TAP

No matter what *Resident Evil 4* throws at you, the game knows you can take on the danger. *Resident Evil 4* didn't just mix up the story and environment, it also totally revamped the control scheme. Goodbye, tank controls and fixed camera angles. The game places the camera behind Leon's shoulders as you move around. Whip out your gun and aim at everything in front of you with intuitive FPS precision, while also still seeing enough space around Leon to know if he's in immediate danger. *Resident Evil 4* is a stellar survival horror game, but it's also a hugely influential third-person shooter. Divorced from the campaign's horror, the shooting holds up well enough to sustain a shooting gallery minigame called the Mercenaries, where you and your friends can brag over high scores.

Granted, this gameplay shift does make you feel more powerful and in control. *Resident Evil 4* pushes the franchise even more toward action, with dramatic quick-time events and roundhouse kick melee attacks. However, clever design decisions still keep tension at the forefront. You can't move and shoot at the same time. In the heat of battle, you have to carefully choose a vantage point and plant your feet as you pop off shots. Enemies may be slow, but they still easily overwhelm you. When that spot becomes compromised, know when to bail and repeat the process. It feels a bit like an on-rails shooter, like fellow zombie franchise *The House of the Dead*, except you have more control over your position. Firefights get even more nerve-racking when you have to worry about protecting the vulnerable Ashley along with yourself. Like previous games, you also have to carefully manage your resources. Every weapon, bullet, and healing item takes up physical space in your inventory. To maximize your efficiency, you basically play a little puzzle game. Want to buy new gear? Talk to the merchant, who might be the spookiest, and kookiest, guy in the whole game.

Resident Evil 4 expertly tailored its gunplay to suit its horror needs, but the potential of third-person shooters blossomed well beyond this one subgenre. Today's blockbuster games more often than not have third-person shooter elements, if only to keep the char-

acter on-screen for when they perform actions other than shooting. *Dead Space*, *Gears of War*, and Mikami's own *Vanquish* build on *RE4*'s foundations.

Resident Evil is the Sylvester Stallone of video games. Bear with me for a second. The franchise isn't afraid to get corny. The first game includes infamous lines like, "You were almost a Jill sandwich," and Leon himself spouts plenty of dopey action movie one-liners. The *Resident Evil* name also appears on plenty of garbage. *Resident Evil 5* and *6* became full-on action shooters, and bad ones at that. *Resident Evil 5* in particular may be the most racist game since *Custer's Revenge*, with 99 percent of the gameplay revolving around slaughtering "savage" Africans.

However, just like Rocky and Rambo, two names capable of both art and schlock, you can never count out *Resident Evil*. No franchise has managed to reinvent itself so masterfully so many times. *Resident Evil 4* is a masterpiece, but so is the remake of Leon's first undead encounter, *Resident Evil 2*. Much like *Resident Evil 4*, *Resident Evil 7* created a whole new murky mythology for its first-person southern grindhouse swamp horror before pivoting back to eerie Europe vibes in *Resident Evil Village*. And in 2023, *Resident Evil 4* got remade for new consoles. The franchise itself is a zombie; even when you think you've killed it, it rises from the dead more gruesome than ever. But whether you engage with the rest of the series or not, *Resident Evil 4* stands alone as a testament to the power of fresh ideas, a singularly terrific triumph in terror.

GOD OF WAR, THE ANGRY EPIC

Before *God of War*, director David Jaffe was most famous for *Twisted Metal*, a car combat game starring an evil clown with a flaming skull who drives an ice cream truck with bolted-on miniguns. *God of War* takes Jaffe's raging, violent little boy impulses and blows them up to a mythological scale. As bald, wrathful, ash-covered Spartan warrior Kratos, you'll scream, rip, and tear your way through the entire Greek pantheon. From the depths of Hades to the peak of Mount Olympus, you achieve your blood-soaked revenge. With your deadly arsenal, including two jagged blades you swing from chains wrapped around your arms, no enemies can stand against you. Huge set pieces turn your fights against petty deities (Zeus is such a dick) into truly titanic struggles, especially once the literal Titans enter the picture. You pound Hercules's face into mush!

We call these games character action games, games about lone heroes demolishing rooms full of foes through intricate, almost fighting-game-like combat. Think of them as the 3D descendants of beat-'em-ups. Famous Japanese character action games include *Bayonetta*, *Ninja Gaiden*, and former *Resident Evil 4* prototype *Devil May Cry*. When it comes to Western character action games, though, few rival *God of War*.

Sony debuted some marquee franchises from its best developers during the red-hot PlayStation 2 era, including Naughty Dog's *Jak and Daxter*, Insomniac's *Ratchet & Clank*, and Sucker Punch's *Sly Cooper*. But *God of War* from the Santa Monica team feels like the biggest, most epic, and most important. It foreshadows Sony's later obsession with turning all its output into gaming blockbusters. *God of War* sits at the top of the mountain, ready to murder all challengers.

SILENT HILL 2 (2001)

When was the last time you were both frightened and moved by a video game? For me, it was *Silent Hill 2*. The story of James Sunderland, who goes to the town of Silent Hill after receiving a letter from his dead wife, is full of twists about all the characters we meet in this abandoned, foggy town filled with monsters. And what you learn is that the monsters aren't just horrible for the sake of it. Sure, it's a game with scary moments, but it's about how our inner demons affect us and those around us, and isn't that the most terrifying thing of all?

—CARLI VELOCCI,
   games and culture editor

SOMA (2015)

The ending of a game—most stories, really—involves catharsis. You're released from the tension that's guided everything leading to this moment, and the credits roll. But with *Soma*, you're left with an existential crisis. With *Soma*, you're left to ponder the meaning of life and personhood and its connection to one's fragile sense of reality—and inevitably realize you have no answers because the answers in front of you are too nightmarish to fully accept. All I wanted to do when the screen cut to black in *Soma* was sit in the dark and scream.

So that's what I did.

—PATRICK KLEPEK,
   senior writer at Waypoint

2006

Wii Sports

THE LOCOMOTION OF THE YEAR

PLAY TENNIS, BASEBALL, GOLF, BOXING, AND
BOWLING BY SIMPLY WAVING YOUR ARMS TO MIMIC
THE MOTION OF THE REAL SPORT USING THE WII
REMOTE'S NEWFANGLED MOTION-SENSING TECHNOLOGY.

PRESS START

I love the Nintendo Wii, and I'm tired of pretending that I don't. Hard-core gamers constantly try to dismiss the console's undeniable success. They stick on some qualifier like, "The Wii sold a lot, but it's not good," or, "The Wii is good, but only for casual gamers, not real ones." Enough! Gaming is too old to tolerate this childish, joy-killing gatekeeping. You don't have to think the Wii is as awesome as I do, but when a console sells more than 100 million units and pulls an entire company out of a financial nosedive, clearly it did something right. With the Wii, that something came right in the box: the motion-controlled magic of Wii Sports.

WII WANT A REVOLUTION

Calling the pre-Wii Nintendo "hard-core" never seemed quite right. Sure, the company developed many challenging games that primarily appealed to people who already enjoyed gaming. We still call extremely difficult old-school games "Nintendo hard." Compared to competitors, however, Nintendo also strove to maintain a family-friendly image. Despite Nintendo literally running fan clubs, from the Nintendo Fun Club to Club Nintendo, the games themselves never gave the impression that only a super-special group could enjoy them. Nintendo games were for everyone, including people who didn't play games. We now call those players casual gamers, and when Nintendo decided to chase after that market more aggressively, it was more of a natural evolution than a hard pivot.

Still, Nintendo did change. Following the Game-Cube's middling sales, new president Satoru Iwata and the executive team adopted a marketing plan called the Blue Ocean Strategy. Coined by business professors W. Chan Kim and Renée Mauborgne, the idea posits that instead of competing with rivals like Microsoft and Sony for the limited number of core consumers in the "red ocean," Nintendo would cultivate vast, new, untapped potential audiences in the blue ocean. Nintendo simply had to build a console that could convince millions of regular people to consider playing video games for the first time in their lives. Easy.

And so, we got the Wii. When it's not being used in cheap punch lines, the name Wii reflects the sense of plurality and inclusion Nintendo hoped would draw curious casual gamers into the fold. The console's code name, Revolution, may have sounded too harsh to achieve this effect, but it's also an accurate description of the machine. While the Wii's raw power only slightly bests the GameCube's, and paled in comparison to the high-definition visuals on PlayStation 3 and Xbox 360, the Wii allows for previously impossible new kinds of games thanks to its innovative and intuitive motion controls.

The Wii Remote sits naturally in your hand like a TV remote. You have only a few buttons to worry about and get a bothersome analog stick only when you plug in the optional Nunchuk accessory. But don't let the simplicity fool you. The Wii Remote offers control options no other controller could match. Point at the screen to guide a mouselike cursor. When you move the remote, accelerometers translate that information into actions in the game. Control the game by moving your hands. Like a magic trick, the line between your physical body and the virtual world shatters, drawing you deeper into the immersion. The Wii Remote isn't a piece of plastic, it's a weapon or a tool or just an extension of your own arm. No wonder then that today's virtual reality headsets use Wii-style motion controls.

Motion controls as a pitch have so much childlike wonder that they sound like a dream that's too good to be true. Many bad Wii games with clunky, inaccurate controls prove that the dream definitely doesn't always match up with reality. However, if Nintendo could just make one game well-crafted enough to perfectly sell the illusion, a game that made all skeptics believe in the Wii the instant they played it, then the console would at least start off on the best foot possible. *Wii Sports* was that game, and Nintendo made sure everyone knew it. At launch, *Wii Sports* came packed in with every Wii (except in Japan), so you had no excuse not to play it. Nintendo hadn't packed in games with its new consoles since the SNES, but the Wii marked the beginning of a new era for the company. We soon found out just how entertaining that era would be for you, your friends, your golf-obsessed dad, and even your bowling-loving grandma.

IF YOU BUILD IT,
THEY WILL COME

Sports games work so well for the mainstream because you only barely need to explain them. *Wii Sports* puts an imaginary tennis racket, golf club, or baseball bat in your hands, and you immediately swing. Seeing your character, your adorable Mii avatar customized to resemble your face, perform your same action in the game pierces through the layer of controller abstraction that previously kept so many people away from gaming. *Wii Sports'* fuzzy, not-exactly-accurate controls actually make the fantasy even more intoxicating. You can flail around in boxing and still believe you're punching with skill. I've gotten way more strikes in *Wii Sports* bowling than I ever will in real life. In tennis, you only have to worry about timing your swing, not the all-important footwork you have to do in a real match. *Wii Sports* is not a fact that is true, it's a fiction that *feels* true, and that's more bewitching than even the fanciest HD visuals.

Wii Sports radiated so much sunny power, put so many smiles on faces, that for millions of Wii owners it was the only game they ever needed. The 2006 holiday season introduced countless families to Wii's possibilities, and we couldn't get enough. For months the Wii was impossible to find on store shelves as word of mouth spread not just through gamer circles, but into that big, beautiful blue ocean. Parents played more often than their children. News stations ran feel-good stories about *Wii Sports* taking retirement homes across the country by storm. The physical aspect didn't just entertain, it also provided precious, if mild, exercise to anyone concerned that video games forced you to sit on your butt all day. Everyone knew what Nintendo was, whether they had bought the GameCube or not, and the Wii certainly traded on some of that nostalgia. Alongside motion controls, the Wii also allowed you to download retro games from the NES, SNES, N64, and more through its Virtual Console service. Regardless, the Wii phenomenon quickly eclipsed its own parent corporation as a gaming and cultural force. What was Nintendo? The Wii Company.

Nintendo carried the *Wii Sports* philosophy forward into other Wii-branded games released throughout the system's life, like minigame collection *Wii Play*, *Wii Fit* and its exercise balance board, and the mediocre *Wii Music*. The best Wii series game was the true *Wii Sports* sequel, the tropical *Wii Sports Resort*. Thanks to the gyroscopic Wii MotionPlus accessory, the game detected your movements, from slashing a sword to rowing a canoe, far more accurately than before. *Wii Sports* sold nearly 83 million copies, but as a pack-in game that's not really a fair number. However, except for *Wii Music*, all of these other Wii games cracked the 20 million mark at least. Iwata passed away in 2015, but he saw his strategy vindicated.

Nintendo's blue ocean left Nintendo's rivals green with envy. If the Wii didn't achieve the massive success that hard-core gamers try to deny it, then why did these other hard-core gaming companies immediately try to copy it? Despite advanced motion tracking, the PlayStation 3's Move controllers didn't truly take off until Sony repurposed them as PlayStation VR controllers. Microsoft had initial success with its Kinect body-tracking camera for Xbox 360, but making the accessory mandatory on Xbox One nearly doomed that console before Microsoft reversed its stance. Even Nintendo couldn't make the Wii lightning strike twice with the failed Wii U. Try as you might, there's something about the Wii's approach you just can't replicate. All these imitators overcomplicated a concept whose strength lies in its balanced simplicity. Take away too much from *Wii Sports* and it becomes a basic, boring toy. Add too much and it becomes another alienating video game. *Wii Sports* is just right for just about everyone.

While the Wii had plenty of other great games (*Super Mario Galaxy*! *Metroid Prime: Trilogy*! *Kirby's Epic Yarn*!), none of those games are *Wii Sports*. *Wii Sports* turned so many people, however temporarily, into gamers with far more grace than the exploitative cell phone games that soon followed. It blew apart old, ossified notions about what a controller should be and connected us even more directly into the action and the fun. Whether you take games too seriously or seriously hate them, when you swing for the fences, hear the crack of the bat, and hit a home run, you get up and cheer. As the commercial says, when it comes to *Wii Sports*, yes, we would like to play.

THE DAWNING OF A NEW BRAIN AGE

As big as the Wii was, the Nintendo DS was even bigger. Nintendo's experimental Game Boy successor, with weird gimmicks like a touch screen and a microphone and a second screen, wound up selling more than 150 million units. That puts it neck and neck with the PlayStation 2 for most successful game system ever. With those features, the DS gave you early smartphone technology before we had smartphones, and games like *Brain Age* were basically our first apps.

Based on the work of the actual neuroscientist Dr. Ryuta Kawashima, *Brain Age* is a minigame collection in which the minigames are short exercises designed to keep your mind sharp. Solve a series of fast math puzzles. Remember short words. Follow basic patterns. None of these pose a challenge for anyone out of elementary school, but by training their brain for just a few minutes a day, older adults may stave off certain neurological disorders later in life. Just remember, a video game shouldn't substitute for a doctor.

Gaming grows by getting more games into as many hands as possible. If someone wants to keep their quick wits with *Brain Age*, or play with some virtual pups in the DS's other casual hit *Nintendogs*, maybe they'll consider checking out some other games, too. After all, they already bought a whole system. Perhaps they'll dip into *Professor Layton*'s puzzle adventures or a full-on RPG like the *Chrono Trigger* remake. Only tiny minds gatekeep. Galaxy brains open up gaming for everyone.

ŌKAMI (2006)

The crowning achievement of short-lived Capcom subsidiary Clover Studio, *ōkami* represents the pinnacle of the pre–*Breath of the Wild* era of 3D *Zelda* game design. That's no coincidence: industry luminary Hideki Kamiya, *ōkami*'s director and a self-proclaimed *Zelda* fan, has openly admitted Nintendo's legendary franchise influenced the game's development.

Due to those design parallels, and particularly its lupine protagonist Amaterasu, *ōkami* was initially compared offhand to *Twilight Princess*, the actual *Zelda* game released just a couple of months after *ōkami* in late 2006. But *ōkami* carves its own identity, thanks in part to its brilliant Celestial Brush mechanic, enabling players to draw miracles like gusts of wind directly into the world for use in puzzle solving and combat. Its breathtaking art style, inspired by traditional ink wash paintings, has only improved with age and multiple HD rereleases. *ōkami* ultimately eclipses superficial comparisons and outshines its contemporaries to stand the test of time as a genuine masterpiece.

—ASH PAULSEN,
creator and cofounder of
Good Vibes Gaming

THE WONDERFUL 101 (2013)

In a year dominated by lofty, mature blockbusters, *The Wonderful 101* was a breath of fresh air—a widely underappreciated and misunderstood masterpiece from the mind behind *ōkami* and *Viewtiful Joe*. Hideki Kamiya's fingerprints are all over this deceptively deep, mechanically dense, superheroic action title. Its AAA production values and Nintendo involvement bely a game that feels personal and distinctly Kamiya: from its self-aware sense of humor and well-written character arcs to its expertly choreographed set pieces. The only downside is that the unforgettably massive finale will make any future action game feel quaint by comparison.

—LIAM ROBERTSON,
video game historian

2007

THE JAM OF THE YEAR

LIVE OUT YOUR ROCK-AND-ROLL FANTASIES
AND PERFORM YOUR FAVORITE SONGS ON
PLASTIC GUITAR AND DRUM CONTROLLERS.

PRESS START

Music comes in eras. Rock-and-roll music sounded a lot different in the 1950s compared with the 1970s. In the 1990s, hip-hop artists had no idea what "dubstep" even meant. We've now gone through about enough different gaming eras to distinctly recognize them. A 1980s platformer, 1990s shooter, or 2010s open-world game each brings specific examples to mind. Like the subject of a musical biopic, few gaming eras rose as quickly, shined as brightly, and burned out as intensely as the 2000s music game boom. **Rock Band** lived, partied, and died like a real rock star.

FEEL THE BEAT

When you really think about it, most video games boil down to hitting the right buttons at the right time. Games are rhythmic by nature. So why not make games about hitting buttons in sync with real music? The late nineties saw an explosion of rhythm games following the success of NanaOn-Sha's quirky cartoon hip-hop game *PaRappa the Rapper* (your karate mentor, Chop Master Onion, is literally a Rap Scallion). This established the basic formula: notes on-screen fly toward you, and you press the correct button on beat as cool visuals play out in the background. Konami soon spawned a small empire of arcade rhythm games in its Bemani franchise, which included everything from *Beatmania* to *Pop'n Music* to the world-famous *Dance Dance Revolution* series.

As cool as these games were, they were also quite abstract and hard-core. Unless you go to some very specific clubs (like my *DDR*-loving wife), stomping on four directional arrows in time with intense Japanese pop music isn't everyone's idea of dancing. As arcade games, these early rhythm games often featured punishingly high difficulty with tight timing windows to hit each beat. You couldn't even play them on HDTVs because the slight added lag from the display made some challenges impossible. Music games as an idea had plenty of mainstream appeal. Music, like sports, is something everyone understands. We just needed the right groove.

Harmonix, as its name suggests, develops only music games. Few developers boast such a singular focus. I don't think you *have* to join a band when you start working there, but you probably should. The company's first games, the lo-fi *Frequency* and *Amplitude*, featured similar vibes to music games of the time. You traveled along neon techno tubes blasting beats in time with club bangers. After that came the *Karaoke Revolution* series (another Konami Bemani series), and here's when the shift happens. A whole lot of people, whether they admit it or not, want to perform. They want to sing for their friends. They want to participate with the music, not be passive. You can listen to music at home, but you go to concerts to feel connected to the band and to the crowd. Music, like video games, begs to be interactive. Sometimes people just need an easier jumping-on point.

What if instead of asking players to sing, which opens them up to judgment over their relative real talent, Harmonix made a different kind of music performance game? After all, it takes a plethora of musical instruments to make our favorite songs. Some of the biggest rock stars speak to us not by flapping their lips but by shredding on their axes. With 2005's *Guitar Hero*, made in partnership with Activision, everyone could tap into that six-string power.

In practice, *Guitar Hero*'s gameplay doesn't deviate too much from rhythm game formula. You still hit buttons in time with the music. However, the big plastic guitar controller itself sells a much stronger ego trip. It removes the abstraction. Plus, the fact that you have to strum and move your fingers on the fretboard in a vaguely accurate guitar-ish motion gives players the slight hope that playing the game also serves as practice for learning real guitar. Later rhythm games like *Rocksmith* fully explored these educational possibilities. *Guitar Hero* broke through the mainstream and became a huge success. Folks lined up to get their hands on this hot guitar toy, even if it meant paying a little extra. Harmonix knew it had a special concept on its hands, but what was the next step? If *Guitar Hero* was a hit single, what did the whole album sound like?

COME TOGETHER

Whatever the future held for Harmonix, it wouldn't be at Activision. As the publisher, Activision held on to the *Guitar Hero* brand, and handed it off to the development team at Neversoft that made the musically superb *Tony Hawk* games. Meanwhile, original developer Harmonix got bought by none other than MTV (at one point a music television channel) to expand its plastic-instrument vision even further. *Guitar Hero*'s multiplayer modes let two players play the same song, one player on lead guitar with the other on bass. *Rock Band* finally brought the whole band together.

Along with the two guitars (lead and bass), *Rock Band* lets players perform vocals (like in *Karaoke Revolution*) and play the drums. While you didn't receive a full drum kit, banging on plastic cymbals and snares blurred the line between fake and real instruments even more. *Guitar Hero* celebrated the individual, the front man, the showboat. *Rock Band* and its four-piece ensembles widened the scope to celebrate the collaboration at the heart of music as performance art. Plus, more instruments to buy meant even more cash to rake in.

Rock Band made *Guitar Hero* look like a warm-up act, and not just because it had real songs instead of covers. By making multiplayer the star, the game became an absolute social phenomenon. Friend groups gathered for regular jam sessions hosted by whomever had the biggest apartment. Bars hosted *Rock Band* parties. Now that Harmonix had established the foundation, it treated *Rock Band* as a platform to build upon. Players gobbled up the constant stream of songs to buy in the marketplace, from "Gimme Shelter" by the Rolling Stones to "Dance, Dance" by Fall Out Boy. People spent thousands of dollars on these songs, and the franchise made more than $1 billion in revenue in its first two years. Along with these downloadable tracks, Harmonix released whole sequels centered around specific bands. The *New York Times* calling *The Beatles: Rock Band* "the most important video game ever made" may be a slight exaggeration, but it was a pretty big deal.

With *Rock Band*, the floodgates opened, and plastic-instrument music games burned up the charts. *Guitar Hero*, which began to get annual releases, eventually added drums and vocals. Later *Rock Band* games added keyboards and music-writing functionality. The excellent and experimental *DJ Hero* featured a plastic turntable to mash up songs from a more diverse library of genres beyond rock. Nintendo not only put out a plastic set of conga drums to play its music game *Donkey Konga*, but also localized a rhythm game about Japanese musical cheerleaders called *Elite Beat Agents*.

Unfortunately, so many of these games came so fast that the public simply grew sick of them. We ran out of room in our houses for more instruments. Retailers didn't want to keep these huge boxes clogging their shelves if people weren't buying them. After Harmonix released *Rock Band 3* in 2010, MTV and Harmonix went through a contentious, litigious breakup, leaving Harmonix as an independent company. Harmonix returned to the *Rock Band* well again in 2015 with *Rock Band 4*, eerily enough the same year Activision tried to resurrect *Guitar Hero* as *Guitar Hero Live*, but tepid response to both products proved the fad was over. In 2021, Harmonix got acquired by Epic Games to create "immersive music experiences" for *Fortnite*, whatever that means.

But don't mourn the music because it died. Be glad that it lived. No one's rushing to buy new plastic instruments, but there's nothing stopping you from busting out your old ones whenever the music game mood strikes you. It's okay for something, a game or a whole genre, to be tied to a single moment in time. We cherish *Rock Band* memories as the gaming equivalent of dusting off an old record player. Besides, if you love music, you love to complain that music used to be better back in the day.

ENLIST WITH CALL OF DUTY 4: MODERN WARFARE

Call of Duty 4: Modern Warfare sparked a multiplayer revolution. After a trilogy of first-person shooters set during World War II, Modern Warfare set its action firmly in a post-9/11 landscape. Now you fought a war on terror, wherever it may lurk.

Call of Duty 4 cemented the franchise as the most important shooter series of the decade, and it's easy to see why. Snappy gunplay forced you to always stay alert lest you lose a firefight in mere seconds, and racking up a killstreak enabled you to unleash unique perks like calling in air strikes. Through the new ranking system, you leveled up after each multiplayer match and gained access to better weapons, and real badasses reset their ranks once they'd reached the top in exchange for Prestige bragging rights. For solo players, the campaign took you through a dramatic playable action movie with tight pacing, thrilling set pieces, and Captain Price's excellent mustache. Call of Duty 4 is a fantastic shooter from the best of the best at developer Infinity Ward.

And yet, it remains difficult to separate Call of Duty 4's gameplay excellence from its troubling politics. This is a game that turns one of the United States' most morally dubious recent military misadventures into a binary struggle between good guys and bad guys. Activision recruited actual war criminal Oliver North (convicted of felonies for his role in the Iran-Contra affair, charges later dropped) to shill for the franchise. Modern Warfare 2 asks you to gun down innocent bystanders at a Russian airport. The 2019 Modern Warfare reboot blames Russia for American war crimes. Don't even get me started on the photorealistic Ronald Reagan.

Millions of people enjoy Call of Duty, including me! They're great games, and I don't need all my media to fit my exact worldview. Would-be soldiers should just remember that despite how modern this warfare may look, Call of Duty does not reflect the real world as it is or as it should be.

ROCK BAND (2007)

Fissures had emerged in our friendship by November. We were sixteen. The power trio that spent all summer doodling band logos in anticipation was breaking up. The day Rock Band dropped, one friend stopped answering our calls. We went to the mall as a duo, gritting our teeth with forced enthusiasm. Then I locked my keys in my car. We waited in a freezing Michigan parking lot for my dad to bail us out, nauseous.

My fondest memory of Rock Band came later, playing with my uncle Steve and cousin Sara. We were dorks, and we were unashamed. I played the hell out of that game—I just didn't get to play it as a child. I'm cool with that.

—JON OLIVER,
writer

PIXELJUNK 4AM (2012)

Being a gamer is like a lifelong game of double Dutch. Finding the perfect spots where you can jump in and find your groove is what most people want. But sometimes technology and the theories of why or how you should play are weirdly at odds with each other.

A game came into my life in 2012 and erased any and all invisible barriers I had to feel like one with a piece of technology. That game is PixelJunk 4am. This music-conducting game gave me my first sense of what a flow state could be and not only what that state would mean for my love of music but how technology, gamification, and letting go in a virtual space could be beautiful.

—KAHLIEF ADAMS,
founder of Spawn On Me with Kahlief Adams

2008

THE PIPE DREAM OF THE YEAR

BECOME A GOD AND CREATE LIFE! THEN GUIDE IT
FROM SINGLE-CELL SURVIVAL TO INTELLIGENT
ENLIGHTENMENT . . . IN THEORY.

PRESS START

I'm not mad at **Spore**, I'm just disappointed. Video games can offer infinite possibilities, a power that easily turns from a blessing into a curse. Creators need to find the balance between giving players all that they can while having the restraint to not promise what they ultimately can't deliver. It takes skill, discipline, self-awareness, and a lot of luck. You can feel this tension in even the best games, and no amount of talent and good intentions can save a game that bites off way more than it can chew. Combine that with a gaming audience totally unwilling to keep expectations in check and you get an inevitable yet informative example of a game whose reality could never measure up with its impossible dream: **Spore.**

GOD LOVES, MAN KILLS

After taking over the planet with *The Sims* and other god games, Will Wright and developer Maxis became gods themselves. With so much power to flex, how could the team possibly challenge itself? How do you top a game about simulating a human life? For its next major project, completely separate from *The Sims* franchise, Maxis gave itself a modest goal with a narrow scope: simulate *all* life. Maxis announced *Spore* in 2005, but its development started five years earlier, and its earliest ideas first cropped up in the mid-nineties as Wright's *SimEverything* concept. Even as the genre was just beginning, Wright knew that simulating all life around us all at once was the logical end goal of the sim genre itself.

To create the most complete and comprehensive sim game there ever was, that there ever could be, *Spore* starts with the micro and blossoms out into the macro. According to the pitch, players begin as omniscient caretakers of simple single-cell organisms. Under your eye, your species adapts, evolves, and expands. Eventually, your creatures rise from the primordial ocean to form tribes, societies, and nations with as many diverse cultures and political complexities as great human civilizations. At the end, you gaze upon your work with pride as these life-forms, once too weak to stand against aquatic predators, become scientifically advanced enough to travel to the stars. Perhaps they'll help lesser creatures on other planets reach their full potential just as you did for them. Millennia of evolution and a future even humanity has yet to reach, all captured in one PC gaming session. Thanks to procedural generation (a computing technique that creates infinite unique creature elements through math rather than by hand), no two playthroughs would ever be the same. *Spore* sounded unbelievably awesome.

Emphasis on "unbelievably." Maxis could tease all the incredible features it wanted, from the grandest plans to the tiniest details. However, eventually *Spore* needed to be an actual game and not just a series of what-ifs. *Spore* hype grew exponentially. Between Maxis's promises and fans' pressure, the public col-

lectively envisioned a game that could never possibly exist. Throughout any game development process, developers trim down and simplify their design ideas as they approach the finish line. It's the only way to keep things doable. Unfortunately, *Spore* fell into a trap where the slightest appearance of being dumbed down would shatter the entire premise, even if dumbing down had to happen no matter what to ship a finished product. Following a few delays, *Spore* finally launched in September 2008. After dealing with its obtrusive digital rights management copyright protection (a whole separate discussion), players stopped dreaming and saw the truth.

If you squint, *Spore* does stick to its intriguing, life-creating conceit. You do uplift your own species across several evolutionary phases. Plus you can make a really nice variety of Muppet-looking monsters, from scaly orange bipeds with extra eyes and back spikes to purple apes that walk on six webbed feet. *Spore* isn't an awful game, but few games have such a stark contrast between what they promised and what they delivered.

The shallow gameplay leaves much to be desired. Each stage plays like a truncated version of a different, deeper game. Guide your single-cell creature in a 2D plane like an undersea arcade game. Control tribes of creatures with real-time strategy mechanics. The civilization stage plays a whole lot like a certain other PC strategy game about civilizations, complete with multiple ways to exert power and influence. Stringing these distinct gameplay styles together didn't make *Spore* the simulation epic we hoped for, but a weirdly disjointed and clearly compromised take on a vision that maybe was never clear enough to start with. It's impressive that *Spore* even exists and achieves as much as it does, but this was not the next *Sims*.

To its credit, Maxis didn't give up on *Spore* after launch. You don't spend that many years working on one game only to instantly walk away, and *Spore* got an expansion. Maxis chopped up and sold some of the phases as individual games. The inexplicable spin-off *Darkspore* used the game's creature-creation technology to make totally tubular alien heroes for an action RPG. Someone somewhere even tried to make a

Spore movie happen. However, Maxis soon went back to being the *Sims* factory. In 2009, Will Wright left Maxis to pursue his own, smaller think tank projects. He's on the board of directors of Linden Lab, the developers of *Second Life*, which might be the actual final form for simulation games that *Spore* could never be. After a legacy of games that tested new sim possibilities, Maxis finally found its limit.

GREAT EXPECTATIONS

It may be among the most high-profile, but *Spore* is hardly the only video game that wrote a check it definitely could not cash. *Duke Nukem Forever* spent fifteen years in development hell as nonexistent vaporware before emerging at last as . . . just another first-person shooter where you kill aliens and crack bad jokes. *No Man's Sky* teased a *Spore*-like, infinite, procedurally generated universe to explore, and only after years of free updates has that vision finally started to mostly come true. Peter Molyneux is famous for making his own sim and god games like *Populous*, *Black & White*, and *The Movies*, but he's equally famous for passionately making ludicrous claims about his upcoming projects that anyone with a brain will instantly realize simply aren't feasible. The Twitter account @PeterMolydeux shares joke premises for games Molyneux might pitch.

The fraught relationship between fan desires and creators' capabilities exists across all art, and has for decades, centuries even. Today, crowdfunding has made this whole dilemma trickier than ever. To succeed on sites like Kickstarter, you have to promise potential fans features so cool that they're willing to spend real money on a hypothetical game. Even when crowdfunding campaigns raise millions of dollars, that's still usually not enough to fund the game from start to finish. Rather, it shows enough interest for investors to swoop in with the rest of the required capital. Sometimes it works out. *Bloodstained*, *Broken Age*, *Pillars of Eternity*, and *Shovel Knight* are niche but great games that wouldn't exist without crowdfunding showing there was an audience waiting for them. On the other hand, there are awful games like *Mega Man* successor *Mighty No. 9* and games like space sim *Star Citizen*, which has raised more than $400 million over the course of the decade and still hasn't yet fully come to fruition. At least *Spore* came out.

Spore teaches us how important it is to remember and accept that games will always have limits, to set reasonable expectations. The technology powering them may improve, and the people behind them may grow more skilled, but they'll never be all-powerful. Great games sell us a convincing illusion, but it's just that, an illusion. They'll always be bound to reality. We'll never be gods.

FAR CRY 2 'S
HEART OF DARKNESS

Snobby video game critics will never shut up about *Far Cry 2*. While the first *Far Cry* impressed, the developers at Crytek had nothing to do with this sequel, instead working on *Crysis*, aka the game only the most powerful computers could run without melting. *Far Cry 2* seemed like Ubisoft cashing in on the name, and maybe that's all the publisher wanted, but Clint Hocking and the team smuggled in a work of gaming art.

After getting his start with Ubisoft's *Tom Clancy* military action games, Hocking coined the controversial phrase "ludonarrative dissonance," which refers to when the actions your character performs in a story clash against the actions you make them perform as the player. Ludonarrative dissonance is when you go on a killing spree in *GTA*, and then watch your character become sad after killing a single person in a cutscene. What makes *Far Cry 2* so fascinating is how it turns the struggle against this phenomenon, an uncanny issue unique to gaming, into text. In this action-packed first-person shooter, you feel the same emotions your character feels.

Many of those emotions aren't positive! In *Far Cry 2* you play as a mercenary tracking down an elusive arms dealer during an African civil war. The scenario goes out of its way to show just how dangerous, stressful, and bleak this would be, not just with its burning jungles and arid savannas but with gameplay unafraid to inconvenience and actively frustrate you. Uncontrollable fire destroys your flimsy cover. Unreliable smuggled guns jam and break during firefights. You contract malaria and have to regularly take medicine to stay alive. *Far Cry 2* treats you with so much hostility it makes you realize how much even hard-core games coddle and flatter players.

Ubisoft's later *Far Cry* games abandoned all this friction, this wider spectrum of evocative feelings and larger truths, to focus on pure open-world fun. But *Far Cry 2* courageously demonstrates the raw, radical power of baking meaning into the mechanics, of treating gameplay itself as art to deliver a message, even if you must leave fun by the wayside.

FALLOUT 3 (2008)

I'm in Megaton, standing in the kitchen of a house I was not invited into, where a local citizen is puttering around in the background and grumbling about my presence. I open the fridge and discover that it contains, among other items, an apple. Glancing at my health and seeing that I could use a quick pick-me-up, I ignore the fact that the prompt for taking said apple is highlighted in red, toss it into my bag, and head for the door. Whoever lives here ain't happy about it—in fact, sounds like they're following me out the door—but I am unconcerned. Who cares?

Turns out, many people in Megaton care about the stolen apple. Upon exiting the residence I find myself back in what passes for this hellhole's town square, the whole thing loosely assembled around an undetonated, two-story nuclear warhead, and quite literally everyone on-screen is mad at me. Guns are drawn, bats come out, and before long I am massacred by the townsfolk for my apple-related transgression. I sit there watching *Fallout 3*'s in-game camera swooping around my dead body as Megaton's citizens go back to doing whatever they'd been doing before I launched my crime wave.

These events represent my first real foray into the world of then-modern RPGs. I'd been having a good time in *Fallout 3* up until that point, but this was a level of interactivity and responsiveness I simply had not anticipated. I was uneducated, I was a fool, and I was utterly enchanted. I've experienced many revelatory moments while gaming over the years, but stealing that apple in *Fallout 3* had invested me with a particular sort of forbidden knowledge, a gateway drug to an entirely new game genre that I'd either ignored or willfully avoided for years. Good god, I realized, I've been wasting my life. No more.

—SCOTT WAMPLER,
cohost of *The Kingcast*

2009

THE SONY BLOCKBUSTER OF THE YEAR

THE PINNACLE OF THE UNCHARTED SERIES,
THIS GLOBE-HOPPING ADVENTURE HAS YOU RUNNING
ACROSS BUILDINGS, SHOOTING YOUR WAY OUT
OF DANGER, AND FINDING ANCIENT RELICS
ALONGSIDE YOUR WELL-ACTED ALLIES.

PRESS START

In 2006, Ken Kutaragi stepped down as CEO of Sony Interactive Entertainment, and he retired the year after that. "The Father of the PlayStation," Kutaragi led engineering on the consoles that turned the company into a gaming giant. But that kind of success breeds arrogance, and between its absurdly expensive price and needlessly complicated hardware, the PlayStation 3 didn't launch with nearly as much momentum as its predecessors. Also, despite being a Japanese company, Sony's American and European gaming divisions were quickly gaining power and influence within the organization. All these changes set the stage for the most significant identity shift we've ever seen from a first-party console maker. Uncharted 2: Among Thieves gave Sony the homegrown blockbuster template it desperately needed to usher in a new era of PlayStation domination. PlayStation needed a fresh face, and that face was Nathan Drake.

RAIDERS

When *Uncharted: Drake's Fortune* launched in 2007 on PS3, the snarky headlines wrote themselves. *Uncharted* boldly asked, "What if *Tomb Raider* starred a man?" For more than a decade, *Tomb Raider* had already been an extremely popular franchise about exploring tombs, climbing around jungles, solving ancient puzzles, and shooting guys. If you wanted to play a game about doing Indiana Jones stuff in the modern day, just call up Lara Croft. So when *Uncharted* swapped out "Angelina Jolie action hero" with "generic, scruffy white guy," gamers didn't suddenly rush out to drop $599 on Sony's next-gen console.

Still, there was good reason to be at least curious. *Uncharted* didn't come out of nowhere. Santa Monica–based Sony subsidiary Naughty Dog developed not one but two of PlayStation's most defining franchises: *Crash Bandicoot* and *Jak and Daxter*. But *Uncharted* bore only slight resemblance to those cartoony platformers. Under director Amy Hennig, *Uncharted* revealed Naughty Dog's unparalleled skill at creating rollicking single-player adventures that surpass even the most epic and action-packed blockbusters. Through its sheer quality, *Uncharted* narrowly avoided looking like a rip-off and became a beloved property in its own right.

Drake's Fortune received good reviews and impressive sales, but it wasn't until two years later when the sequel *Among Thieves*, a *Mega Man 2*–level upgrade over the original, dropped that we really appreciated what this series had going for it. Although *Tomb Raider* had name-brand recognition, its quality had gone down the drain (until getting an *Uncharted*-esque reboot in 2013). So what *Uncharted* really asked was, "What if *Tomb Raider* was good?" *Uncharted 2* isn't just good; it's one of the greatest games of all time.

OUT OF THE FRYING PAN

What *Uncharted 2* does that even your favorite flicks can't is put you directly in the action. *Uncharted* isn't *Dragon's Lair*; you fully interact with your environment. You aim guns and shimmy across ledges. *Uncharted 2* didn't just look better; it controlled better, even if it's still not the best shooter in the world. However, although you do have agency, the game guides you through its nonstop flow of varied action like a tightly paced film. You act with as much urgency and investment as the characters and barely have enough time to catch your breath before you get tossed into the next set piece.

Consider the Nepal train sequence late in the game. As rebellious treasure hunter Nathan Drake you hop through windows and hang on to side railings en route to the front of the locomotive. Every moment feels as clear and choreographed as an action movie beat despite being (mostly) under your control. Once you get spotted, you shoot back at the mercenaries, all while the train keeps moving through the jungle and the action escalates. Helicopters swoop in to hunt you down. Train tracks carry you over treacherous waters. You detach cars behind you before they explode. Drake casually commandeers a turret and lets out a sardonic quip. The fight continues into dark tunnels and back up onto snowy peaks until, well, you'll have to play for yourself to see what happens next.

Uncharted 2 doesn't just use its gameplay to replicate the look and feel of a blockbuster movie. The PS3 may have been infamously tricky to develop for, but Naughty Dog tapped into the machine's considerable power to give the game lush environments and gorgeous, HD photorealistic visuals. With motion-captured animations, characters look and emote like real people. But that's not enough. Stellar writing and performances that do the material justice elevate Drake, his love interests Chloe and Elena, his mentor Sully, and dastardly villain Zoran from stock archetypes into human characters we love hanging out with. Nolan North may be the most overexposed voice actor in gaming, but after hearing him as Drake you get why developers love casting him. He keeps up the everyman charm during the chases as well as the slower dramatic scenes that add crucial depth to what so easily could've been the most uninspired premise imaginable.

Uncharted 2 also has a multiplayer mode, perhaps to give the PS3 a third-person shooter to compete with *Gears of War* on Xbox, but the game shines as a solo journey. After years of bad, cheap tie-in games based on Hollywood blockbusters, *Uncharted 2: Among Thieves* gave gaming an outstanding blockbuster of ts own. If you're a Sony fan you'd better like it—basically every PlayStation game is *Uncharted* now.

PLAYSTATION ALL-STARS

Among Thieves enshrined *Uncharted* as PlayStation's crown jewel franchise. Of course we got sequels and spin-offs, not just on the PS3 but on the PS4 and the doomed Vita handheld. Meanwhile, Naughty Dog developed another acclaimed cinematic action-shooter franchise, *The Last of Us*. Instead of pulp adventure fare, this dramatic and harrowing series takes inspiration from zombie survival fiction and brutally violent revenge stories. But when I say that every Sony game is *Uncharted* now, I'm talking about how Sony almost overnight pivoted its entire internal creative process, across all of its teams, toward making blockbuster games in this Naughty Dog mold. When you think PlayStation game, Sony wants you to think "huge, expensive, movie-style action adventure" and nothing else. They want you to think of *Uncharted*.

Days Gone, *Ghost of Tsushima*, *Horizon Zero Dawn*, *Spider-Man*, the *God of War* reboot. In many ways, these games are very different. Some are open-world games while others are linear. Some star famous superheroes while others take place in a postapocalyptic world where everyone looks like *Flintstones* cavepeople wearing Bluetooth headsets. But they all share a Sony aesthetic, an *Uncharted* aesthetic, that blurs them all together. Maybe it's because all their art styles trend toward realism despite vastly different settings. Maybe it's because they all use similar third-person camera setups for their standard blends of shooting, climbing, and chasing. Their technical craft is undeniable, but there's just a bit of soul and individual identity missing that you see in Nintendo mascot platformers or even Xbox bro shooters.

Notice that all these games come from Western studios, in North America or Europe. Hermen Hulst, formerly of Amsterdam-based Sony team Guerilla Games, now heads up the PlayStation Studios enterprise. Of nearly twenty teams, only two are Japanese. It's telling that Sony, a Japanese company, commissioned the Washington team at Sucker Punch to make the Japan-set *Ghost of Tsushima*. The PS4 itself, which benefited from this modern wave of Western Sony blockbusters, featured a revamped, PC-like architecture to make it much friendlier to Western devs burned by the PS3. Who designed that architecture? Mark Cerny, the American engineer behind *Marble Madness*.

But what actually unites these Sony games, and why they turn me off, frankly, is that at some point Sony decided being like a movie means stuffing games full of belabored, self-serious cutscenes. The Norse-themed *God of War* reboot seamlessly swaps between enjoyable melee and projectile combat using the axe. It's also a pretentious TV show about the angry Greek warrior's oh-so-important fatherhood feelings. While Naughty Dog is undeniably talented, the industry's obsession with chasing the studio's style (along with allegations of its punishingly taxing working conditions—allegations Naughty Dog creative director Neil Druckmann hasn't entirely denied) makes it, to me, the single most overrated studio. But based on earth-shattering sales, for the games and for PlayStation hardware, clearly fans disagree.

Years of video games trying to ape movies would naturally lead to a game like *Uncharted 2: Among Thieves*. And now this relationship goes both ways; we've come full circle with an *Uncharted* movie. Without the novelty of its being a game, a cynical critic (like me) might call the *Uncharted* movie a faded copy of a copy, but it speaks to the strength of the brand that the adaptation even got a chance. Blockbuster movies are big business for a reason. People love them. The same goes for high-quality blockbuster games. People love *Uncharted*. They love its thrilling action, compelling characters, and globe-trotting delights. *Uncharted 2* convinced millions of players to stick with PlayStation for years to come.

BECOME THE BAT IN
BATMAN: ARKHAM ASYLUM

Batman: Arkham Asylum gave DC's Caped Crusader the phenomenal video game he always deserved, and gave us the chance to act out our Bat fantasies like never before. Thanks to a series of smart choices, *Arkham Asylum* stood out from other, mediocre comic book games. While it draws inspiration from specific comic books, it tells an original story. The developers at Rocksteady didn't have to rush to coincide with a movie release, which is what killed the *Dark Knight* game planned alongside the Christopher Nolan movie in 2008. Instead, Rocksteady crafted a yarn that was best for gameplay. Batman finds himself locked inside Arkham Asylum, trapped with his vast and deadly rogues' gallery. What more do you need?

Imagine a list of everything you would want to do in a Batman video game, and *Arkham Asylum* checks it off. Use gadgets like Batarangs and hacking devices. Sneak around in the dark and perch on top of gargoyles to scare criminals through stealth. Beat up whole hordes of henchmen using an innovative, flowing, rhythmic combat system that feels as awesome as it looks. Fight over-the-top bosses like the Joker and Bane and Poison Ivy, with multiple voice ac-

tors reprising their roles from the beloved *Batman: The Animated Series*. Never ever fire a gun.

Arkham Asylum spawned its own universe of high-quality Batman games, but this first one is still the best one. The dense, interconnected space feels more intelligently designed than the sprawling Gotham City open worlds, despite the awesome cape gliding. Later games also do a questionable job mixing Burton gothic, Schumacher gaudy, and Nolan gritty into a single aesthetic. Still, *Batman: Arkham Asylum* remains one of the very best pieces of Batman media, period. When you consider how much Batman stuff is out there, that's really saying something.

THE LAST OF US PART II (2020)

Few games combine narrative and gameplay as masterfully as *The Last of Us Part II*. Its combat is brutal and engrossing. Its story is composed of pain and love. Its cyclical violence left me feeling weighed down by what could've been and empty when I see what remains.

When I think back on *TLOU 2* I'm flooded with memories of gorgeous yet gruesome cinematics and horrifying encounters, but also empty queer bookstores, abandoned breweries, and acoustic guitar covers. This game may be one bloody tragedy, but it's balanced by the quiet moments (an owl mug . . . a dream of outer space . . .) and human vulnerability (a fear of heights . . . a back covered in blood and bruises).

All of this is complemented by fantastic gameplay, from carefully laying traps and pulling back that familiar bow to heart-pounding chase sequences and battles with the most terrifying, disgusting things you've ever seen. *TLOU 2* can stand among the greats as a game that manages to be even better than its iconic predecessor.

—JANET GARCIA,
game critic

2010

THE FLASH GAME OF THE YEAR

THIS SCATOLOGICAL SIDESCROLLING PLATFORMER GIVES YOU IMPECCABLY PRECISE CONTROLS AND THROWS YOU INTO BRUTALLY DIFFICULT LEVELS THAT PUSH THOSE CONTROLS TO THE LIMIT. THE FAST PACE AND INSTANT RESPAWNS WILL HAVE YOU SAYING ~JUST ONE MORE TRY~ UNTIL YOU REACH BLOODY VICTORY.

PRESS START

Indie gaming, as a category, could easily fill an entire book on its own. No one video game could encapsulate something as broad as "games made by independent creators, not massive corporate studios." But Team Meat's pitch-perfect platformer Super Meat Boy is at once a highly specific artistic vision as well as a reflection of larger, underappreciated indie Flash gaming roots. Plus, you fight a bad guy named Dr. Fetus.

BREAKING NEW GROUND

In the early 2000s, no program let young computer nerds express their creativity like Flash. Acquired and bounced around between several companies before settling at Adobe, Flash let web developers add interactivity to their websites. Early YouTube relied on Flash to create video players. Flash was so robust and powerful that you could use it to do anything from animating your own cartoons to programming your own video games. As a creative software suite it stood right alongside other Adobe products like Premiere video editing and Photoshop image manipulation. Thanks to Flash, *Homestar Runner* web cartoons defined an entire generation of online humor. Some actual TV shows that air on real networks, like *Teen Titans Go!*, use Flash animation techniques. Flash was magic.

If you wanted to see just how magical Flash could be, Newgrounds had your back. Flash let anyone with a computer make their own games and cartoons, and Newgrounds celebrated that democracy by providing a platform for anyone and everyone to share their material. Founded by Tom Fulp in 1995, the website was unpolished, juvenile, and proud of it. Honestly, Newgrounds had a lot of garbage, one-note joke games and animations only meant to shock you with violence and bad taste. Murder a bunch of terrorist stick figures or watch Nintendo characters curse. I made a cartoon where the Kool-Aid Man guns down the Lorax, and that was relatively wholesome.

However, if you searched for it, you found real, raw, youthful art flowering from Newgrounds' mud. After releasing *Alien Hominid* as a Flash game, Tom Fulp and his team at the Behemoth went on to make "real" games like *Castle Crashers* and *Pit People*. Newgrounds was the online equivalent of a seedy comedy club or punk bar where undiscovered acts went to perform just before blowing up. Millions of fans love Arin "Egoraptor" Hanson as one-half of the wildly popular streaming duo *Game Grumps*, but I saw his first cartoons on Newgrounds. When so many ambitious, aspiring indie artists have a space to freely collaborate and hone their talents, eventually something will break through. *Meat Boy* was a cool Flash game. *Super Meat Boy* is an amazing game, period.

MEAT ON THE BONES

Super Meat Boy may have launched on PC and consoles, but its young Flash game soul shines bright. Edmund McMillen's art and Tommy Refenes's programming feel like something straight out of a browser, and the lightning-fast levels are practically begging to be secretly played on school computers. Everything is flat and bright and square and cartoony . . . with an enthusiastically icky edge. Like *Wolfenstein* or *Doom*, *Super Meat Boy* has an almost transgressive grindhouse quality—Meat Boy isn't a boy made of meat, he's a boy with no skin! As for his nemesis? An evil baby in a jar, of course. The cheeky decision to have the same initials as Nintendo's wholesome, omnipresent *Super Mario Bros.* furthers its gross-out parody status. This kid sticks it to the man. *Super Meat Boy* could only exist as an indie game because no big company would touch it.

That's their loss, though, because if you can stomach *Super Meat Boy*, it's a flat-out incredible game. Unlike Flash games that wear thin after you see the gag, *Super Meat Boy*'s pure platforming gameplay stands at the top of the genre. The sense of control you have over Meat Boy himself, from his running acceleration to his air speed to his wall jumps, satisfies immensely with its pinpoint precision. Meat Boy becomes a divine extension of your will. You'll quickly realize you need that precision, because *Super Meat Boy*'s levels are downright devious. They constantly ask you to make impossible long jumps, avoid overwhelming obstacles, time your movements exactly, run like your life depends on it, and cling to surfaces while praying you'll soon find safe ground.

Super Meat Boy is an excellent example of the masocore game, or games where you derive pleasure from masochist levels of punishment. It uses several key design tricks now common to the genre to keep the constant deaths fun and funny rather than frustrating. The first essential element is the perfect controls, meaning failure is always your fault, not the game's. Next, by keeping levels short, you never lose much progress when you die, so you don't feel like you've wasted too much time. You'll also immediately begin again at the start of the level. If you had to sit through loading screens to try again, even for a few seconds, each death would tempt you to quit instead of making you say, "One more try." Finally, *Super Meat Boy* provides wonderful catharsis when you do succeed. After completing a level, the game replays all your attempts at once, so depending on how many times you retried you'll see this horde of Meat Boys all running forward and dying at various parts of the level before one ultimately makes it.

Super Meat Boy released in an era when indie games finally started getting real visibility. The Xbox 360 in particular did a fantastic job bringing smaller games to mass audiences. With the Xbox Live Arcade service, you could download games over the Internet, and small teams could find fans without relying on big brick-and-mortar stores or weird websites where indie gems like *Cave Story* used to live. So *Super Meat Boy* actually achieved the financial success it deserved, unlike most other indie games before it. Team Meat has since split up to work on other projects. McMillen dove deeper into his love of the grotesque with the profane, roguelike *The Binding of Isaac*, while Refenes headed up *Super Meat Boy Forever*, a sequel that forces Meat Boy to keep running no matter what.

Flash's spirit may live on, but Flash itself is extremely dead. Apple's refusal to allow Flash on iPhones back in 2007 kicked off a slow demise the software never recovered from. It's now been completely scrubbed from the Internet, replaced by the similar HTML5 language and Adobe Animate program. Flash certainly had its problems, from security holes to inefficient power usage, but it's a bummer to see so many tech pundits celebrate its death. Flash wasn't just obsolete tech, it was a tool for vibrant online creative expression. Fortunately, heroic volunteers are working to preserve as many works of Flash indie art as possible for future appreciation.

Super Meat Boy may have helped father a generation, but indie gaming is way bigger than one game. The documentary *Indie Game: The Movie* highlights not just *Super Meat Boy* but also the minds behind other influential indie hits like *Braid* and *Fez*. Indie games serve so many important roles in the current gaming landscape. They filled in the gap left when publishers abandoned mid-tier games to exclusively pursue big-budget blockbusters. They showcase wildly experimental ideas too risky for the mainstream but adored by gaming enthusiasts. They push boundaries forward not just in their designs but in providing crucial entry points for outsider voices and marginalized groups to start demonstrating their unique talents in the industry. And in indie games like *Super Meat Boy*, we see everything that made an entire online art community so special, every flying freak flag that made it too good to exist in this world, kept alive and gifted to us in one meaty package.

MASS EFFECT 2 STRIKES BACK

After the success of *Star Wars: Knights of the Old Republic*, the RPG masters at BioWare set out to create their own sci-fi saga, with EA footing the bill. *Mass Effect*'s universe takes as much influence from *Star Trek*'s intense scientific nerdiness as it does from *Star Wars*' operatic space fantasy, but this is ultimately BioWare's original epic trilogy, and *Mass Effect 2* is gaming's own *The Empire Strikes Back*.

The first *Mass Effect* spent a lot of time diving deep into its own lore, and the gameplay leaned more toward BioWare's dorkier role-playing roots than the action and shooting elements. While many players enjoyed that style, *Mass Effect 2* hits the ground running in a way that immediately roped in far more players. The third-person shooting feels better. You don't have to drive the stupid Mako vehicle. The plot ramps up the interstellar intrigue as you recruit and prepare teammates for a potential suicide mission. That overarching goal allows for a more episodic plot structure as you form bonds, including romantic bonds, with memorable characters. Choose dialogue that pushes your morality in lighter or darker directions, Paragon or Renegade. Commander Shepard feels like your own personal creation, the best feeling a role-playing game can provide.

Let's not argue about *Mass Effect 3*'s ending or the embarrassing entitled gamer backlash. Even if you don't like how a story ends that doesn't make it a defective product, so stop whining to the Better Business Bureau of all places. And let's just pretend *Mass Effect: Andromeda* never happened. But whether we're gunning down Geth troopers or just hanging out on the bridge of the starship *Normandy*, we can all agree that *Mass Effect 2* is one of the greatest games in this or any other galaxy.

DRAGON AGE II (2011)

Dragon Age II often gets a bad rap for repetition of maps, being developed so quickly on the heels of *Dragon Age: Origins*, but it's a game that will always have my heart. From the narrative of Hawke escaping a literally blighted wasteland to starting all over with new friends and found family. The party you gather is lively; they go about their days and talk about it when in a group with you. They have agency outside of waiting around for you to just show up and drag them around on adventures.

It's a complex tale when you dig in, a digital life led in three acts but always different, depending on how you run through Kirkwall with your companions in tow. It's an older game, with a bit of wear and tear after being out in the world for so long, but I encourage you to visit Thedas and spend a while in Kirkwall getting to know Hawke and company.

—TANYA DEPASS,
founder and director of I Need Diverse Games

Dragon Age II is imperfect. Unavoidable, awful things will happen, and no wiki or BradyGames strategy guide will save you.

Kirkwall isn't a sandcastle for you to build. It's a city of stone that stood long before your arrival. Your companions aren't heroes. They can be reckless, destructive, and angry. But aren't you tired of running around open-world RPGs, making all the right choices, waiting for everyone to love you?

Yes, the combat is boring. But playing a BioWare RPG solely for the combat is like eating carrot cake for the fiber content. Sure, it's in there, but that's not why you came to this bakery. Eat up.

—TRIN GARRITANO, writer of games and half a book

2011

MINECRAFT

THE BUILDING BLOCKS OF THE YEAR

CREATE AND LIVE INSIDE ENTIRE WORLDS
MADE OUT OF COLORFUL BLOCKS. WHETHER YOU
WANT TO SURVIVE THE ELEMENTS OR GOOF AROUND
IN THE SANDBOX, YOU'RE FREE TO EXPRESS
YOURSELF HOWEVER YOU WANT.

PRESS START

Minecraft is infinite, digital building blocks. It's Lego in video game form, more so than even the vast number of actual Lego games. With a pitch that potent, of course literally every child on the planet loves **Minecraft**. No wonder it's the single best-selling game of all time, at more than 238 million copies sold. **Minecraft** lets anyone create and share any kind of space they can imagine. It makes you the master, the author, of your own boxy world. As the game of the year, it's a piece of pure light, and when you consider the darkness behind **Minecraft**'s actual author, seizing ownership yourself goes from fun to downright necessary.

BRICK HOUSE

It's funny: for a game so beloved by children, *Minecraft* started off as something only hard-core PC dorks could possibly know about. It was the kind of game you heard about through updates listed on weird web forums. The person who created *Minecraft* (whom we'll discuss in *much* greater detail later) drew inspiration from impressive but absolutely inscrutable games like *Dwarf Fortress*, which uses algorithms to generate and manage complex infinite worlds displayed as text-based art. *Minecraft* took that concept into the third dimension. By rendering its worlds through nothing but big, smooth blocks with basic N64-era textures, *Minecraft* sprawled on forever and took on any shape it wanted.

When you actually play *Minecraft*, those janky PC roots are still super obvious. Its most structured game mode is a survival mode, a mode modders love to hack into existing PC games. Wander the pixelated wilderness gathering resources and turning them into the tools you'll need to make it through the night. Put another way, you mine and then you craft. Eat livestock to replenish your health. Carve weapons out of wood and diamonds. Fend off shambling zombies and exploding Creepers. Eventually, things will go wrong, either because you didn't understand something and made a mistake or the game's various systems collided in a strange and unexpected way. But that's also part of the fun, and you wind up with crazy stories to tell, like, "I dug too deep into the center of the Earth and died in magma." *Minecraft* is experimental, both in its existence and in what it asks players to do.

The creative mode brings that experimentation to the forefront. Without having to worry about enemies or health or even the laws of gravity, players purely focus on sculpting the playground world as they see fit. Carefully place, destroy, and rearrange every single block until you've created an exact re-creation of Westeros from *Game of Thrones*, a modern metropolitan city full of skyscrapers, a humongous hedge maze, or a series of mechanisms that power a working calculator. They may not exist in physical space, but the craziest *Minecraft* constructions surpass the most absurd Lego builds in terms of wild scope and ambition. Also like Lego, *Minecraft* features official licensed partners like *Star Wars* and Mario to add those extra toyetic touches to your creations.

But *Minecraft* doesn't pressure you to make anything this elaborate. There's no way to play it wrong. All that matters is the open-ended freedom to build as you please. The cubist abstract art style is a technical necessity for ensuring the game runs well on everything from high-end PCs to cheap phones. But it also keeps everything cute and cohesive. Put a few dots on a pink square and call it a pig. *Minecraft Dungeons* and *Minecraft: Story Mode* may be an action RPG and adventure game, respectively, but the iconic art style lets us know they're still *Minecraft* games. Massive *Minecraft* landscapes actually look quite stunning at 4K resolution with ray tracing casting natural light and shadows across every box's corners.

Minecraft impacted a gaming generation just a bit younger than my own. So I can't exactly speak from experience as to why kids love it so much. But here's an educated guess: Kids love *Minecraft* because it lets them express themselves. It gives them control. They can even play older versions of the game for free. In *Minecraft*, children can explore without restraints and manipulate their surroundings in ways they could never safely do in the real world. You can get lost in the adventure alone, but friends can also make their own shared *Minecraft* servers to explore and socialize together. We all crave power, and young people have so little of it they flock to any space they can have it, if only to pretend. *Minecraft* turbocharges childhood imaginations, as do other kid-friendly creative software and toys like *Roblox* and, yes, Lego blocks.

No one saw *Minecraft* coming, but it brings so much joy let's be glad it's here. There's only one problem. *Minecraft* was created by a developer named Markus "Notch" Persson, and sadly, unlike *Minecraft*, he sucks.

DEATH OF THE AUTHOR

Notch created *Minecraft*. We can't avoid this fact. When we learned about the game's various updates, as it went from a beta in 2009 all the way up to its full PC and mobile game launch in 2011, we heard about it from him. This Swedish programmer got his start making text adventures, and worked for developer King right before it released its own mega-hit *Candy Crush Saga*. But when Notch made *Minecraft*, and founded developer Mojang, he became a gaming celebrity. Why shouldn't he? He's responsible for perhaps the most formative game of the current era, an original modern classic beloved by generations. He earned a massive platform with an especially high amount of impressionable kids. So what does he do with it? He calls feminism a "social disease" and claims transgender people are mentally ill. He tweets bigoted garbage like this:

"Privilege is a made up metric used to silence and repress."

"It's ok to be white."

"Q is legit. Don't trust the media." ("Q," of course, referring to the delusional, fascist, Trump-loving right-wing pedophile-cabal conspiracy cult QAnon.)

Understandably, most players don't want to support, or even think about, someone as bad as Notch while enjoying something as good as *Minecraft*. These days, you don't really need to. In 2014, Microsoft bought Mojang and *Minecraft* for $2.5 billion. Instead of being locked on the PC and Xbox, *Minecraft* thrives anywhere and everywhere Microsoft can put it. Forget console wars, *Minecraft* belongs in the classroom. Meanwhile, Notch took his gargantuan payday and stopped working on the game. When he's not firing off ignorant tweets, he's outbidding the likes of Beyoncé and Jay-Z for extravagant Beverly Hills mansions and filling them with candy rooms. Following so many controversies, Notch can't come to *Minecraft* conventions anymore, and the game scrubbed all traces of his name even from loading screen jokes. Those loading screens now include messages like "Black Lives Matter" and "Be anti-racist," a big improvement.

This wasn't and won't be the only time the gaming community will need to question if and how we should distance phenomenal games from problem-atic creators. Scott Cawthon developed *Five Nights at Freddy's*, a deviously effective series of horror games that recognizes the sheer terror of animatronic animal mascots. Palmer Luckey's Oculus Rift headset paved the way for virtual reality tech more immersive than ever. Cawthon and Luckey also both heavily support the worst of the worst when it comes to anti-LGBT, anti-immigrant, and climate-change-denying politicians. The problem isn't unique to video games. Some of the most acclaimed movie directors of all time are total scumbags, and Harry Potter–worshipping millennials still can't process just how horrible J. K. Rowling turned out to be. And really, in a world smothered by capitalism, any time you spend money on anything, chances are some of it will go to somebody who really shouldn't have it. There's a reason why we joke about "no ethical choices."

In general, erasing original creator ownership in favor of corporations is a troubling trend. Again, Notch did make *Minecraft*. But he doesn't deserve a platform. Imagine the crushing disappointment of being, say, a trans kid who loves expressing themselves in *Minecraft* only to find out the person who made the thing you enjoy so much may actually hate you for being who you are. Maybe there is something to this new Internet myth that says Hatsune Miku, a Vocaloid singing software represented as a digital anime girl, really created *Minecraft*. Or maybe we should show more appreciation to Mojang's Jens Bergensten, *Minecraft*'s lead designer since 2011.

In the real world, we need to take things as they are, in their totality. We have to accept the good, like *Minecraft*, along with the bad, like *Minecraft*'s creator. However, *Minecraft* itself lets us live and play in a world without this baggage. In *Minecraft*, we build the world; we pick what to include and what not to include.

Huge profits may be great for Microsoft's shareholders, but *Minecraft*'s real lasting impact will be on the minds it has already molded. The game will inspire millions of young people to enter creative, design, and engineering fields. It demonstrates the value of expression for its own sake, and how not every game needs pointless competition. *Minecraft* shows us the joys and possibilities of reshaping the world around us, one digital brick at a time.

FOR THE FIRST TIME, BUT NOT THE LAST, THE ELDER SCROLLS V: SKYRIM

The *Elder Scrolls V: Skyrim* will never ever leave us. *The Elder Scrolls* is Bethesda's flagship franchise alongside *Fallout*, and these fantasy role-playing games are where Todd Howard and his team show off their distinct game design philosophies. The sprawling, open medieval landscapes bombard players with choices, quests, and people to interact with. You feel like you can poke at almost anything, so much so that you're willing to forgive glitches as the game occasionally struggles to keep its clockwork world spinning. This is true of every Bethesda RPG, and *Skyrim* more than most.

But *Skyrim* is where the series really exploded for a lot of people. Old-school *Elder Scrolls* fans will tell you why earlier entries like *Morrowind* and *Oblivion* are better, but *Skyrim* captured the public's imagination. Even non-fantasy fans dug the game's mechanics and approach to exploration. Getting better at skills the more you use them encourages you to pursue playstyles you naturally enjoy. The radiant quest system generates interesting challenges to tackle just about anywhere. Learning the dragons' language and shouting it back at them is hilarious (funnier than any arrow-to-the-knee jokes).

Skyrim itself, the icy and mountainous northern region that serves as the main locale, begs you to wander through its harsh yet natural beauty. Even at its most aimless, the game compels you to keep playing.

More than a decade later, we're still waiting for *The Elder Scrolls VI*. But in the meantime, Bethesda (now owned by Microsoft) has released and rereleased *Skyrim* on every device imaginable. Play it with PC mods. Play it with better graphics on new consoles. Play it on handhelds. Play a version of *Skyrim* by talking to your Amazon Alexa voice assistant. There's even a *Skyrim* tenth anniversary edition. This may all sound like overkill, but *Skyrim* has become exactly the kind of grand myth that deserves to get told and retold until the end of time.

THE ELDER SCROLLS V: SKYRIM (2011)

When you're a kid, fantasy role-playing (or rather, "playing pretend") comes easily, and there are minimal repercussions for gallivanting around outside battling the deadliest foes your imagination can conjure. As an adult, it's different; disbelief is harder to suspend, and brandishing homemade polearms or hurling invisible fireballs at nonexistent enemies outdoors can have unwanted results, like ridicule or getting the cops called.

Skyrim nailed the act of playing pretend, striking a brilliant balance that combined the best of RPGs and open-world action games, while offering plenty of other stuff to do in between. Make your own armor, become a chef, buy a house, get married to a lizard, turn into a werewolf, adopt an unkillable orphan, collect all the cheese wheels in the land and throw them off a cliff. If you want more, install a mod where you're a giant sexy Waluigi and all the dragons are "Macho Man" Randy Savage. Too often video games conflate fantasy and role-playing with lore and stats, but *Skyrim* was a nice reminder that freedom to run around like an idiot is just as important.

—MAX SCOVILLE,
host and producer at IGN

2012

THE WALKING
DEAD

THE ZOMBIE OF THE YEAR

IN THIS EPISODIC ADVENTURE GAME ADAPTATION
OF THE FAMOUS ZOMBIE FRANCHISE, YOU TAKE A
DIRECT HAND IN CRAFTING THE SURVIVAL STORY BY
CHOOSING DIALOGUE, MAKING CRUCIAL PLOT DECISIONS,
AND FORMING CHARACTER RELATIONSHIPS.

PRESS START

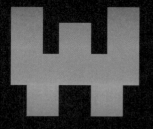hen you buy a Nintendo game, you can generally assume what you're in for. A Harmonix game? You can probably make a safe bet. But a Telltale game? You *know* exactly what to expect: an episodic approach to story-driven adventure games you won't find anywhere else. In fact, you won't even find them at Telltale anymore. After years of growing success and rapid expansion, the studio met a violent and undignified end, not unlike a victim in a zombie movie. It's only fitting then that the absolute best example of the Telltale formula remains Telltale's The Walking Dead.

LET ME TELL YOU A TALE

Telltale Games was founded in 2004 by former LucasArts developers, and the company's first games unapologetically carried that classic adventure game torch. Imaginative settings, rich stories, memorable characters, and puzzles so hilarious you could forgive how obtuse they were. With expensive, modern games putting a premium on action like never before, Telltale games served as modest counterprogramming for folks who preferred great writing to great explosions. The types of licenses Telltale acquired for its games gave you a big clue that these were meant for somewhat quirkier audiences. Telltale made games based on indie comics (*Bone*), underground web cartoons (*Homestar Runner*), landmark stop-motion shorts (*Wallace and Gromit*), network procedurals (*CSI*), and revivals of old LucasArts properties (*Sam & Max*, *Monkey Island*).

While adventure games have devoted fan bases, they tend to be quite small. If Telltale was going to devote itself to pretty much one genre, it needed to rethink what that genre could be and hopefully expand its appeal. Adventure games value story like few other games, so early Telltale games experimented with bringing concepts from other storytelling mediums into the adventure game formula. Like a season of television, Telltale broke up its games into episodes, bite-size chunks you could play in a few hours. Dramatic cliffhangers left you on the edge of your seat waiting for the next episode. And while a typical Telltale season lasted only five episodes, with each episode released about two months after the previous one, this presentation got players to engage with the story first and foremost, to gather around the watercooler in between episodes to react and discuss theories.

Presentation can go only so far, though. To truly reimagine adventure games from the inside out, Telltale's breakthrough project questioned the genre's every tenet and asked, "How can we make this better?" or "Do we even need this at all?" So, did these cunning survivors succeed? Find out the answers to all these burning questions, and more, next time on . . . Telltale's *The Walking Dead*.

MY DARLING CLEMENTINE

In a media landscape drowning in zombie stories, a *Walking Dead* video game sounds about as soulless as a shambling corpse, and most games based on the franchise should've stayed buried. Fortunately, Telltale's *The Walking Dead* more than clears the arguably low bar of "best *Walking Dead* adaptation." Aside from adopting the comic book's stark, stylized art and southern setting, you can and should view the game as an original and completely separate zombie survival yarn. Rick Grimes? Never heard of him.

What matters is that the zombie apocalypse provides the perfect backdrop for Telltale's bold reworking of crusty adventure game tropes. As Lee Everett, you'll first wander the wasteland alone, occasionally shooting at zombies with appropriately clunky controls. However, as you meet more survivors, you quickly learn that the real path to survival lies in keeping this group together. You're constantly faced with high-stakes, life-or-death decisions with no good options. As the leader, your fellow survivors expect you to listen to their concerns, and they remember when you ignore them. When zombies attack your safe house on Hershel's farm, you have time to save only one little boy, Duck or Shawn. I saved Duck, which pleased his father and Lee's friend Kenny, but caused Hershel, Shawn's father, to kick us out. Oh, and you have to make these decisions in real time. If I'd waited too long, both boys might've bitten the dust.

Then there's Clementine, a little girl who lost her family to the zombie horde and the first survivor you encounter. As you watch over her, you don't just make short-term choices to keep her alive but long-term choices to mold her into a woman strong enough to survive in this hell. Teach her to fire a gun, give her a hat, and cut her hair so zombies can't grab it. Demonstrate the value of selflessness in a world where it's everyone for themselves. Since you control Lee, his heartwarming fatherly relationship to Clem becomes your own heartwarming fatherly relationship to Clem. Your investment in her future becomes the powerful emotional center the entire game revolves around. There's even a surprisingly sophisticated racial undercurrent. Lee is a Black history professor who, before all the zombies attacked, was on his way to prison for accidentally killing a state senator who slept with his wife. Taking care of surrogate daughter Clem, who is also Black, provides a sense of redemption. Although it's worth mentioning only Lee is voiced by a Black actor, Dave Fennoy, while white actress Melissa Hutchison voices Clem.

Led by Sean Vanaman and Jake Rodkin, the team behind *The Walking Dead*'s first season finally gave Telltale the adventure game it was searching for. Stellar performances elevated the great, character-centric dialogue adventure games thrive on. The dramatic choice-based gameplay was far more enjoyable, and relevant to the story, than random point-and-click puzzles. Each journey felt unique—if you talked to friends who made different decisions, it sounded like they played an almost entirely different game. The episodic structure kept the game fresh in everyone's mind as buzz grew throughout the weeks. The mega-hot *Walking Dead* license encouraged casual players to give this a shot. More people care about *The Walking Dead* than *Monkey Island*. The future may look bleak for *Walking Dead* survivors, but *The Walking Dead* game promised a very bright future for Telltale . . . until it didn't.

DON'T OPEN, DEAD INSIDE

If someone told me a licensed point-and-click adventure game would be nominated for top awards I would have laughed. But that's how hard critics and audiences fell in love with what Telltale created in *The Walking Dead*. With the formula firmly established, Telltale produced three more full seasons of *The Walking Dead*, as well as a few one-off episodes and shorter miniseries. To bring things full circle, you wind up helping an older Clem take care of her own young ward.

But for Telltale, *The Walking Dead* was just the beginning. The beauty of this template is that it allowed Telltale to make games out of franchises that didn't make sense as other kinds of video games. Sure you could turn *Game of Thrones* into some generic fantasy RPG, but what fans really care about are the characters and shocking twists. They care about the stories, and

Telltale games, like their adventure game ancestors, put stories at the forefront. Plus, no one else could match the publisher when it came to consistent episodic releases. Quickly, all sorts of franchises got the Telltale game treatment. Comic books like *Batman*, *Guardians of the Galaxy*, and *Fables*. Other video games like *Borderlands* and *Minecraft*. Soon "Blank: A Telltale Games Series" became a running joke.

Unfortunately, all this success set Telltale on a course for disaster. Even though only Telltale made these kinds of games, the studio flooded the market with so many of them the public lost its appetite. Their quality also got a lot spottier; few seasons reached the same heights as *The Walking Dead*. And even now the first *Walking Dead* season is still considered the best by far. Behind the scenes, a hidden rot slowly ate the company from within. Management gobbled up expensive licenses that left little budget for other resources. Impossible deadlines, aging technical tools, and the loss of key talent like Vanaman and Rodkin greatly hurt the development process. In 2018, all these problems became too much to bear when Telltale laid off 250 employees, 90 percent of the company, and basically shut down until a new company revived the name. *Walking Dead* creator Robert Kirkman and his Skybound Entertainment company swooped in to finish the final *Walking Dead* season.

As *The Walking Dead* teaches us, everyone dies, some just sooner and more violently than others. So let's celebrate the game's life, not just its death. Actively shaping the narrative through your choices remains a brilliant gameplay mechanic. The writers creatively crafted plots that allowed for the most enjoyable and dramatic decisions possible while still organically hitting the same major plot beats in all playthroughs. Playing these games alongside other people only adds to the sense of shared storytelling. Even haters get on board. I've played Telltale games in massive theaters, where the audience got to vote on what to do next. I've also played these games with my wife, where she makes every decision. Although its leaders drove the developer into an early grave, Telltale's *The Walking Dead* perfected the modern adventure game formula.

FORZA HORIZON'S OPEN ROADS

By bringing together nearly every disparate piece of the racing genre, *Forza Horizon* is a car lover's dream. Open-world games like *Grand Theft Auto* have you frequently driving cars, but what about an open world exclusively about driving cars? Instead of racing down linear, preset tracks, you can discover your own courses on the roads surrounding you in all directions. *Burnout Paradise* nailed this concept as well, but its emphasis on wicked-cool destruction meant it only featured fake car brands. Ferrari won't let some lowly game developers demolish its merchandise. *Burnout* studio Criterion later developed some decent *Need for Speed* games in the same style, which featured real cars, but those games simply felt like diet versions of the real *Burnout* experience. Meanwhile, the mainline *Forza* series was Microsoft's answer to Sony's *Gran Turismo*. They aren't accessible arcade racers but highly technical simulation games, appealing to experts but off-putting to everyone else, games you buy steering wheel controllers for. Each game has what the others lack.

Miraculously, *Forza Horizon* pulls this all together. Developed by Playground Games, *Forza Horizon* still has one foot in that sim world. However, you can tweak the controls to your liking to get a far more forgiving ride. You also get all the benefits of real cars, as the game depicts your luxury vehicles with a beautiful, almost erotic attention to detail. And like *Burnout Paradise*, you're free to drive wherever you want, finding all sorts of mayhem and challenges in the twisting, open terrains. Throughout the years, *Forza Horizon* has taken us from Australia to the United Kingdom to Mexico to a world made of Lego blocks. A visual showpiece and one of Xbox's most dependable franchises, *Forza Horizon* has outgrown its spin-off status. *Forza Horizon* is the only *Forza* that matters.

JOURNEY (2012)

Gaming can be an abrasive and toxic place, but *Journey* by Thatgamecompany is a shining example of the good that games can do. Partly a game and partly a social experiment, *Journey* famously pairs you with a random stranger who just happens to also be playing the game. Under normal circumstances, this would open up endless opportunities for trolling and abuse, but *Journey*'s uniquely cooperative design shows what we're capable of when we work together.

Nothing will ever match the emotional response I had playing *Journey* for the first time. My roommate at the time watched my entire playthrough from start to finish, and once I finished she asked what the name on the screen meant. I replied, "Oh, that's the person that was playing with me."

Her jaw dropped. With a look that landed somewhere between wonder and disbelief she asked, "Wait a minute, scarf buddy is real?!" Before I had time to finish explaining, as if to prove my point, I got a DM from the person I had been playing with . . . in Japanese. Through some clever work-arounds, we were able to put the text into Google Translate. The message simply read, "Thank you for the wonderful journey."

—ALICE NEWCOME-BEILL,
  game critic and contributor for
  the Verge

2013

Depression Quest

an interactive
(non)fiction
about living with
depression

THE FIRESTORM GAME OF THE YEAR

SIMULATE THE EVERYDAY STRUGGLES OF
LIFE WITH MENTAL ILLNESS IN THIS TEXT
ADVENTURE BASED ON PERSONAL EXPERIENCES

PRESS START

The indie game boom elevated marginalized creators, and we're all better off for it. Finally, more artists freely made games that reflected their own personal and political identities. Gaming became a broader tapestry of perspectives than "white guy with a gun." Gaming became a place that allowed for excellent emotional experiences like Depression Quest.

Unfortunately, Depression Quest's significance is unfairly, inescapably linked to the fact that it also inadvertently caused a chaotic controversy, Gamergate, that revealed the darkest realities of video game culture itself. As some championed new voices, others attempted to shout them down.

INTERACTIVE (NON)FICTION

Before we get into all the . . . unpleasantness, *Depression Quest* deserves to be talked about on its own merits, to have its legacy reclaimed from the shadows surrounding it. An interactive fiction game, *Depression Quest* was made using the Twine engine. Twine makes it incredibly easy for anyone to develop games in the text adventure genre. Advanced users can implement all sorts of nifty tricks, but even if you have zero coding experience you can make your own interactive short story. Twine puts the emphasis on narrative, a rarity in video game engines. Twine also makes it quick and easy to publish your games. Designer Zoë Quinn gave away *Depression Quest* for free, and if you did choose to pay them money, part of the proceeds went to the National Suicide Prevention Lifeline.

By stripping away complex mechanics and arbitrary paywalls, *Depression Quest* gets right to its serious point. Written by Quinn and Patrick Lindsey, with music by Isaac Schankler, *Depression Quest* puts you in the headspace of someone experiencing the titular mental disorder. The intro spells out the purpose perfectly.

"The goal of this game is twofold: firstly, we want to illustrate as clearly as possible what depression is like, so that it may be better understood by people without depression. Hopefully this can be something to spread awareness and fight against the social stigma and misunderstandings that depression sufferers face. Secondly, our hope is that in presenting as real a simulation of depression as possible, other sufferers will come to know that they aren't alone, and hopefully derive some measure of comfort from that."

Quinn uses the text adventure format, where players technically make decisions but are still bound by the story, as a metaphor. Although you should have complete agency in your own life, depression robs you of those choices and forces you down bleaker and bleaker holes. For example, the game spells out how your rational mind realizes that you should catch up on work you're behind on, but that option is crossed out.

The choking brain fog only lets you watch TV, crawl into bed, or make an attempt at work that inevitably fails. The static gray background art reflects a constant, hopeless, low-energy malaise. The path to healing is hard, but you don't need to travel it alone. *Depression Quest* makes it clear how therapy and medication can save your life.

Recently, we've heard a lot about the idea of video games as empathy machines, as ways to understand others by literally walking in their virtual shoes. You should be able to care about other people without needing to become them by strapping on virtual reality goggles or whatever. However, games that do successfully let you experience the world from another perspective leave incredibly powerful lasting effects. *Depression Quest* walks you through real-life depression. *Papers, Please* casts you as an immigration officer forced to decide who can and can't enter the country. *Gone Home* slowly turns what looks like a haunted house story into a burgeoning young queer romance in 1990s Oregon.

Make no mistake, the desire to convince others to see the world from other points of view is a political stance. It's a stance meant to remind you that other people also matter, and that we should improve society by helping everyone, not just ourselves. It's a progressive stance. Tragically, there are those who view this progressive power, fearlessly wielded by *Depression Quest* and others, as an unwelcome and unacceptable intruder in their precious gaming hobby. They're wrong; we cannot and will not go backward. But the fight for the future that followed left a lasting scar on gaming, and on actual lives, that we still haven't recovered from.

THAT HORRIBLE HASHTAG

You may have heard a lot of hand-wringing about how "complicated" or "nuanced" Gamergate was, so let's cut through that noise. Gamergate was an online reactionary hate campaign whose end goal was to harass women, LGBT people, ethnic minorities, and pretty much anyone with left-of-center politics out of the video game industry, full stop. That's it. Now, someone might try to convince you that Gamergate was actually about ethics in video game journalism. Media ethics are very much worth discussing, but with Gamergate, those "concerns" were a smoke screen, a lie some supporters perhaps told themselves, but a lie nonetheless. Gamergate wasn't a Watergate-style exposé; it wasn't a crusade against corruption. Gamergate was a hate movement, period.

To understand what happened, to separate truths from lies, you need to understand what any of this has to do with *Depression Quest*. In 2014, Zoë Quinn's bitter ex-boyfriend wrote a blog post imagining a vast conspiracy in which *Depression Quest* succeeded only because of the crooked video game journalism clique. A horrible, false smear, it claimed that Quinn and the media were literally in bed together to drum up sales and trick the public into thinking the game was better than it actually was. It didn't matter that this made no sense. If all you wanted was money, why give the game away for free? But to many gamers, Zoë Quinn's status as a marginalized person making indie games about mental health was already more than enough reason to hate them. Gamergate provided the excuse, and it didn't stop there.

It also didn't really start there. Gamergate gave shape and a name to an alarming amount of regressive elements that had festered in gaming for a very long time. Take it from me, a Black guy who knows what happens when you tell other gamers online that you're a Black guy. A Black guy who's been on 4chan. *Depression Quest* may have been the inciting incident, but it was the inevitable end point of an industry dominated by white boys who worship corporations and see themselves as perpetual nerdy victims of censorship by the government/jocks/their moms. Before Gamergate, gamers already had little tolerance for any criticism of the medium, not just dumb criticism but also criticism that was thoughtful and only sought to improve video games for everyone.

However, in 2014 Gamergate brought these issues out into the open so violently we could no longer ignore them. Mainstream news outlets covered how thoroughly, embarrassingly childish games culture still was. Video game websites, who previously maintained plausible deniability for the harassment that happens (mostly to women and people of color) in their anonymous forums, got dragged into making milquetoast calls for peace. Gamergate claimed to want a video game industry free of a nebulous, nefarious political agenda, but that in itself is a deeply political position. If you think that video games without politics means video games without diverse voices, what you really think is that video games should have only bigoted, right-wing, fascist politics. If you're going to be scum, at least be honest.

Throughout this online drama, real human beings suffered immense actual harm. Zoë Quinn and many other talented developers who aren't boring straight white men were harassed and threatened. The kind of developers the industry desperately needs more of were shoved back onto the sidelines. Gamergate wanted to kill Zoë Quinn, to the point where Quinn had to change addresses and warn their family and cooperate with federal law enforcement. Quinn survived, fortunately, and wrote a book called *Crash Override* detailing the experience while offering advice to anyone else staring down online abuse.

All these years later, one of the most upsetting aspects of Gamergate (as someone who was an observer and not a direct victim) was how it gave us in gaming a sneak preview of forces gathering behind the scenes to destroy the world. Gamergate pioneered the tactics that young, Internet-savvy, alt-right trolls later used to wage the online disinformation wars that no doubt helped put Trump in office. I love video games, but I hate that they played any role in that living nightmare, no matter how small. However, we can't cede gaming to the worst among us. Try as some might to fight against it, progress by definition is the future. And the future must have room for creators who don't fit into the mainstream and games with stories about difficult topics. Zoë Quinn matters. *Depression Quest* matters.

FIRE EMBLEM AWAKENING'S BATTLEFIELD OF LOVE

Think of *Fire Emblem* (from Nintendo and developer Intelligent Systems) like chess but with sweeping narratives and boards that change in every match.

In a strategy RPG, you need to worry about not only your character's abilities and stats, but also where they're physically located in relation to opponents on the grid. Strategy games like *Fire Emblem* and *XCOM* ratchet up their tactical tension with permanent death. If a unit dies, no matter how much you relied on their skills or how attached you were to them as a person, they stay dead for the rest of the game. So think carefully before each move.

Fire Emblem Awakening on the Nintendo 3DS used the same rock-solid formula the franchise introduced in the NES days. Swords beat axes, axes beat lances, lances beat swords. But what made this entry so brilliant was how it turned your relationships with the cast into a metagame unto itself. It turned *Fire Emblem* into a dating sim. If you paired units next to one another in battle, their bond increased with each victory. When certain pairs bonded, they got married. Eventually, you can even recruit their children from the future. Sure, you could be a heartless robot and try to breed the strongest warriors possible, but Chrom and Olivia just make a great couple. These mechanics exponentially increase your investment in the game. Permanent character death becomes so much more devastating (though, in a first for the series, this mechanic could be turned off). *Fire Emblem Awakening* is its own kind of empathy machine, and its surprise popularity saved the niche franchise from extinction.

PAPERS, PLEASE (2013)

A strange, otherworldly thing happens at borders: Everyone stops being human.

For as long as I can remember, we were alien numbers to the American immigration officers scrutinizing only our papers as we smiled back nervously. Each time, Mom handed them that thick, neatly filed binder of documents proving our existence, our worthiness to reenter, and become human again. But they can send you back anyway, she warned sharply when we acted outside the programming of a model minority while waiting in line. They don't need reason—just a mistake.

But playing *Papers, Please*, a realization dawned. Those officers croaking mundane questions like accusations weren't allowed to be any more human than we were.

In the liminal space of a border, we are all automatons. Identity dissolves, reducing every being to a set of predetermined inputs and outputs. You are either the well-oiled cogs toiling inside the machine of nationalism, or the cogs outside shaving themselves down in hopes of fitting well enough to toil.

I am another stack of papers to be organized on your desk. You are one more semi-sentient firewall to bypass. There is a sick satisfaction to serving our functions in such a well-designed system working precisely as it was engineered to.

At times it is a relief to leave behind the burden of humanity. The machine depends on that.

—JESS JOHO,
media and culture critic

2014

DESTINY™

THE (EVENTUAL) GAME OF THE YEAR

TEAM UP WITH FRIENDS IN A PERSISTENT ONLINE
WORLD TO SHOOT ALIENS AND COLLECT INCREASINGLY
VALUABLE AND STYLISH WEAPONS AND ARMOR.

PRESS START

You can't play 2014's Destiny anymore. You can play a game called Destiny, but the game you'll play today just barely resembles the game that launched years ago. Thank god. After a promising but botched debut, why do we now look back at Destiny as 2014's game of the year? Despite its failed first attempt to fuse together multiple familiar formulas, Destiny never stopped updating itself until it got it right. In the process, Destiny created a new type of game, an evolving and ongoing way of delivering a game, a game that major rivals can't help but chase after. While Destiny's inspirations are obvious, as is its impact on future games, it remains king of its own genre through its sheer craft and commitment to creative self-improvement. Destiny shows how, in gaming, original ideas never stay exclusive for long, but execution lasts forever.

THAT WIZARD CAME
FROM THE MOON

It's not like *Destiny*'s developers planned on screwing up the launch. As the next game from Bungie, *Destiny* sounded like the surest of surefire hits. After revolutionizing the console shooter and single-handedly saving Microsoft's inaugural Xbox console with the *Halo* franchise, the folks at Bungie freed themselves from Bill Gates and sought to carve a new path. Being the latest project from the minds behind *Halo*, a game so popular it has its own 7-Eleven sweepstakes, *Destiny* arose from appropriately ambitious beginnings. Bungie signed an unprecedented ten-year, $500 million deal with Activision as the *Call of Duty* publisher looked to further tighten its shooter market stranglehold. There's no bigger, better example of writing your own check in game development.

To a casual observer, *Destiny*'s screenshots look like something from *Halo*. You and your vaguely militarized space friends with shiny armor and dusty capes run around attractive, open environments shooting alien armies in first person. Despite superficial similarities, drastically different structures completely change how you play each game. *Halo* offers multiplayer modes, where you battle against other players, and a campaign, where you alone play through thoughtfully designed linear levels and absorb a story. *Destiny* blurs these lines. The game persists as a cooperative or competitive online social space even when you're flying solo. Add in a fresh layer of role-playing concepts, like leveling up your character the more you play and looting better equipment with more power, and you're left with the shooter equivalent of an MMORPG, like fellow Activision game *World of Warcraft*. Reminder that *World of Warcraft* is so astronomically popular it's less a game and more an alternate, superior plane of reality for millions of subscribers across two decades. These aren't new ideas, but *Destiny* set out to transform them into a new experience.

A huge and expensive next-gen sci-fi shooter from the *Halo* people (the *Halo* people!) could never fail. If the *Halo* people (the *Halo* people!) came up to me and said, "We need half a billion dollars to make *World of Warcraft* with sci-fi guns," I would also say yes because that's a fantastic pitch. In practice, though, the mash-up created surprising and unfortunate dissonance. Due to immense internal and external pressure on Bungie, the game went through an infamously rocky development process, and it showed. *Destiny* didn't fail exactly, but the game that launched in 2014 was a qualified success at best.

There's hardly any story beyond "check out this cool giant sky ball" and other hidden nonsense lore. The action smears together into too much mindless repetitive blasting in the same locations, occasionally broken up by flashy melee attacks. My hands had a lot of fun playing *Destiny* in 2014, but my bored brain never stopped thinking, "Why am I even playing this?" The most hilariously sad part of the preview beta, where it became distressingly obvious how little real content the game had at launch, was when your mystical floating robotic companion, voiced by *Game of Thrones*' Peter Dinklage, said, "That wizard came from the moon," with not nearly the passion one should have when saying, "That wizard came from the moon."

RELOAD

So why didn't *Destiny* simply perish like countless other well-pedigreed disasters? The game did get one thing spectacularly right: the guns. Here's some advice for envious game designers. If you're going to copy *Destiny*, copy the guns. Coming from a team with a historically strong first-person shooter legacy, no video game guns shoot better than *Destiny*'s deliriously ornate and wacky video game space guns. The handling and weight, the precision and performance, the satisfying collision as projectiles crackle and explode with pulsating energy you'll never get from boring Earth bullets. It's all near perfect. Not only that, but the gunplay elevates other parts of the experience. Excellent controls allow for tactical individual enemy encounters that make the game feel smarter than it is. You love the guns, so you want to scavenge for more of them and get sucked into the rewarding loot loop with your friends.

As a game 99 percent about shooting, *Destiny* would fall apart if its otherworldly weapons disappointed. But because those guns rule so hard, and everything surrounding them was just competent enough, many people played and loved countless hours of *Destiny* without questioning it, despite the glaring flaws. For them, the shooting and looting masterfully fed into each other, creating a potent and entertaining mix greater than the sum of its recognizable parts.

That mix also left a lasting impression. By applying MMORPG concepts to a different and more mainstream game genre, in this case a shooter, *Destiny* innovated and popularized the games as a service formula, or GaaS. Side note, GaaS has to be one of the most unfortunate acronyms in an industry full of unfortunate acronyms. Games as a service aren't merely static products you enjoy for a few days and sell back at GameStop. With their constant Internet connections, these ever-changing games breathe, mature, and expand as living platforms. They're meant to take over your whole life through a careful combo of FOMO-fomenting online social features, consistent content updates, microtransactions, and addictive core gameplay hooks.

Once a live service game like *Destiny* gets going, once enough players invest into the ecosystem, its momentum becomes self-sustaining. Nimble developers take advantage of this flexible format to quickly brainstorm and toss in cool concepts, original or taken from elsewhere, to tinker and see what sticks. Live service games take the idea of patches, postlaunch fixes for a game's problems rolled out after hearing feedback, and crank them up exponentially.

GaaS saved *Destiny*. The empty *Destiny* that barely clung to life in 2014 faded into a distant memory as Bungie regularly added tiny tweaks and acclaimed epic expansions. Hoverbike races? Sure! Halloween masquerade parties? Go nuts! There's a lot less Peter Dinklage and a lot more Lance Reddick. A full-on sequel in 2017 gave curious players the perfect excuse to jump into the community. How radically did *Destiny* rehabilitate and revitalize itself? After Bungie ended its deal with Activision and took *Destiny* with them to become fully independent, *Destiny 2* relaunched as a free-to-play smash hit where players choose to spend money only if they want to. Trust me, they spend money. Bungie then got acquired by Sony, putting Microsoft's former favorite child in the PlayStation family.

Depending on whom you ask, *Destiny* is still either too complex to be a game you don't think about, or too dumb to be a game worth thinking about. However, with its state-of-the-art GaaS package of remixed parts, Bungie (eventually) built something undeniably original, impressive, and capable of growing even stronger. Movies may get director's cuts and albums may get remastered, but only video games can and will wholly reinvent themselves if that's what it takes to survive, especially in the online twenty-first century. In time, *Destiny* resonated with not only millions of players, but also fellow game designers. And those designers took notes.

STOP ME IF YOU'VE
PLAYED THIS ONE BEFORE

Because modern game development lasts so long, it takes years before we see certain games' immediate impact. But soon enough the *Destiny* clones came rolling in, looting the game without mercy. Ubisoft's *Tom Clancy's The Division* trades space battles across different planets for uncomfortably realistic war-torn American cities. EA's *Anthem* gives you a slick robot suit, complete with jet pack, to fly around in as you loot and shoot. If that's not enough Iron Man for you, the most recent *Marvel's Avengers* game from Square Enix is literally *Destiny* but with superhero punching instead of gun shooting. When the Avengers copy your idea, you've made it.

Granted, most if not all of these games launched with even more problems than *Destiny* did. The thing about GaaS (ugh) is that they're really complicated and hard to get right. Developers must plan and generate enough compelling content for the long term, and squash endless technical bugs as soon as they appear. These games take time, and everyone's watching you. Understandably, players don't want to waste so much of their precious limited time on something bad on the shaky promise it may get better months or years later. So if a service game releases in a truly horrific state, not even the greatest comeback in history may remove that stink.

Nevertheless, even just the alluring opportunity to monopolize online players' lives and wallets with GaaS tempts publishers so much they can't help themselves, despite the costly risks. They keep trying, even if they can't get the guns right. And when they do manage to introduce a worthwhile addition or change, like *Rocket League* using GaaS structure to promote its kick-ass arcade car soccer game, then the whole genre moves forward. That's how GaaS goes from an intriguing trend to gaming's new model.

Besides, it's not like *Destiny* is the first game to get instantly imitated. Walk through any arcade and you'll see walls of poorly disguised clones. Take Konami's *Teenage Mutant Ninja Turtles* game, swap in *The Simpsons*, and you, my friend, have got yourself another, totally different, beat-'em-up game. Entire game genres get their names from the original games that inspired them, from *Doom*(clones) to *Rogue*(likes) to Metroidvanias (*Metroid* + *Castlevania*). *Destiny* didn't invent *Halo*-style first-person shooting or *Diablo*-style, loot-driven, action RPG progression. It wasn't even the first to combine them. *Borderlands* did that in 2009.

The unique ways games can rip one another off create unique dilemmas. The way a game controls and feels arguably does more to define its identity than its narrative or aesthetic. However, it's a lot easier for audiences and lawyers alike to recognize a stolen character or plot point or art style than it is to recognize something as intangible as stolen mechanics. Still, from bold remakes to brazen burglary, turning old influences into something fresh is key to making not just games but any art. *Destiny* and its imitators demonstrate how no games are wholly original, but also no games are wholly without at least some originality. There's value and validity in both inventing from the ground up and improving what already works.

That process, that invention and improvement, can continue even after a game's release, however bad that release is. Not all games get second chances, so we congratulate the ones that do. They give us hope that even the worst games may (eventually) turn things around and make good on their initial promises or fulfill their unexplored potential. We definitely didn't know this in 2014, but *Destiny* has now become a quality game, a pioneer for the ascendant games as a service model, and an icon that's original . . . enough.

THE TRAGEDY OF THREES

In this puzzle game for phones, players slide number tiles around the screen to create the biggest multiples of three possible before running out of room. It requires strategic thinking and spatial reasoning totally different from standard block-dropping puzzle games. After the game's February release, my friends and I spent weeks beating each other's high scores and gloating about it. Adorable sound effects and soft pastel graphics add layers of aesthetic charm and personality that tip an already great game into a mobile masterpiece. It's absolutely worth the $6 asking price.

One month later, *2048* seemingly stole everything wonderful about *Threes*, made it dumber and faster, and gave it away for free. As a result, way more people played it. *2048* achieved the cultural phenomenon status, however fleeting, *Threes* deserved. Again, video game rip-offs are nothing surprising, especially on phones where free-to-play clones notoriously reign supreme. Regardless, the shamelessness of this theft really bothered me, not just because I love *Threes*, but because the game also came from the overlooked Chicago indie game development community, a community I was slowly partying my way into at the time. Only good manners stop me from walking up to every person playing *2048* on the subway and evangelizing to them about *Threes*.

What happened to *Threes* is a tragedy that can happen only in gaming. The game did do well critically, and continues to rank high on App Store sales charts. Still, how much more successful could it have been if the tiny team (Ashmer Vollmer, Greg Wohlwend, and Jimmy Hinson) had patented their mechanics the way console makers like Nintendo and Sony patent analog sticks, motion controls, and other hardware gimmicks? Then again, patenting mechanics creates potentially worse problems, like denying other developers the opportunity to build on brilliant emerging ideas. So how can a game acknowledge its influences, protect its own legacy, and avoid greed that stifles gaming as a whole? Beats me, but there must be a better solution than simply accepting this apparent robbery.

DESTINY 2: THE WITCH QUEEN (2022)

As someone who mostly plays AAA and indie single-player games, it took a while for me to get into multiplayer first-person shooters. Connecting with those games' stories just wasn't as easy. But *Destiny 2: The Witch Queen*'s story felt fulfilling. It meshed the FPS quality with intricate lore. New combat methods, combined with puzzle mechanics, maintain that grind-y, loot-based *Destiny* structure. Even hearing the melancholy soundtrack made the magical realm of Savathûn's Throne World even more alluring. With its sense of immersion, *The Witch Queen* exhibits how a multiplayer FPS can transcend into a breathtaking experience.

—SANIYA AHMED,
freelance writer at GameSpot

2015

THE TOME OF THE YEAR

TAKE CONTROL OF GERALT OF RIVIA, A GRIZZLED
MONSTER HUNTER, AS YOU TRAVEL A VAST LAND BASED
ON ANDRZEJ SAPKOWSKI`S POLISH FANTASY SERIES.
IN THIS EPIC OPEN-WORLD RPG, YOU`LL FIND YOURSELF
AT THE CENTER OF MANY STORIES, LARGE AND SMALL,
AS YOU TRY TO RESCUE YOUR SURROGATE DAUGHTER, CIRI.

PRESS START

If video games are the medium that everyone thinks is dumb until proven otherwise, then books are the polar opposite. There are some spectacularly stupid books, especially in the sci-fi and fantasy genres. But fairly or not, something about reading a book just feels smarter than playing a video game. What makes **The Witcher 3: Wild Hunt** so miraculous then is how it leverages the strength of its literary source material while still remembering to be a phenomenal video game. With **The Witcher 3: Wild Hunt**, words come alive.

BOOK SMART

Successfully adapting books into video games is no easy feat. Technically, something like *Middle-earth: Shadow of Mordor* counts, but it draws more inspiration from the *Lord of the Rings* movies (and other popular games) than from any of the Tolkien novels. Tom Clancy was an author, but when Ubisoft slaps his name on a game, all it means is there's military stuff in it. EA turned *The Divine Comedy*, Dante Alighieri's fourteenth-century imagining of the Christian afterlife, into *Dante's Inferno*, a bog-standard action game where you slash Lucifer with your big sword like a big man.

The fact that we're starting with the third *Witcher* game should tell you just how hard this nut is to crack. Polish developer CD Projekt Red's first two stabs at translating Andrzej Sapkowski's acclaimed Polish fantasy novels were far from horrible. Released in 2007 and 2011, respectively, *The Witcher* and *The Witcher 2: Assassins of Kings* earned strong reviews. President Obama received a copy of *The Witcher 2* from Polish prime minister Donald Tusk as an example of the country's vibrant cultural exports.

However, with its next *Witcher* game, CD Projekt Red wanted to deliver not just another eastern European "Eurojank" game whose ambitions outstripped its technical ability, but an experience that stood shoulder to shoulder with top-tier games from any country. The company wanted to be famous for more than its digital vintage games storefront, Good Old Games. The team set out to make the next *Mass Effect* or *Skyrim*. That's really hard. There's no secret trick or shortcut to creating a game with a scale this massive. It just takes a lot of work and a lot of time. In 2015, our patience and CD Projekt Red's labor were rewarded with the absolute masterpiece that is *The Witcher 3: Wild Hunt*.

CONTINENTAL

The first two *Witcher* games gave you pockets of exploration inside a largely linear structure. So *The Witcher 3*'s shift to full-on open-world RPG is already an enormous evolution. But even compared with contemporary open-world games, *The Witcher 3*'s world (the Continent) combines huge scope with handcrafted care you consistently get only from, say, Nintendo or Rockstar. The map consists of three major zones—little open worlds unto themselves. The scenery shifts so dramatically you'll feel like you've started playing the sequel to the game you're already in. Velen's lush forests and humble villages couldn't feel more different than Novigrad's dense, bustling city life or the seafaring culture in the Skellige Isles. You don't need to be an expert on Slavic mythology to appreciate the Polish approach to European mythology compared with what a British or French developer might have come up with.

You'll have plenty of reasons to travel back and forth across the land, whether it's tracking down a character, following a story thread, or just sightseeing. When you need to intensely focus on an investigation, activate your Witcher Senses to tune out distractions and follow scents and auras. This detective vision mechanic has become a bit of a cliché, but here it makes the environment itself an important player in the story, not just a backdrop. Plus, patiently tracking prey makes the buildup to the fight all the more enticing.

The combat is the closest thing *The Witcher 3* has to a weakness, but that's only because it's just pretty darn fun instead of the best thing ever. As a Witcher, a mutated monster hunter, you need to always have two swords at the ready: a silver sword to fight monsters and a steel sword to fight men. The game automatically gives you the proper weapon so you can focus on evading attacks and striking back. Witchers aren't the strongest magic users, but you can also upgrade a handful of tactical spells, Signs, to suit your playstyle. Shoot fireballs with Igni, shield yourself with Quen, or confuse foes with Axii.

With just these elements, *The Witcher 3: Wild Hunt* already has a solid open-world RPG structure, leagues ahead of the first two games in ambition and execution. If *The Witcher 3* didn't succeed as a video game, it wouldn't succeed, period. But as fantastic, fun, and functional as its gameplay is, it's ultimately a means to an end. What truly makes *The Witcher 3* so special is its beating, literary, hardcover heart.

THE LAST WISH

The Witcher 3 sits near the end of the *Witcher* timeline, after the first two games and well after the Netflix show. The added sense of history enriches the experience. However, at the beginning of the adventure Geralt suffers from some amnesia, so feel free to start with this game because the hero will be as confused as you are. This is more than just a convenient contrivance, though. This is how *The Witcher 3* begins to thread the needle of its own inherent contradictions.

Novels are written. They are authored works with a set story that never changes. You sit back and read what the storyteller tells you. Video games, though, empower you to make choices. As an open-world game, *The Witcher 3* grants you the freedom to go wherever you want. So how do you respect Sapkowski's work, without watering it down, while still encouraging player freedom? You have to do both at the same time. You have to know when to let players loose and when to subtly rein them back in. It's more hard work for developers, but *The Witcher 3* makes it look so effortless it's practically magic. It's like living inside a tome.

Take Geralt himself. Your decisions will shape his personality to a degree. You can make him gruffer or sweeter, more willing to help people or happier to ignore them. Decide whether he's the kind of person who participates in community theater. Making these choices makes the character your own, which is good because you'll be stuck with him for dozens of hours. But Geralt of Rivia is no blank cipher; he's an actual character. With so many fixed traits, he's closer to a JRPG hero than a Western RPG hero, a set of defined lines you can color inside. Geralt is more than a horny dude with white hair and cat eyes who hangs out in bathtubs. He's a Witcher, so he's intimately familiar with the customs and traditions of that lifestyle, the prejudices it comes with. You can't change his past romantic entanglements with witches like Yennefer of Vengerberg and Triss Merigold; only whether or not to pursue them into the future.

Above all else, Geralt is Ciri's guardian. No matter how many tangents you go down, your goal always remains the same: rescue Ciri. As a player, you mold Geralt into whatever kind of father figure you think he should be, and see how that impacts Ciri's destiny. In an aging games industry overrun with daddy-daughter simulators, *The Witcher 3* is by far the least cloying and most genuinely emotional.

The luxurious world-building and novelistic writing taken from Sapkowski's oeuvre flesh out and enhance the rest of the game surrounding you. Lengthy sequences like the Bloody Baron's dark family drama or the political intrigue surrounding King Radovid showcase maturity and sophistication, a desire to walk players through a narrative that makes them feel something. It's also frequently hilarious. Geralt is a sassy icon. This is the kind of game where Uma isn't a generic fantasy name, but an acronym for "ugliest man alive."

Even side quests and monster hunts, typically the most tedious padding in an open-world game, constantly shock and amaze with their depth. There are one-off encounters with werewolves, water hags, godlings, and something called a lubberkin with higher-quality stories and more compelling characters than whole entire games. DLC expansions introduce elements like vampires and colorful fairy-tale lands like something out of *Shrek*. True to its source material while never forgetting its immediate interactive needs, *The Witcher 3: Wild Hunt* is the video game equivalent of reading a dense and brilliant fantasy novel or short-story collection. The gaming community responded with rave reviews and ongoing sales success. *The Witcher 2* sold just under two million copies; *The Witcher 3* is at more than forty million and counting.

CD Projekt Red isn't perfect—just look at *Cyberpunk 2077*'s disastrous launch— but *The Witcher 3* showed us the dizzying heights these creators are capable of. Geralt's odyssey delivers stories within stories with the skill and confidence of a seasoned fantasy author while granting players more than enough space to express themselves, as in any proper video game. *The Witcher 3: Wild Hunt* gives us everything.

YAKUZA 0 CHASES THE DRAGON

A smash hit in Japan for years, the *Yakuza* series finally broke through in the United States with *Yakuza 0*. The 1980s prequel welcomed newcomers into the elaborate soap opera plot. But really, what's wonderful about one *Yakuza* applies to all of them.

Japanese *Grand Theft Auto* is a somewhat accurate but largely reductive take on *Yakuza*. Really, it's more like a spiritual successor to Yu Suzuki's cult hit Sega series *Shenmue*. Instead of dropping players in a sprawling open world, it places them in a small environment, the fictional Kamurochō district, simulated with unreal detail and full of tiny things to do. As up-and-coming gangster Kazuma Kiryu, you'll fight punks in 3D beat-'em-up battles, but you'll also sing in karaoke minigames and play actual working *OutRun* and *Virtua Fighter* arcade cabinets. Before his gritty *Yakuza* reinvention, producer Toshihiro Nagoshi worked on the *Super Monkey Ball* series, and despite the dark crime flick exterior, *Yakuza* has a proudly wacky, anime sensibility.

Yakuza's gameplay keeps you entertained as you push forward through the story, the real reason you're here. If you continue with the *Yakuza* saga past *0* it's because you too have fallen in love with Kazuma Kiryu and Goro Majima. You want to see their macho drama play out in lengthy cutscenes punctuated by flashy fistfights. In Japan, the *Yakuza* series is called "Like a Dragon," and these games sure make you want to chase that dragon.

ASURA'S WRATH (2012)

To love *Asura's Wrath* is to love something that shunts typical standards for what makes a video game good on several levels. Basically a lengthy series of extraordinary quick-time events, it almost totally lacks the things that $60 games were supposed to have in 2012. The combat is simplistic and messy, only there seemingly to get the game green-lit. Its best and final chapter was locked behind $10 DLC.

Asura's Wrath's greatness lies instead in its embrace of escalation as storytelling, with men ballooning to the size of planets, swords piercing entire worlds, and the very nature of button prompts shifting in its conclusion. Like its rage-powered protagonist, *Asura's Wrath* powered through market forces and conventional wisdom that sought to warp its incredible vision with nothing but sheer force of will to become my favorite video game of 2012.

—ALEX PERRY,
tech reporter at Mashable

THE WITCHER 3: WILD HUNT (2015)

For all the main plot's drama and well-crafted set pieces, the small moments are the heart of CD Projekt Red's masterpiece, *The Witcher 3: Wild Hunt*. Subtle expressions and slight glances tell the real story. Trees convincingly stir in the wind like a daydream, or bend low to a sudden storm, giving life to the land. Perfectly melancholy music hums in the lulls.

Western studios chased the potential of the fully realized open-world RPG in the decade-plus prior, but this game sits alone as the spiritual culmination of those efforts. Much is owed to the excellent writing: Humble quests blossom into memorable tales, actors big and small are given surprising depth, and our protagonist's stoicism waxes and wanes. I felt lucky to inhabit its world in every moment, equally drawn into each conversation, village, and dark forest.

Wind's howling.

—MATTHEW BUZZI,
senior analyst at PCMag

the witcher 3: wild hunt

2016

THE PHENOMENON OF THE YEAR

HUNT AND CAPTURE YOUR FAVORITE POKÉMON IN
THE REAL WORLD USING YOUR MOBILE PHONE
IN THIS AUGMENTED REALITY EXPERIENCE.

PRESS START

"**I** don't know who created **Pokémon Go**, but I'm trying to figure out how we get them to have **Pokémon Go** to the polls." —Hillary Clinton, 2016

Look, you already know that **Pokémon Go** is a big deal. There's not a person on the planet who isn't at least vaguely aware of this mobile monster-catching sensation. At the height of **Pokémon Go**, people became so invested in hunting for little fake creatures that they stumbled across real dead bodies and into traffic. What's left to say?

A lot, actually. **Pokémon Go** isn't just one big deal but the confluence of several other preexisting big deals, all leading to an absolutely huge deal. Let's **Pokémon Go** into it.

PART ONE: POKÉMON

By 2016, Pokémon had already existed for two decades, and as the highest-grossing media franchise of all time it lived firmly inside the imaginations of multiple generations. New love became old nostalgia in a self-perpetuating cycle. None of this would have been possible if the original *Pokémon Red* and *Blue* Game Boy games weren't legit classics. Satoshi Tajiri miraculously convinced little kids to fall in love with relatively complex, traditional, turn-based RPG concepts by dressing them up with superpowered animals. Even JRPG haters can easily fall right back into *Pokémon* whenever a new mainline game comes out and only barely tweaks the proven formula. There's something about hunting Pokémon in the wild, on your intimate portable Game Boy you take with you anywhere, that adds to the sense of adventure, but when those games launched (1996 in Japan and 1998 in North America), we didn't yet have the technology to fully realize the potential.

As awesome as the games are, the Pokémon brand's goal is to conquer any and all forms of entertainment. Every single Pokémon, from Pikachu in a college graduation robe to smug duck Sirfetch'd holding an onion as a sword, is available for purchase as an adorable stuffed animal. The Pokémon trading card game proves kids would rather talk about Charizard than some baseball player. We've watched Ash Ketchum pursue his dream of becoming a Pokémon master for years in the anime. The live-action *Detective Pikachu* movie, where Ryan Reynolds voices Pikachu and says "hell," is better and more beautiful than it has any right to be.

But Pokémon never forgets its gaming roots. The Pokémon Company eagerly expands into all game genres to the point of feeling experimental. They capitalized on the nineties Tamagotchi craze with Pokémon virtual pets. On your Nintendo Switch, you can play a Pokémon MOBA, a Pokémon fighting game, and a Pokémon photography adventure. Pokémon has always been willing to go anywhere. *Pokémon Go*'s crossover into the real world was just the next evolution.

PART TWO: MOBILE GAMING AND VIRTUAL REALITY

If you need a reminder that we are actually living in the future, every day we now carry immensely powerful supercomputers in our pockets. The term "phone" doesn't do these devices justice anymore. Whether you're an iPhone lover or an Android acolyte, you can use a little slab of metal and glass to instantly connect with the rest of the world. Not only that, but all sorts of experiences, from productivity apps to silly time wasters, are just a tap away.

The mobile landscape promised to revolutionize gaming like never before. Nintendo had to desperately convince nongamers to bring Wii consoles into their homes, but everyone already has a phone, so why not download a game or two? There are some real gems. *Threes*, *Plants vs. Zombies*, *Spaceteam*, *Florence*. Even *Angry Birds*, overexposed as it is, got that way by being a pretty fun time.

Unfortunately, mobile gaming's reality never caught up with the dream. It's not because of the casual audience—the Wii has plenty of great games. And it's not because of the lack of proper controls—developers find plenty of fascinating touch-only interfaces. Rather, the mobile market has become a wasteland where only exploitative free-to-play games (games that cost nothing upfront but demand money later) can survive. It's a huge bummer that devalues mobile as a healthy platform for great games. Apple had to create a whole separate subscription service, Apple Arcade, to subsidize high-quality mobile games again.

Even the free *Pokémon Go* uses these gotcha tactics. Nintendo doesn't fully own Pokémon, which is why the franchise could come to mobile instead of staying exclusive to Nintendo hardware. But for the longest time Nintendo resisted mobile because of its player-hostile economy, before eventually giving in to shareholder pressure and releasing textbook mobile game scams like *Mario Kart Tour*. Still, making your mobile game free-to-play will help it get in front of millions of players extremely quickly. It's a smart way to take advantage of the platform.

Mobile gaming's omnipresence also solved a problem tech enthusiasts had struggled with for decades: virtual reality. By the mid-2010s, viable virtual reality finally became a possibility. When tethered to a powerful PC, devices like the Oculus Rift render high-quality graphics at high resolutions beamed into each eye. Combine that with smooth movement and intuitive controls, and at last you had a VR headset that wouldn't make you vomit. VR cleared one hurdle but now faced another. These headsets worked, but they were expensive.

Enter mobile VR. Why spend thousands of dollars on a computer and a VR headset when you could slot your phone into a piece of Google Cardboard, hold it up to your face, and get basically the same novelty experience? Alongside VR, mobile devices also introduced millions of people to augmented reality, or AR. With AR, you point your phone's camera at your surroundings. As you look at your screen while moving your view, the app simulates virtual elements around you. For developer Niantic, augmented reality opened up new possibilities for mobile game design, the immersion of VR with more freedom, less sickness, and more mainstream accessibility. Augmented reality turned the real world into a digital canvas, and what did we want to paint on it? Pokémon!

PART THREE: GOTTA CATCH 'EM ALL

With *Pokémon Go*, Niantic synergized these three trends (Pokémon, mobile gaming, and augmented reality) at the exact correct moment. Pokémon is so popular that everyone knows how it works. Its specific exploration monster-catching mechanics worked like a dream with augmented reality, something only GPS-equipped mobile phones could pull off at that scale. Catch wild Bulbasaur that emerge from the bushes onto the sidewalk. Head down to your local bodega and suddenly begin a gym leader battle. Join teams (Team Instinct!) and try to cover the most territory in your region. Meet up with other trainers to take down one massive Mewtwo in the middle of town. Become the ten-year-old you always wanted to be, the one who roams the world alone picking fights with godlike monsters.

The rest is history. *Pokémon Go* took over the world so thoroughly that it didn't even matter that the creatures technically didn't exist. We all spent summer 2016 running through parks and streets trying to track down Ponyta, a horse on fire, or Butterfree, a butterfly but different. *Pokémon Go* fever raged so hard that every single website, from gaming sites to political blogs, wrote *Pokémon Go* tips and guides to scoop up that sweet Internet search traffic. Meanwhile, the game brought in billions of dollars and temporarily caused Nintendo's stock to surge, before investors realized that Nintendo and Pokémon aren't the same company despite their close partnership.

Pokémon Go may not show up in quite as many headlines these days, but its player base still thrives. Millions of people still play every day. Years later, Niantic supports the game with new features like a photo mode and new Pokémon pulled from later generations. Finally, catch Trubbish, a cute little garbage-bag boy. *Pokémon Go* influenced the design of future core Pokémon games. Connect your phone to your Nintendo Switch to import your *Pokémon Go* collection into *Pokémon: Let's Go, Pikachu!* and *Eevee!* During the COVID-19 pandemic, Niantic introduced updates to make *Pokémon Go* just as fun even while indoors. More than an intense fad, *Pokémon Go* lives on as arguably the best way for anyone to casually enjoy the world of Pokémon.

Pokémon evolve once they reach the right level, but real evolution is the result of multiple forces swirling in the background for years to shape a life-form into its perfect self. *Pokémon Go* combined cutting-edge mobile augmented reality functionality with the well-worn Pokémon formula to literally make dreams come true. Following *Pokémon Go*'s success, we got more AR mobile games based on popular franchises like *Minecraft* and *Dragon Quest*, as well as more Pokémon mobile spin-offs. But *Pokémon Go* reigns as the king, the apex predator, that will never be topped. We'll see Pikachu for the rest of our lives, but *Pokémon Go* is a singular phenomenon that may never happen again.

BE THE LIFE OF THE JACKBOX PARTY

Party games get a bad rap for being lazy, throwaway garbage you only play with casual friends who don't know any better. Sometimes that's true. But the *Jackbox Party Pack* series proves that with just a little effort, smart developers can make party games so deliriously enjoyable that hard-core gamers and casual players alike will never want the good times to end.

Each *Jackbox Party Pack* consists of five or so different individual games. Instead of using awkward controllers, up to eight players connect to a network to play using their phones. Quality varies between games, but the best ones encourage wildly entertaining and borderline evil forms of socializing nothing else offers. New packs release annually, but all these years later *The Jackbox Party Pack 3* remains a personal favorite.

Quiplash turns you into hacky comedy writers as you attempt to come up with clever responses to humorous prompts. What do unicorn farts smell like? Probably some kind of inside joke that only makes sense in your office group chat. In *Fakin' It*, everyone responds to personal prompts like, "Raise your hand if your underwear has holes in it," except for the one liar who must respond without knowing the prompt and concoct an explanation for any suspicious responses. *Tee K.O.*, where players match one another's drawings and slogans to create T-shirts, produces hilarious genuine works of art. I loved it so much I bought a T-shirt from Jackbox covered in hand-drawn Twitter memes.

Beyond the games themselves, other genius touches elevate the whole *Jackbox* experience, from the charming narrator to special modes for inviting audiences and streaming viewers into the action. Like the perfect party host, *The Jackbox Party Pack* sets up the right ridiculous environment for guests, and lets our natural naughty shenanigans take it from there.

POKÉMON GOLD AND SILVER (1999)

While *Pokémon Red* and *Blue* may have been the games that started it all, *Gold* and *Silver* cemented the future of the franchise by being the perfect embodiment of a video game sequel. They cleaned up much of the mechanical messiness of their predecessors by introducing new Pokémon, new moves, new types, and new systems. They set that improvement in Johto, a vast and distinct expansion set alongside the Kanto we'd already visited, giving both regions their share of adventure and new discovery. They implemented an impressive internal clock that changed the world's monsters and events based on both time of day and day of the week. And they filled that world with intricately designed new monster sprites that remain standouts even among today's 3D models. Nothing in 1999 came close to the ambition and adventurous expansion present in *Pokémon Gold* and *Silver*. Arguably, at least in the Pokémon franchise, nothing has come close since.

—REBEKAH VALENTINE,
reporter at IGN

2017

THE BLOB OF THE YEAR

ONE HUNDRED PLAYERS PARACHUTE ONTO AN
ISLAND AND COMPETE TO BECOME THE LAST PERSON
STANDING IN THIS BATTLE ROYALE SHOOTER.

PRESS START

Not to brag, but I actually saw an early version of Fortnite years before it became, well, Fortnite. Sometime in 2012, a Fortnite trailer aired alongside some other game's demo at a local Chicago game development community event. I walked away unimpressed. The game had been announced a year prior, but the creators didn't know what they were making yet. A game where you build forts? To keep out zombies at night? I thought I could safely ignore Fortnite.

What a fool I was. Little did we know that as soon as Fortnite figured out exactly what it wanted to be (by taking more than a little inspiration from an emerging new genre's pioneer) no one could possibly ignore it. Everything is now Fortnite.

EPIC ORIGINS

Fortnite didn't come from some little company that broke big. It's not an inspirational underdog that triumphed despite all odds and proved the naysayers wrong. No, *Fortnite* is an unbelievably successful video game product from a company that already had a long track record of unbelievably successful video game products.

Founded by Tim Sweeney in 1991, Epic Games developed multiple hit franchises including shooters *Unreal Tournament* and *Gears of War*. Those brands alone could sustain most other whole companies, but Epic's tendrils extend even further. The company also creates the Unreal Engine, a set of standardized tools for streamlining and optimizing the game development process. One of the most popular game engines by far, everyone from tiny indie studios to massive publishers license the Unreal Engine for their projects.

At first, *Fortnite* appeared to be yet another Epic game that only existed to show off what the next engine, Unreal Engine 4, was capable of on a technical level. But the game spent so long in development that by the time *Fortnite: Save the World* began entering closed beta tests in 2015, Unreal Engine 4 had already been around for years. So what was *Fortnite* now? A middling mix of cooperative third-person shooting and base building to defend yourself from zombies, with a stylish but generic art style you'd see in any mobile game. Hardly sounds like the biggest game in the world. *Fortnite* needed a hook, or rather, it needed someone else's hook.

TOMB OF THE UNKNOWN PLAYER

This story's real underdog is Brendan Greene, aka PlayerUnknown. He earned that nickname by making popular mods for janky PC military shooters and survival games like *Arma 2* and *DayZ* (itself an *Arma 2* mod). However, by spinning off his battle royale mod into its own game, he changed gaming forever. In 2017, he released *PlayerUnknown's Battlegrounds*, or *PUBG*, and kicked off the battle royale revolution, the most radical shift in multiplayer gaming in a decade.

If you've seen *The Hunger Games* or the Japanese movie *Battle Royale* (from which this genre takes its name), you get the idea. A horde of contestants descend upon a wide-open space cut off from the outside world. They must frantically, desperately search for supplies and weapons to stay alive while killing other players. The hunters and the hunted swap places at a moment's notice. Violent, victorious satisfaction immediately gives way to paranoia and terror.

PUBG not only captured these potent emotions with its killer premise but enhanced them through brilliant, tension-raising, heart-pumping mechanics. As funny as it is to win by hiding in a bathtub, eventually you'll need to leave your safe house to avoid the deadly circle constantly closing in on you. This forces the final players into the same cramped area for the last bloodbath. Strict bullet physics reward skillful shooting, but the sheer amount of potential random chaos means anyone could win at any moment. Scream as you whack your foe upside the head with a frying pan. Never take your eyes off the chicken-dinner prize. Playing by yourself almost feels like a survival horror game full of real humans out to slaughter you, with dread enhanced by long stretches of boring nothingness, but when you squad up with your friends, *PUBG* pivots into a goofy good time.

In a matter of weeks, *PUBG* totally consumed the gaming world. All anyone could play or talk about was this battle royale concept. As an especially entertaining game for a live streaming audience, word of mouth spread quickly through Twitch and YouTube. *PUBG* sold millions more copies each month throughout the rest of the year. *PUBG* was one of the freshest and most immediately significant games to hit in a long time.

And *Fortnite* just stole its whole idea! With *Fortnite: Save the World* failing to garner much interest, Epic Games did something fast and drastic. In July 2017, just a few months after *PUBG* exploded onto the market, Epic launched *Fortnite Battle Royale*. A companion to the original *Fortnite*, this battle royale mode was *PUBG* but remade in Epic's new world. A hundred players descend on an island and murder one another until only one remains, all while avoiding the deadly surrounding storm.

A handful of crucial differences separate the two games. For starters, *Fortnite Battle Royale* was free from the beginning, unlike *PUBG*, which took years to adopt a free-to-play model. *Fortnite Battle Royale* also soon came to consoles and mobile phones, alongside PC. These two selling points massively expanded the game's potential audience, and you need as many players as possible to quickly populate hundred-player matches. *Fortnite Battle Royale* also retains *Fortnite*'s base-building powers. You still harvest material to build defense structures like walls and stairs around yourself. The shooting controls are looser and more forgiving compared with *PUBG*'s military realism. And instead of stalking your prey in a depressing wasteland, Fortnite's island is colorful and cartoony and inviting. You fall from a vehicle called the Battle Bus. *PUBG* is a game about shooting, while *Fortnite* is a party that happens to have shooting.

But superficial differences can't hide what certainly seemed like *Fortnite* totally ripping off *PUBG*. Making matters even fishier, *PUBG* runs on Epic's Unreal Engine. Imagine being copied by your own landlord. *PUBG*'s creators actually sued Epic, but neither side decisively won (the case ended in a "draw"). At least *PUBG* is also a huge hit in its own right. It's not as big as *Fortnite*, but at more than 75 million copies sold, it's still one of the best-selling games of all time, and it earned that success all on its own. Consumers don't care about who came first, though. They just play the games they want to play. It turns out pouring on a heaping spoonful of *PUBG*'s secret battle royale sauce was the one thing *Fortnite* needed to leapfrog over everyone and become the unstoppable gaming juggernaut we all know and love today.

THE METAVERSE

Since 2017, more than 350 million people have played *Fortnite*. As the game's popularity grew exponentially, the game itself expanded to keep up. At this point, calling it a battle royale only captures a fraction of what *Fortnite* actually is, what it has evolved into. *Fortnite* now exists as a separate social space, an alternate online reality like *World of Warcraft* but more amorphous and freed from the limits of the MMORPG genre label. Alongside *Battle Royale* and the *Save the World* mode it eclipsed, *Fortnite* also includes a creative mode just for hanging out and building.

Pundits like to call this a metaverse, a new kind of Internet where we all vibe in a persistent, living online world instead of visiting flat websites. *Fortnite* doesn't just constantly introduce new weapons and other content; it goes through seasons where the island itself changes and never looks back. Goodbye, Tilted Towers. Hello, Salty Towers. Your goals change, too. Obviously, you want to win your match, but what keeps you coming back are longer-term challenges and weekly tasks like riding motorboats or killing players at certain locations. *Fortnite* even sort of has a story, with absurd blockbuster cutscenes about superspies and interdimensional portals. The Russo brothers, fresh off directing Marvel's *Avengers: Endgame*, helmed a *Fortnite* commercial.

Constant changes also mean constant opportunities to ask players for money. *Fortnite* is a "free game," but to make the most of your time you'll need to subscribe to the Battle Pass every season. Not only that, the shop rotates new outfits to buy, but only for a limited time, so act now. Every brand in existence wants a piece of *Fortnite*'s action. You can dress up like Iron Man, Harley Quinn, John Wick, Kylo Ren, Lara Croft, Chun-Li, and even real-life people like multimil-lionaire competitive player and professional Twitch streamer Tyler "Ninja" Blevins. Along with powering *Fortnite*'s self-sustaining economy, watching all these characters collide only adds to the metaverse quality, the *Ready Player One* of it all.

But just because *Fortnite* is as fascinating as it is popular doesn't mean there's no dark side. The term "metaverse" itself actually comes from Neal Stephenson's seminal cyberpunk novel *Snow Crash* and is very much meant to be seen as the ultimate expression of corporate dystopia superseding reality. As with all free-to-play games, the microtransactions exploit people who just want to have fun without paying more for the privilege. *Fortnite*'s paywalls feel especially gross when all the branded skins already make matches feel like living advertisements you can't opt out of.

Perhaps trying to replicate its success ripping off *PUBG*, *Fortnite* occasionally rolls out radically new modes for a limited time, some of which clearly reference other popular games. During the height of the pandemic, indie game *Among Us* (inspired by card games like Mafia or Werewolf) captured our hearts by convincing us to distrust our friends and find the fakers. A few months later, *Fortnite* introduced a very similar mode called Impostors, and didn't acknowledge the inspiration until months after that. Pretty sus.

NOW LET'S TALK ABOUT FORTNITE AND RACE

Fortnite sells popular dances as emotes, dances originally created and popularized by Black dancers. The problem? Those dancers don't get any cut of the profit. Actor Alfonso Ribeiro sued *Fortnite* for selling his famous Carlton dance from *The Fresh Prince of Bel-Air*. Ribeiro later voluntarily dropped the lawsuit, but the whole spectacle pointed out how *Fortnite* continues a long, shameful tradition of corporations profiting off underappreciated Black artists. After all, *Fortnite* also seemingly took material from young dancers in niche TikTok communities, not just famous former sitcom actors.

It only gets weirder. When you fire up *Fortnite*, you don't have to play a game. Epic hosts virtual live concerts with musicians like Ariana Grande and Travis Scott (presented as holographic giants wreathed in energy), as well as screenings for movies like *Inception*. However, following George Floyd's murder in May 2020, Epic aired We the People x More Than a Vote, a conversation on race in America. Sometime after that, *Fortnite* re-created Dr. Martin Luther King Jr.'s "I Have a Dream" speech during the March on Washington as an interactive museum on the island. Players could walk through the memories and inhabit that moment in history. While Epic may have had its heart in the right place, it's super strange and, honestly, borderline offensive to be hanging out at the fake version of a place known for the struggle over real human rights while dressed up like the *Terminator* robot or Mancake, a man with a pancake head.

Fortnite has problems that you couldn't even fathom if we were talking about literally any other video game. Only a game this huge and unprecedented could spark debates about both proper ways to honor victims of racist violence and whether or not it's cool to pay for Superman holding a gun. Like a true metaverse, *Fortnite* absorbs the real world into itself, of course we'd feel some growing pains.

THANK THE BUS DRIVER

Fortnite will never go away. It may fade from the headlines, but like fellow aspiring metaverse Facebook (which went so far as to rename the company itself Meta), it will exist forever as digital background noise. Flush with cash and investments from Chinese megacorporation Tencent, Epic Games is bigger than ever, with its own PC gaming storefront. *Fortnite* even made Epic cocky enough to pick a legal fight with Apple over the revenue split on iOS apps. (After a judge initially ruled in favor of Apple, Epic appealed, and the legal battle has continued. Fortnite remains unavailable on the iOS App Store.) As *Fortnite* lives on, it will keep changing. The *Fortnite* of 2030 may look as unrecognizable compared with today's *Fortnite* as today's *Fortnite* looks compared with the *Fortnite* I first saw in 2012. We may not be ready for Epic's metaverse at full power, but our kids will love it.

THE LEGEND OF ZELDA: BREATH OF THE WILD, WHAT ELSE?

As discussed all the way back in the 1987 chapter, *The Legend of Zelda: Breath of the Wild* is a masterful reinvention of the open-world game filtered through Nintendo's singular philosophy of fun. Whether at home or on the go, you owe it to yourself to take a leap off the Great Plateau and play the one true video game of the year.

THE LEGEND OF ZELDA: MAJORA'S MASK (2000)

The Legend of Zelda: Majora's Mask is a haunting meditation on isolation, regret, and loss. Most of your playtime is just that—playing classic *Zelda*. You gather rupees, solve puzzles, and open chests like always. This adventure, though, flirts with—and at times relishes—its cartoonish pensive melancholy.

The awkward marriage works because of a masterful execution of nearly every component. Characters conduct their lives on layered schedules crossing a variety of regions, each with its own aesthetics and leitmotifs. Their stories and themes blend and emerge countless times as you reset the game's internal clock in a surreal, time-bending quest. Your goal isn't to save a princess or even the world, but to free yourself and your friends from the lingering, ethereal grip of timeworn trauma. You're just here to break the cycle and then be okay. Not all at once,

but over a lifetime, your relationships with mortality and relationships themselves evolve.

—STARKEY B., *writer*

THE EVIL WITHIN 2 (2017)

It can feel like the worlds that fill our beautifully rendered landscapes grow stagnant. There are corridors. There are checklists. There are daisy chains. *The Evil Within 2* breaks this pattern in an increasingly standardized genre, by designing an open world to take things from you rather than give them. Encountering nightmares in this survival horror title expends resources. So you explore, and getting that next precious box of ammo unfolds yet another delicious box of consequences. In this cycle, *The Evil Within 2* manages to evoke the magic that accompanied early open-world titles: the question of what games can become next.

—XALAVIER NELSON JR., *creative director at Strange Scaffold*

BROTHERS: A TALE OF TWO SONS (2013)

Like the name implies, *Brothers: A Tale of Two Sons* focuses on the journey of two siblings as they venture through a fairy-tale world to find a cure for their ailing father. Its unique control scheme tasks the player with using separate thumbsticks to control the younger brother or older brother.

The controls wind up being more than just a mechanical quirk. Through them, this game asks the player to rethink their relationships with things they probably know consummately. The symbiotic connections between the left and right hemispheres of the brain, different generations of family, rivalry and affection . . . between tears and growth.

—EVAN NARCISSE, *senior writer at Brass Lion Entertainment*

2018

SUPER SMASH BROS.™
ULTIMATE

THE MUSEUM OF THE YEAR

THIS MASSIVE CROSSOVER FIGHTING GAME
PITS DOZENS OF CHARACTERS FROM
COUNTLESS GAMING FRANCHISES AGAINST ONE
ANOTHER IN THE BRAWL TO END THEM ALL.

PRESS START

e need more video game museums. The lack of proper preservation continues to plague this industry, and what better way to motivate us than to provide more space to curate, safeguard, and share our history with the public? Institutions like the Strong National Museum of Play, Museum of the Moving Image, and Video Game History Foundation do wonderful work, but they can't do it alone. To truly appreciate video game history, you can't just read about it, watch some clips, or even play a short demo out of context. You have to immerse yourself in that history, experience what it must have felt like to play these games when they were shiny and special and new. A video game museum should be immediate and interactive. It should be a game unto itself. No one game celebrates the history of all games with more respect and reverence than Super Smash Bros. Ultimate.

MASCOT MELEE

When you think of museums, you think of quiet temples of artistic reflection, not a madcap fighting arena. But that's exactly what *Super Smash Bros. Ultimate* is. Yes, the best-selling fighting game of all time (more than thirty million copies) is, in fact, a fighting game. That shouldn't sound controversial, but, well, Nintendo's epic crossover loves subverting expectations.

The first *Super Smash Bros.*, released on the Nintendo 64 in 1999, didn't play like a traditional fighting game, and not just because Donkey Kong can body-slam Pikachu. Instead of executing a needlessly complex button combination to make Mario shoot a fireball at Link, you just press one button. This simplicity felt appropriate for a game about cuddly mascots pummeling one another. But just because you can easily perform the moves doesn't mean you don't need skill. If anything, *Smash Bros.*' unconventional mechanics demand even more unconventional strategies.

In a normal fighting game like *Street Fighter II*, the two characters stay locked in a relatively tight arena and don't jump too far off the ground. In *Smash Bros.*, Nintendo calls upon its 2D platforming heritage to create a fighting system that makes frantic movement just as crucial as landing attacks. Up to four characters run around oddly shaped stages, positioning themselves on platforms while avoiding obstacles. Fall off the stage and you lose a life. Characters don't have life bars. The more damage you take, the more vulnerable you are to getting knocked off the stage by a strong move like a smash attack. Think of it like exaggerated sumo wrestling.

Before *Smash Bros.* became a Nintendo mash-up, the game's creator, Masahiro Sakurai, came up with these mechanics for *Dragon King*, an alternate, more accessible take on a prototype fighting game. You can see the influence from Sakurai's earlier *Kirby* games. Fights feel more satisfying when you can spend more time thinking of creative tactics instead of memorizing annoyingly rote combos. Some characters do have more complicated special moves, like guest characters imported from *Street Fighter*, but *Smash Bros.* aims to be fun for everyone while still allowing for a high skill ceiling. "Can you perform this move?" is a boring question. "Do you know the right way to use this move?" is what should really matter in a fighting game. It's the mind games, the punches you don't throw.

Because *Smash Bros.* casually rejects so much fighting game dogma, an unfortunate number of the players in the community don't see *Smash Bros.* as a real fighting game, even as it draws in huge crowds at tournaments. This obnoxious gatekeeping attitude isn't helped by the fact that Nintendo itself has a rather chilly relationship with the largely grassroots competitive *Smash Bros.* community, a community that actively rejects the game's wackier aspects like random power-up items in the name of fair balance. And while I love to watch world-class *Smash Bros.* matches, I don't love that some of the best *Smash Bros.* players have been at the center of some disturbing abuse allegations. But that's hardly the game's fault.

You don't have to like S*mash Bros.* But after more than twenty years and six games with this same basic fighting framework, clearly it appeals to people. *Smash Bros.* works even without the Nintendo nostalgia and insistence on GameCube controllers. It spawned an entirely new fighting game subgenre called platform fighters. So questioning its legitimacy, in an attempt to dismiss it, just reflects a narrow, closed-minded view of what game genres can be. It sucks! So for the final time, yes, *Super Smash Bros.* is a fighting game, period.

But it's also more than that. *Smash Bros.*' mechanics and absurd character rosters have sparked enjoyment since day one. As time goes by, however, it becomes clear that *Smash Bros.* exudes a pure affection for the medium of gaming that's all too rare. Nowhere is this more obvious than in the care and attention to detail contained in 2018's *Super Smash Bros. Ultimate* for Nintendo Switch.

COLORS WEAVE INTO A SPIRE OF FLAME

"Everyone is here!" That's how Nintendo revealed *Super Smash Bros. Ultimate* to the world. How do you top a franchise built on providing the world's wackiest "Who would win in a fight?" scenarios? Pack in every single character who has ever been in the series, and then some. Deliver an all-star lineup of gaming greats all together for the first time. *Ultimate*'s unmatched roster pulls from every corner of the gaming universe. Obviously, Nintendo stars make up the bulk of the cast. *Mario*, *The Legend of Zelda*, *Pokémon*, and *Metroid* have strong presences alongside smaller franchises like *Star Fox* and *Kirby* or newer faces from *Splatoon* and *Xenoblade Chronicles*. Characters like Mr. Game & Watch, the *Duck Hunt* dog, and R.O.B. the robot bring deep-cut retro flair.

Ultimate also recruits beloved third-party gaming icons, including *Metal Gear*'s Solid Snake, *Final Fantasy VII*'s Cloud and Sephiroth, and Mario's eternal rival Sonic the Hedgehog. Disney played ball and loaned Sora from *Kingdom Hearts*, complete with Mickey Mouse key chain. Nintendo even cut a deal with Microsoft, a direct American competitor, to bring Rare's Banjo and Kazooie along with Steve from *Minecraft* into the battle. Watch as a cartoon man made out of children's blocks battles Bayonetta, an erotic witch who slays angels with her own hair. That's *Smash Bros.*!

More than raw quantity, *Ultimate* portrays its cast with such quality you almost take it for granted. While everyone uses the same basic controls, each fighter plays exactly how you expect them to if you're familiar with their original games. Samus Aran jumps and floats like a bounty hunter in low gravity. Min Min extends her ridiculously long arms. Kazuya has combos ripped straight out of *Tekken*. This adds entertaining variety and makes you feel like you truly are playing as these characters. They aren't just skins slapped onto generic fighting game templates. *Ultimate* does a better job honoring characters most famous for PlayStation games, like *Persona 5* and *Castlevania: Symphony of the Night*, than PlayStation's own platform fighter, *PlayStation All-Stars Battle Royale*.

It doesn't stop there. Beyond its massive cast of more than eighty playable fighters, *Ultimate* turns every aspect of its design into a chance to reference and resurrect gaming's past. More than one hundred stages guide players throughout landmark locales like *Fire Emblem*'s battlefields and *Pac-Man*'s mazes. On certain stages, audience members provide snarky commentary and explain character histories. Customize your own Mii fighters with costumes from folks who didn't make the cut, like Bomberman, Travis Touchdown from *No More Heroes,* or the *Doom* guy. Summon assist trophies like the meddlesome Waluigi or crack open a Poké Ball with the fearsome Kyurem inside to aid you in battle. More than one thousand music tracks combine to make *Ultimate* the single greatest video game remix soundtrack of all time. Previous games let you unlock trophies and stickers depicting different characters, but in *Ultimate* you collect them as spirits. Equip spirits to tweak your fighter's stats, and spirit battles remix the rules to make you feel like you're fighting someone who isn't actually playable. That's not Mario wearing rabbit ears and shooting a laser gun. That's Rabbid Mario from *Mario + Rabbids: Kingdom Battle*. Keeping track of just how much *Ultimate* packs in is as exhausting as it is exhilarating.

Even when a game promises to give you everything you want, you'll always want more. No game causes as much feverish fan speculation as *Super Smash Bros.*, with everyone hoping their favorite character will make the cut. It can feel annoying and even a little entitled. No one cares about Geno from *Super Mario RPG*. But when you see just how well *Smash Bros.* treats its stars, who wouldn't want to see a gaming icon they love get that same treatment? *Smash Bros.* kept niche franchises like *Ice Climber* and *EarthBound* from falling into oblivion. More people have used Captain Falcon's Falcon Punch than have ever played an *F-Zero* game. *Smash* directly led to the creation of a new *Kid Icarus* game after twenty-five years. Some *Smash Bros.* games offer playable demos of highlighted games, like watching a solo Marvel movie after falling in love with a superhero in an *Avengers* team-up. You may laugh at people who strongly wanted someone as forgotten as King K. Rool to join the battle, but seeing him kicking Donkey Kong's butt will reignite a passion for the past you never knew existed within yourself. That's what *Super Smash Bros. Ultimate* does; that's how it makes gaming history come alive.

Super Smash Bros. Ultimate's peculiar tone also deserves some recognition for what it adds to the experience. This is a party fighting game, but it reveres its heroes with a somber, solemn dignity typically saved for Greek statues honoring heroes of epic wars. The art style tends to add more realism than these characters usually have—Mario's jeans sport denim textures. In the game's fiction, you control living toys under the command of Master Hand. In the real world, you literally buy these toys, Nintendo's NFC Amiibo figures. *Smash Bros.* itself is a magic diorama containing all of video game history, all the world's a stage set for this majestic pageant of modern myths and legends. Latin choirs chant the theme song. Fates collide in explosive, over-the-top cutscenes way crazier than *Avengers: Infinity War*. Is this all incredibly goofy? Absolutely yes! But so are video games as a whole! *Super Smash Bros. Ultimate*'s cheeky, fun sense of humor doesn't mock the medium—it's the only accurate way to honor it.

The most important name you'll find in *Super Smash Bros. Ultimate* isn't a mascot, but a man. Masahiro Sakurai made the impossible possible, properly portraying more than forty years of diverse gaming history. He negotiated the deals with publishers and ensured their creations didn't get disrespected. He speaks with a depth of knowledge you'd expect from a museum curator. *Super Smash Bros. Ultimate* wouldn't be what it is without the legions of creators who made the important works that inspired it, but no one can tie something this comprehensive together with as much grace and cohesion as Sakurai. Through *Super Smash Bros. Ultimate*, video game history lives on not just as memories in our heads but as an awesome fighting game in our hands and an emotional experience in our hearts.

EXTRA LIFE

ON TOP OF THE
MONSTER HUNTER WORLD

For the longest time, Capcom's monster-slaying role-playing game, *Monster Hunter*, was popular only in Japan. American players couldn't understand how something this inscrutable was so beloved. That all changed with *Monster Hunter: World*.

The core *Monster Hunter* loop remains intact. Hunt monsters, from the lowly Jaggi bird to the menacing Rathalos dragon, and harvest their parts. Use those parts to craft better weapons and armor to hunt stronger monsters. Each weapon handles extremely differently with many tricks and techniques to learn. Switching from the slow but straightforward hammer to the nimble and complex bug-powered insect glaive feels like picking a new character in a fighting game. Once you learn your role, though, you can synergize with your team to deliver overwhelming damage.

What *World* did was finally strip out most of the frustrating cruft that made this franchise so off-putting for so long. Instead of loading between separate zones, you hunt the monster on a single seamless map. You can also see the monster on the map, instead of throwing paintballs to track it. Using items is less fiddly, you don't have to worry about running out of weapon-sharpening whetstones, and in general

the game just makes more sense. Plus, thanks to next-gen console power, *Monster Hunter: World* features gorgeous blockbuster visuals and production values the series had never previously enjoyed.

Removing this unnecessary tedium lets you focus on the tedium that actually matters in *Monster Hunter*, the frustrating parts that serve a point. The deliberate, methodical combat locks you into animations, which means you need to commit to an attack and suffer the consequences if you make a mistake. Think, don't flail. It's tough, but so satisfying to master. With the wildly successful *Monster Hunter: World*, players worldwide, even in the United States, took up the challenge.

SUPER SMASH BROS. MELEE (2001)

Everything about the world we lived through in 2021 should have killed *Super Smash Bros. Melee*'s competitive scene. No longer could the twenty-year-old masterpiece's apostles assemble, huddled at their CRTs. No matter: some brilliant minds found a way to bring the game online, and the community adapted. Now, a new generation is finding its way into one of the most shockingly long-lived games of all time, a game that reinvents itself every decade. If 2021 proved anything, it's that *Melee* truly is forever.

—JACK MOORE,
director at PGstats

DRAGON BALL Z: BUDOKAI TENKAICHI 3 (2007)

Dragon Ball Z: Budokai Tenkaichi 3 still stands tall as the best *Dragon Ball Z* game. It has one of the largest rosters to date, and its alternative story lines and customization features add years of replayability. The What If Saga imagined fascinating scenarios like the Saiyans united and fighting Frieza. The Mission 100 mode lets you craft teams to battle opponents in increasingly difficult challenges. The capsule system allowed you to fully customize a character's powers, transformations, and stats.

As a child obsessed with *DBZ*, I wasn't too interested in games that simply let me repeat key battles—although this is the core story mode—but instead preferred games that let me beat the ever-living crap out of my brother and my friends with Future Gohan, SS4 Goku, Metal Cooler, Buu, and any other character I could think of. Darting around the map, destroying the environment, letting off special attack after special attack like we were creating our own special *DBZ* movie. Other *DBZ* games lost sight of the magic. *Budokai Tenkaichi 3* didn't.

—EDWARD ONGWESO JR.,
tech and labor writer at Vice

super smash bros. ultimate   267

2019

SEKIRO
SHADOWS DIE TWICE

THE PUNISHMENT OF THE YEAR

AS A SHINOBI WARRIOR WITH THE POWER TO RISE
FROM THE DEAD, CUT YOUR WAY THROUGH
SEVENTEENTH-CENTURY JAPAN IN THIS BRUTALLY
DIFFICULT ACTION GAME.

PRESS START

Talking about video game difficulty quickly becomes even more frustrating than suffering through the most difficult video games. Arguments follow the same predictable, never-ending patterns. Games are too hard! If a game is too easy, it's boring! Not everyone has the same skills! Artists should stick to their vision! I'm very much in the camp that says a game should be too easy rather than too hard, if only to make the game more accessible to more players. But games by their nature are challenges designed to push you, tests that derive tension from the fact that you might fail. Punishing games, games where you die a lot, games like Sekiro: Shadows Die Twice, are more alive than ever.

SOULFUL

Sekiro: Shadows Die Twice came out in 2019, a full decade after FromSoftware became the developer it is today with *Demon's Souls*. That wasn't the first FromSoftware game; just ask fans of *Armored Core* and *King's Field*. However, FromSoftware blew up with *Demon's Souls* and by making later games very much in that game's style. *Demon's Souls* is a gothic fantasy role-playing game obsessed with powerlessness. The story reveals itself to you in cryptic bits, keeping you ignorant and at arm's length. Class and item descriptions withhold so much crucial information about how everything works that it feels like the game maliciously lies to you. The vague ruined world you walk through suggests a rich history you never got to witness. The best help comes from the literal ghosts of other online players who leave clues as to what to do next, or misinformation meant to send you to your doom.

Demon's Souls* also loves to kill you. A lot. Enemies hit hard. Defensive options come with limits, like shields that break or a stamina bar that depletes with each dodge roll. Lengthy attack animations mean you must commit to your offense with purpose. As an action RPG, technically you can grind to level up, but to do so you need to hold on to harvested souls. When you die, souls you collected get left behind, and if you die again on the way back to retrieve them, all that progress gets wiped out. Death haunts your every waking moment in *Demon's Souls*. Whether taking on the numerous titanic bosses or just picking a fight with the wrong skeleton in a dingy hallway, your demise comes for you no matter what.

After an era of easier games for casual audiences, hard-core gamers ate up this harsh but strangely fair mistress. *Demon's Souls* demands discipline, patience, and perseverance. If you made a real effort to improve, by studying bosses, practicing techniques, and innately understanding the ill-defined systems, you earned a victory more rewarding than any other. You slayed the dragon. After millions of players conquered *Demon's Souls*, director Hidetaka Miyazaki and the team at FromSoftware fed their ravenous new audience more games to prove just how much punishment we could take. *Dark Souls* popularized the format further, while *Bloodborne* mixed things up with firearms and a Lovecraftian horror aesthetic. *Sekiro: Shadows Die Twice* continues this through line. Just saying it's the next FromSoftware game tells you everything you need to know. However, after ten years of refining immaculately excruciating experiences, *Sekiro* somehow finds even more paths to pain.

DEATH BEFORE DISHONOR

Sekiro: Shadows Die Twice brought substantial changes to the FromSoftware formula. Instead of trudging through dank European castles, you control a nimble shinobi named Wolf in seventeenth-century Japan. Use your grapple hook to scale Sengoku-era fortresses and pray at Buddhist shrines. Although it takes place in the past, and is fixated on death, *Sekiro*'s world feels much livelier than the ghostly *Souls* games. The plot actually bothers explaining itself.

Sekiro's gameplay also shifts to match its new settings with combat centering around your sword, making it less of an RPG and more of a pure action game. You don't whittle away health, you quickly but carefully land strikes to knock enemies off-balance. It's a dance where you compete to control the choreography. Break a foe's posture to deliver a decisive strike to kill in one hit. Supplement your attacks with your prosthetic arm loaded with gadgets like shuriken and flamethrowers. As the subtitle implies, you can immediately revive yourself if you've gathered enough energy from fallen opponents. Finally, a FromSoftware game gives you exactly one extra life.

Don't worry, though. None of these changes make *Sekiro* any easier than other *Souls* games. In fact, the opposite is true. At least in an RPG, you can raise your stats to increase your chances. If you can't learn to execute *Sekiro*'s lightning-fast, razor-sharp swordplay, you won't keep up. As a finger-shattering shinobi simulator, it recalls classic action game and fellow cruel master *Ninja Gaiden*. *Sekiro: Shadows Die Twice* shows how FromSoftware can introduce all sorts of fresh ideas into its template while maintaining the spirit that drew fans to it in the first place. *Sekiro: Shadows Die Twice* does right by its legacy. It's a proud member of a long line of important, innovative, influential games of the year. That's undeniable. But if we're being honest, I hate it. I hate these games.

FROMSOFTWARE, WITH LOVE

I first played *Sekiro: Shadows Die Twice* as a demo at a press event, and I walked out after an hour. The event was only halfway over, but I felt relieved to reclaim my time and stop playing something that offered me no joy whatsoever. I respect people who like these games. They somehow turned what should've been a niche cult hit for masochists into one of the most powerful forces in gaming with millions of sales. But *Sekiro* solidified for me that during the past ten years FromSoftware has done nothing but make games I can't stand.

To me, *Sekiro* isn't just hard, it's obnoxious. I enjoy plenty of hard games, but I need them to respect my time. In a game like *Cuphead*, *Hotline Miami*, or *Super Meat Boy*, you'll bang your head against a wall for hours to finish one particularly nightmarish level. But the levels are so short you'll either beat them in a few minutes or die and have the chance to try again. You can practice without worrying about losing much progress. In *Sekiro*, you'll spend an enormous amount of mental energy to defeat a handful of grunt soldiers, and a few slipups erase hours of forward momentum. Some see that as ice-cold motivation to try again, a stressful reminder that death has consequences, but I see it as the game giving me the perfect excuse to dip out. I love myself too much to have my time so disrespectfully wasted by a video game of all things. *Sekiro* isn't a drill sergeant, it's not J. K. Simmons in *Whiplash*. It's just a hard game I can easily turn off.

What's worse, though, are the defensive conversations surrounding FromSoftware games and the question of difficulty. Again, people have every right to enjoy punishing games. But difficulty doesn't always equal quality, and wanting an easier experience doesn't reflect poorly on your gaming tastes. A game like *Celeste* handles it perfectly, encouraging players to try the uncompromised original challenge while also letting them tweak whatever assist options they want to ease their journey up the mountain. Despite what some game menus might mockingly suggest, there's no such thing as a baby mode. You might just be a grown-up who can't devote hours of their life to getting good at one video game.

The snidest purists find the very idea of a *Sekiro* easy mode so insulting, they think players who mod the game on PC forfeit their gamer honor. FromSoftware designs their games with intent. The cruelty is the point. But so what? Players have been breaking game designers' intent ever since the late Kazuhisa Hashimoto gifted us thirty extra lives in *Contra* with the Konami code. Cheating is a vital part of gaming history. Cheat codes make up some of our earliest shared folklore. The only reason they went away is because publishers would rather openly sell you wacky bonuses than lock them behind secret passwords. If you can beat *Sekiro* blindfolded in under two hours, then more power to you. Be as proud as you want about that accomplishment. But let other people play however they like. Shunning easy modes and cheat codes doesn't make you a true gamer, it just makes you a fun-policing chump.

FromSoftware games aren't going anywhere (the PlayStation 5 even launched with a *Demon's Souls* remake), and love them or hate them, their unique gameplay cocktail is, at this point, a genre unto itself. And there's more to it than just difficulty. Games like *Hollow Knight* and *Nioh* also exhibit a *Souls*-style offbeat approach to world building and atmosphere. FromSoftware followed up *Sekiro* with *Elden Ring*, a return to *Dark Souls*–style fantasy made in collaboration with *Game of Thrones* author George R. R. Martin, and its astounding open-world design made it not only the most acclaimed *Souls* game but arguably the most approachable. If you can penetrate something this prickly, enjoy the sweet fruits of success waiting within. But don't feel bad or surprised if you bounced off of *Sekiro: Shadows Die Twice* as hard as I did. Video games can make you feel a lot of things, but never let shame be one of them.

DISCO ELYSIUM,
THE MANIFESTO OF THE YEAR

Disco Elysium is a dense novel. It's so chock-full of ideas, your brain can barely absorb it. But when the ideas are this potent, and delivered in such an expertly literary way, you'll want to push your mind to its limits.

Disco Elysium uses a familiar computer RPG structure found in classics like Baldur's Gate and Planescape: Torment. You won't find any magic or monsters, though. The game takes place in a depressingly dreary and realistic world pulled from the writings of lead designer and Estonian novelist Robert Kurvitz. From labor crises to economic inequality to constant clashes of left-wing and right-wing political ideology, the characters in the game suffer the same problems we do.

You see it all through the lens of your playable character: a bumbling drunk cop and "absolute disaster of a human being." As you talk to witnesses around town, you won't just hear their responses, you'll also hear bickering voices inside your own head tempting you to feed your baser impulses. Depending on what choices you make, your personality mutates accordingly. Become a vagrant hobo cop, an active communist, or an "advanced race theorist." Although you'll spend more time digging for pills in the trash than firing bullets, customizing your cop in wildly different directions is how Disco Elysium offers fascinating RPG gameplay freedom within its otherwise unapologetically authored murder mystery world.

More than a game, Disco Elysium is a hilarious, breathtakingly well-written, and genuinely thought-provoking piece of political art. It feels like a dangerous gateway to a radical awakening, a book you'd better read now before the cops come and burn it.

DISCO ELYSIUM (2019)

To borrow from Timothy Leary: turn on, tune in to the city of Revachol, drop out. "Go within to activate your neural and genetic equipment," Leary also said, and "become sensitive to the many and various levels of consciousness and the specific triggers engaging them . . . Express your new internal perspectives."

Do drugs is what he meant. And Detective Harrier "Harry" Du Bois clearly took that advice to heart. That man has got the internal perspectives to show for it—twenty-four of them, at least, a cacophonous Greek chorus—and they do not tolerate repression.

But one of those voices is Revachol—the city itself, or as close to it as not to matter. "Shivers" is a communion with all of it. The people. The rain. The underworldly thrum of the harbor freight yard. The pockmarks in a concrete wall and the bullets of the firing squad that made them, so many years ago. The effect is lysergic. It dyes Disco Elysium's world with the color of things beyond the visible spectrum.

—NICK CAPOZZOLI,
  critic

BLOODBORNE (2015)

Bloodborne's gothic architecture, foreboding atmosphere, and ghastly monsters make for a game filled with sights and sounds that make the skin crawl. But this is a thin veil that hides something far headier. As the night unfurls, so do its underlying themes: the hubris of man, schisms in the ideals of intellectuals and people of faith, the devastating impact that can have on the ordinary person, and how the blind pursuit of knowledge can shake the foundation of existence.

You arrive in Yharnam when the events that have precipitated these revelations have already come to pass, tasked with piecing together what went wrong. It's a place that treats you like poison in its body and attempts to force you out. But, ultimately, it becomes a place that, through perseverance, you learn to understand. It is hard-fought, but Yharnam can become a reminder that, in the face of adversity, the human spirit can endure and push you to persevere.

This sense of growth is bestowed on you as the player. *Bloodborne*, thus, is a horror game that opens doors to terrifying places and demands you confront daunting challenges that knock you down in-game, so you can stand up stronger in real life.

—TAMOOR HUSSAIN,
managing editor at GameSpot
and Twitch streamer

DEMON'S SOULS (2009)

In games we are used to a sort of gloss on fantasy, a kind of longing to visit this world. The dragons are beautiful even as we must sadly fight them. *Demon's Souls* starts its first level with an ugly dragon slamming into the ground and screaming at you through a mouthful of corpses. This felt, to me, honest.

The year 2009 was an era of widespread, admirable efforts to make games with less friction and more approachability. It was also an era where the United States was in the throes of an economic crash that overturned the lives of millions and led to effects we are still feeling today. I was about to lose my job, and I had a very bad case of the flu the week that *Demon's Souls* came out, and my god, the game felt like 2009. A mouthful-of-corpses game for a mouthful-of-corpses time that we are still in today. Same dragon, newer corpses.

Demon's Souls was a game that seemed like it didn't want to be beaten, but there were wrinkles in that facade, glints of something else. The challenges could seem impossible, but sure enough, you found that they weren't. And beyond that, it was suffused with this thoughtful strangeness. It was, for lack of a better word, sensitive. Vulnerable, even. It was playful, and funny, and it wanted you to try, to engage, to work through it.

Demon's Souls rewarded you not just with loot or heroic cutscenes or guaranteed badassery, but with fleeting adventures with anonymous strangers, odd glimpses of a world that was more weird horror than high fantasy, and some of the most wonderful quiet moments I have ever seen in a game. It didn't want to just beat you down; it wanted to give you the opportunity to not give up.

I lost my job not long after as the company began to go under. I was devastated and scared, with no real prospects and the world seemingly crumbling into the mist around me. I came home and over the next few days plowed through the rest of this game that had so taken over my mind. The odds seemed insurmountable, but the journey was strange and horrifying and funny and beautiful. I finished the game, got up, and went on.

—SCOTT BENSON,
codirector on *Night in the Woods*

2020

Welcome to **Animal Crossing** — New Horizons

THE ESCAPE OF THE YEAR

RELAX AND LIVE YOUR DREAM LIFE ON AN ISLAND
PARADISE SURROUNDED BY ANIMAL FRIENDS.

PRESS START

Animal Crossing: New Horizons would have been a delightful game no matter what year it came out in. Few games make you so aware of time and unaware of time, all at the same time. But in a year as chaotic as 2020, this relaxing safe haven was absolutely essential in ways nobody could have foreseen. It's not just a life sim; it's a lifesaver.

THE GETAWAY OF
A LIFETIME

Animal Crossing is Nintendo's answer to *The Sims*. A casual life sim, *Animal Crossing* focuses more on the simple repetitive pleasures of being alive rather than the annoying minutiae. You can choose to sit on a toilet in *Animal Crossing*, but you don't need to worry about a bladder meter. *Animal Crossing*'s peaceful activities are far more low stakes and low-key than even the gentlest Nintendo games. Befriend the adorable, emoji-esque animals who move in next door, each with their own vocal tics, and throw them going-away parties when it's time to move on. Fall head over heels for a slick, short king of a frog named Huck, like my wife did. Pay off your mortgage to your raccoon landlord, Tom Nook, and decorate your house with furniture and artwork. Go fishing, collect bugs, and dig up fossils to donate to the museum. Celebrate holidays synced to the real-world calendar.

Some impatient players like to change their system's internal clock to speed through *Animal Crossing* as fast as possible. Why wait a week for an apple tree to grow when you can just wait two minutes? But that's missing the point. If you try to reset your save files to undo mistakes, an angry mole named Mr. Resetti pops out of the ground to yell at you. Guitar-playing pooch K.K. Slider is special because he shows up only on Saturdays and doesn't sing until later in the night. *Animal Crossing* wants you to slow down, go with the flow, and take things one day at a time. That's life, dog.

Whereas previous *Animal Crossing* games were set in small towns, *New Horizons* gave players an entire deserted island to call their own. Customize your perfect vacation getaway not just by rearranging your house but by decorating every inch of the land. Build bridges, erect inclines, redirect rivers. Your island provides bountiful raw materials, from cheap wood to precious metals. Learn recipes to craft these materials into new equipment and goodies, from a basic axe to a solid-gold samurai suit. In the *Happy Home Paradise* expansion, you use your newfound interior decorating skills to furnish custom vacation homes for paying customers. Along with these fresh ideas from director Aya Kyogoku, *New Horizons* also looks gorgeous as the first game in the series with HD graphics. And as a Nintendo Switch game, you can enjoy it on your big TV or as a cozy handheld companion in bed. No game gave you an escape this pleasant or powerful.

THE CURE

In 2020, we didn't just want an escape, we needed one. The *Animal Crossing* series has always been successful, but *Animal Crossing: New Horizons* turned the game into a shared cultural event. That's because in March 2020, the definition of life itself drastically changed for just about everyone. The COVID-19 pandemic forced people worldwide to quarantine at home to avoid catching and spreading the disease. Locked down in my apartment, I and millions of other people dove into *New Horizons* as a substitute for the real outdoors we suddenly found ourselves cut off from.

We soaked up the sun on our virtual islands where nobody got sick. We couldn't safely see our friends in person, so we put up with Nintendo's dumb voice chat mobile app to fly over and hang out in each other's villages. Sure beats a Zoom call. Stuck in our pajamas, we took and shared pictures of our avatars' cute and colorful outfits and hairstyles, a sharp contrast to the world around us sinking deeper into ugliness and despair. *Animal Crossing: New Horizons* collectively comforted us at our most uncertain, soothed us at our most vulnerable. That's how a game buries itself in your heart and becomes eternally linked to an unforgettable moment in time.

When Nintendo scheduled *Animal Crossing: New Horizons* for March 2020, the company probably just wanted a big title to end its fiscal year. There's no way Nintendo knew it would be the perfect game to get us through a pandemic. But that's exactly what happened. More than forty million people bought *New Horizons* and played for hundreds of hours. Casual gamers flocked to the Nintendo Switch like it was the Wii all over again. Unlike crowded movie theaters and concerts, games are the perfect hobby to enjoy at home, especially a game like *Animal Crossing* that you can happily play forever. Fan communities created entire online marketplaces, like Nookazon, to trade *Animal Crossing* goods. How much would you fork over to get smug cat Raymond to move to your island? *Animal Crossing* memes dominated social media and spread to real television like *Saturday Night Live*. Couples staged virtual weddings, complete with invited guests, on their islands. Joe Biden's presidential campaign crafted and shared an island to promote the candidate, and he won!

When I think about games that genuinely make the world a better place, games we look back on and say they touched our lives, *Animal Crossing: New Horizons*' impact in 2020 feels impossible to overstate. It's an infinite paradise for the end of the world.

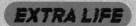

HADES AND THE ENDLESS AFTERLIFE

What other game could possibly represent 2020? Supergiant Games' masterful, roguelike *Hades* comes to mind. *Hades* features not only irresistible combat and stunning artwork but also a narrative that turns its repeated trips through Greek mythology's underworld into a thoughtful thematic point. That's a powerful notion when every day trapped in quarantine blurs together into its own repetitive hell.

MICROSOFT FLIGHT SIMULATOR (2020)

My favorite Christmas ornament is a small piece of metal molded somewhat crudely into the shape of a house. It's stamped, in typewriter font, with "the year we stayed ▢ home" and "2020"—a twee handicraft that, despite the kitsch factor, encapsulates my overriding memory of that year.

What better 2020 GOTY choice could there be than *Microsoft Flight Simulator*? Call it a video game, call it educational software; at heart, it's an astounding monument to wanderlust, that primal human longing that was particularly universal in 2020.

Cooped up inside, unmoored by the divisive, alienating chaos of an endless nightmare, we couldn't see the forest for the trees. *Microsoft Flight Simulator* allowed us to slip the shackles of lockdown and get a thirty-five-thousand-foot view of the world once again.

—SAMIT SARKAR,
deputy managing editor at Polygon

MYST (1993)

Myst is a game about being stuck somewhere, isolated from human interaction, and solving puzzles while periodically enduring the FMV equivalent of bewildering Zoom calls. But I didn't know any of that when I played *Myst* for the first time, nearly thirty years after its release and early in the COVID-19 pandemic. All I knew is that it had a lot of puzzles in it, a delightfully whimsical nineties aesthetic, and no threat of death.

Before the end of 2020 I played all four of its sequels, and then two *Myst* VR remakes. I even attended (virtually) the annual *Myst* fan convention.

Myst is an urtext to video games, invisibly defining much of what followed it, and built with a strange experimental whimsy where even its flaws become a part of the experience. Its shadow is long. For me, it was a patient world to explore, far from the troubles of home.

—MAX EDDY,
journalist and former write-in candidate for Washtenaw County Water Resources Commissioner

SPIRITFARER (2020)

Seems fitting that my pick for game of the year, a game about escorting loved ones into the afterlife, made me sob three full times (only two of which were when I was on my period, thank you very much!).

I first dove into *Spiritfarer* not because of the story, but because of the gameplay. In real life I am a minimalist, so I enjoy games where I can collect, build a house, catch every fish, and farm every fruit. A quick glance into my Switch purchases will show you *Stardew Valley*, *Pokémon Snap*, and some kinky dating sims. Don't judge me! The prospect of building a giant boat with a world of items to collect and errands to run excited me. I expected *Spiritfarer* to scratch my organizational itch.

I didn't expect it to resonate on a deep level with the collective and personal losses I have felt over the past two years of our short, precious lives on this strange, waterlogged planet. If you pick it up, be sure to have a tissue box nearby, and regardless, you should probably go call your mom and tell her you love her.

—MAGGIE MAE FISH,
actor, writer, and video essayist

2021

CO-OP: BONUS ROUND

PSYCHONAUTS 2

KIMARI RENNIS

**senior intern at the New York Videogame Critics Circle
and game design major at New York University**

The year is 2005. I am three years old and unable to comprehend the game series that would change my life. Fast-forward to the summer of 2021, trapped amid a pandemic. I arise from my heat-induced stupor pondering a friend's advice to buy Tim Schafer's *Psychonauts* for $4 in the PlayStation Store.

Immediately I thought back to my childhood, where my immature gamer brain insisted that games with stupid names were unworthy of my attention. Paying $4 for this weird 3D platformer felt like a battle of moral convictions, but as I played, I could only be sucked deeper into the literally mind-bending world of *Psychonauts*, the one thing I had been missing all my life.

Then my sights turned to *Psychonauts 2*. Sixty dollars left my pockets with the utmost ease because I knew I would be playing the best game ever made. I experienced the mental journey of more than fifteen years within a few weeks.

HALO INFINITE

RAHEEM "MEGA RAN" JARBO
rapper and author

November 15, 2001. The day that Gregorian chants hit the hood. As a fresh-faced Penn State graduate, class of 2001, I prepared to embark on my journey into manhood, leaving behind all the things that I just knew I wouldn't need anymore. I left so many things in a Pennsylvania storage locker that I would never look at or touch again:

My sketch pads of drawings.

A ton of athletic gear, memories of my years of intramural sports.

And last but certainly not least by a long shot: my video games.

For as a child I thought like a child, and as a man, I would surely need to move on and grow up. Goodbye, PlayStation . . . so long.

. . . Or so I thought. When the Xbox system launched with *Halo* in 2001, it changed what the first-person-shooter genre could be, and transformed everyone in my middle-class Philadelphia neighborhood into full-on *Halo* junkies. When *Halo* hit, we piled into any home we could, ten to fifteen deep, and would play multiplayer for hours at a time, sometimes well into the night, and even the next morning. When we discovered System Link play, we would bring TVs and additional Xbox consoles to my friend's auntie's house and set up in the basement, playing nonstop. *Halo* had officially seeped into our pores.

Fast-forward and it's twenty years later. The first-person-shooter genre has evolved. There are a few new champions in town. So when *Halo Infinite* was announced and touted as an open-world *Halo* sequel, a lot of people, including myself, wondered if this was a move I should care about. So many games have come and taken so many of *Halo*'s innovative mechanics and pushed them further by leaps and bounds. Would *Halo* continue to innovate, or would it show its age in a world of faster, hotter, and bigger FPS games?

Halo Infinite didn't just come to play; it came to deliver. And it did. It's by far my favorite game of 2021, with beautiful graphics, new innovations like the Grappleshot (if it sounds satisfying to pull yourself toward an enemy and sock them in the nose, just imagine what it *feels* like), and a single-player experience that is masterfully crafted. It's just what the year of 2021 needed.

IT TAKES TWO

VICTORIA SONG AND GABE CAREY

reviewer at the Verge and
commerce editor

We don't really play games together. Gabe's more into action-y games. Victoria plays sims and JRPGs. Co-op games like *WarioWare* are too anxiety-inducing, and Victoria hates being demoted to a simple Waddle Dee in *Kirby Star Allies*. That's why we decided to play *It Takes Two*. It's about married people. We're married. But also, it's about a couple going through magically induced couples therapy—and everyone could use a little bit of that.

The mechanics emphasize teamwork, so you can shine at what you're good at while your partner has your back. It's not just one type of game here, either. You're going to suck at a few of them. Gabe is great at the platformer elements, but he is a dingus at puzzles. Victoria's great at puzzles. Cody and May, the protagonists, are also complementary. She carries a hammer, he's got nails. He turns into flowers. She waters him. Gabe yells at Victoria to jump at the right time. Victoria throws water on him. When one of you sucks at platformers (Victoria) and lags behind (also Victoria), you're not automatically zapped forward. You have to wait for them to catch up because you need to progress together. It also gives the "weaker" player time to actually enjoy that part of the game, at their pace.

Thematically, forcing a struggling couple to save their relationship by working together is cliché. *It Takes Two* keeps it fresh by traumatizing you both after murdering the world's cutest stuffed elephant and doing a celebration dance in your daughter's tears. Nothing beats being absolutely baffled together. At the end of the day, could playing through the vaguely racist Dr. Hakim's Book of Love save your marriage? Yes, and it's cheaper than actual therapy.

2022

THE STANLEY PARABLE
ULTRA DELUXE

THE CHOICE OF THE YEAR

CHOOSE AND CHOOSE AGAIN TO UNRAVEL THE FULL
STORY IN THIS PUZZLING VIDEO GAME METAPHOR.

PRESS START

We all make choices all the time. It's like breathing, second nature. What do you want to eat or wear? Who should you vote for? When's the right time to take your relationship to the next level? With movies, books, and other passive media, the choice is pretty simple: Do you consume this or not? But choosing to play a video game is just the first of many choices the interactive entertainment asks you to make. What do you say? When do you jump? Whom should you shoot? The choices we make as players, as human beings, give meaning to the experience. They define what the game even is. Or rather, at least that's what we like to think. The truth is a far deeper rabbit hole, and no game tackles the treachery of choice like **The Stanley Parable: Ultra Deluxe.**

THIS IS THE STORY OF A MAN NAMED STANLEY

Designed by Davey Wreden and William Pugh, *The Stanley Parable: Ultra Deluxe* is a video game about video games. It's a comedy, a satire of the form. It's also, arguably, a bit pretentious and inaccessible, a video game for fans of Federico Fellini and Charlie Kaufman (or people who like to drop those kinds of references). Talking straight about this infinite fun house mirror requires a lot of honesty, as well as a lot of spoilers. So right now you may want to choose to play the game first before learning anything that ruins the surprises.

Final warning.

The Stanley Parable is a first-person narrative adventure game. You play as Stanley, a typical office drone who one day notices that all of his coworkers have mysteriously disappeared. As you investigate, a wry omnipresent narrator, played brilliantly by Kevan Brighting, describes Stanley's every action. The narrator tells us Stanley's choices before he even makes them. After only a few minutes of searching, Stanley uncovers and shuts down a diabolical mind-control device before stepping into freedom. The end.

But what if you made Stanley do something else? Ironically, the only way to free Stanley's mind is to precisely follow every step told to you, to abandon your own free will. Come to a room with two doors: the narrator says to walk through the left door, and you do. But what if you walk through the right door? Or walk down the stairs? Or click on a random door five times to earn an achievement? Or turn the game off for five years? All these choices trigger radically new stories, some funny and others profound, that form the core of what *The Stanley Parable* truly is: a comedically expressive meditation on gaming's unique illusion of choice.

Stanley isn't just an office drone, he's a person playing a video game, someone who sits down and presses buttons all day. The narrator is the godlike creator, the maker of this world who swings between amused and enraged as you rebel against his lovingly crafted linear design. At one point, the narrator actually paints a big line on the floor for you to follow. You feel alive, like a mischievous cartoon character, every time you zag when the game clearly tells you to zig.

So why don't these choices matter? Paradoxically, it's because you're allowed to make them. Every time you make an alternative choice and something else happens, it's because the game anticipated you might make that choice and planned accordingly. Ultimately, you still followed some part of the plan, even if you changed up the order a bit. That's true in every video game that makes you believe you're doing what you want and not what the designers intended, when you go left instead of right and find a secret stash of coins. That convincing feeling of real freedom is in fact the simulation succeeding. *The Stanley Parable* just highlights the obvious and turns the farce into its own kind of fun. Think about it: If the game really didn't want you to walk through the door on the right, the door wouldn't exist at all.

THE END IS NEVER THE END IS NEVER THE END

The Stanley Parable constantly resets, as every ending encourages you to try again to see where else the story might lead. Each new attempt presents you with a loading screen that says, "The end is never the end is never the end." *The Stanley Parable* keeps going, in more ways than one. The game first released as a *Half-Life 2* mod in 2011. Two years later, it expanded into a stand-alone release. And in 2022, *The Stanley Parable: Ultra Deluxe* continued the cycle.

Ultra Deluxe defies classification. When you start, you'll play everything the original had to offer, now on consoles alongside PC. But soon the fourth wall shatters even further as you walk through a conspicuous new door that's literally labeled "New Content." From there you'll experience more than enough additional material to justify a nine-year wait for a sequel, material that eventually calls itself a sequel to mockingly question the very idea of sequels.

What do we want from our new games—innovative, fresh ideas or more of the same? Fixes for old complaints or extra content for its own sake? A jump button? Do we even want sequels, or are they obligations, more false choices? If the original *Stanley Parable* was *The Matrix* (Stanley himself has very pre-Neo Thomas A. Anderson vibes), then *Ultra Deluxe* is the psychedelically self-aware *The Matrix Resurrections*. The only thing in gaming that even compares is Jim Stormdancer's *Frog Fractions* franchise, and spoiling those masterpieces would be a crime.

In 2015, between *Stanley Parable* releases, Wreden wrote another fascinating first-person narrative game called *The Beginner's Guide*. Trying to definitively claim what that game means would completely miss the point, but here's a pretty safe theory: The game explores the anxieties of a self-critical creator whose project suddenly becomes an acclaimed critical darling. These themes reappear in *Ultra Deluxe*, a game that contains angry user reviews of itself. Creators especially know how scary it is to make choices. In the endless search for vital validation, bad choices leave you at the mercy of hostile critics and uncaring audiences. But to form a positive connection with just one other person through your art, almost anything is worth the risk.

Choices frighten all of us for too many reasons to list. They overwhelm us until we can't decide anything at all. Maybe it would be nice to have a narrator tell us everything to do. But *The Stanley Parable: Ultra Deluxe*'s marvelous maverick metafiction exclaims that we must make choices, even laughably fake ones, in real life and in video games.

AUSTIN WALKER

IP director at Possibility Space, host of
Friends at the Table

es so long to make a game, so it is rare for one to feel like it's speaking to its h
ent. Yet *Umurangi Generation*, a righteously angry photography-at-the-end
 simulator, only grows more relevant with each passing day. Hired to snap
 during the apocalypse, players find a world of blood, bureaucracy, and (sc
atigable vibrance. A high-priced VR pod for dazed and disinterested executiv
ers smoking, shrugging, and sighing, boots ready to be placed on necks. Snap.
eetwear doing their thing under the glow of massive humanoid war machin
r fire in the dark. Snap. Friends piled into a train. Snap. At last, a boiling, b
s protest. Snap. So, how long will *Umurangi Generation* be relevant? Only
 changes.

ETAL GEAR SOLID 2: SONS OF LIBERTY (20

JULIE MUNCY

writer and video game consultant

r wanted to kill him.
Ve were on top of a federal building, all concrete and dread. The voices in my

Despite supply shortages, Microsoft, Sony, and even Valve somehow managed to launch new consoles during the pandemic: the Xbox Series X/S, PlayStation 5, and Steam Deck. Not to mention Nintendo refreshed the Switch with a fancier OLED screen. While development has understandably slowed down, resulting in many delays, 2022 still brought us **Elden Ring, Pokémon Legends: Arceus, Horizon: Forbidden West, Sifu, Lost Ark, Neon White, Kirby and the Forgotten Land, Immortality, God of War Ragnarok, Bayonetta 3, Marvel Snap, Vampire Survivors, Splatoon 3, Pentiment,** and more new games than we know what to do with. Heck, we even got a great new **Teenage Mutant Ninja Turtles** game. The pandemic did not crush our love for gaming. Far from it.

An uncertain future also makes us appreciate the video games we already have, our cherished backlogs. We return to the games we've accumulated over the years, games that have entertained, surprised, and delighted us as far back as 1977. We'll always have new games to anticipate. No industry is as obsessed with looking forward as the gaming industry. But when you remember to also take a look back, you'll discover endless games to love right now.

Video games are the preferred pastime for millions of players all over the world, but they're also the products of proud artists. They're treasures with a rich history, a history I humbly hope you understand and admire just a little better thanks to this book. I don't know when I started loving video games, but I do know that I will never stop. When you get into gaming, you open yourself up to a universe of enriching experiences and entertaining possibilities you won't find anywhere else, from space invaders to Italian plumbers, from epic fantasy battlefields to intimate island getaways.

Curious where you should begin? Let me tell you about a game called **Pong** . . .

ACKNOWLEDGMENTS

Sam(s) of the Year:
Without Sam Morgan and Samantha Weiner, this book wouldn't exist. I'll always be endlessly grateful to them for giving me this opportunity. Hilarious how it all started with a *Street Sharks* lie on Geek.com.

Editor of the Year:
Connor Leonard is the kind of thoughtful, professional editor any writer would dream of working with, regardless of topic. But the gaming knowledge he brought to this project elevated the editing process so much. I didn't expect it, but I very much appreciated it.

Publishing Team of the Year:
The entire team at Abrams Books did a wonderful job guiding me as a first-time author. Seeing everyone perform their role so well inspired me to do better. Thank you to Heesang Lee, Lisa Silverman, Denise LaCongo, Gabby Fisher, Kevin Callahan, and everyone else who helped out in ways I may not even know about.

Artist of the Year:
As you've seen by now, Wren McDonald is a phenomenal artist whose illustrations truly took this book to an entirely new level of quality. I literally gasped the first time I saw them. Really, the pictures are the star of the show. I just wrote some nice words to go along with them.

Contributors of the Year:
Thank you so much to every writer who graciously contributed their own video game of the year picks. You all chose such fascinating games to highlight and offered incredible alternative perspectives. Your cooperation turned this project into the collaborative and comprehensive celebration of gaming history I always wanted it to be. And to the creators behind these games, I hope I did my best to honor the awesome work you do pushing this medium forward.

Leftover Jokes of the Year:

As pleased as I was with my jokes about a *Metal Gear Solid* Broadway musical and a McDonald's Telltale adventure game starring the Hamburglar, sometimes you need to kill your darlings (or sneak them in at the very end).

Family of the Year:

To my parents, who always supported my very peculiar career goals in ways not all parents might. To my sister, who made sure I was surrounded by video games before I even knew what they were. To my aunts and uncles, who gave me every game I put on my Christmas list. To my cousins, who were always ready for multiplayer. To Ashley Santana, a fantastic assistant photographer.

Friends of the Year:

Northwestern University not only provided the journalism education I needed to eventually pull this project off but also introduced me to lifelong friends who still ask me for game recommendations. Shout-out to my colleagues at PCMag and Mashable, my peers at the New York Videogame Critics Circle, all you gorgeous hams and squids in Spectre, and the glorious comrades at the Ziff Davis Creators Guild and the NewsGuild of New York union. Solidarity forever.

Dog of the Year:

Amber Skittles Santana-Minor. No other dog does it better.

Wife of All Time:

To the brilliant and beautiful Romary Santana, who went through law school, wedding planning, apartment hunting, pandemic spikes, election anxiety, union contract negotiations during a Disney World vacation, and countless hours of trash reality television throughout the course of my writing this book. Thank you for everything. I love you, always.

Editor: CONNOR LEONARD
Designer: HEESANG LEE
Managing Editor: LISA SILVERMAN
Production Manager: DENISE LACONGO

Library of Congress Control Number:
2022947229

ISBN: 978-1-4197-6205-5
eISBN: 978-1-64700-680-8

Text copyright © 2023 JORDAN MINOR
Illustrations by WREN MCDONALD
Author photograph by ROMARY SANTANA

Cover © 2023 ABRAMS

Printed and bound in China
10 9 8 7 6 5 4 3 2 1

Abrams Image books are available at
special discounts when purchased in
quantity for premiums and promotions
as well as fundraising or educational
use. Special editions can also be created
to specification. For details, contact
specialsales@abramsbooks.com or the
address below.

To Romary, for loving all of my levels.

ABRAMS The Art of Books
abramsbooks.com